D1316920

TRUTHS MEN LIVE BY

A Philosophy of Religion and Life

I, Lord, went wandering like a strayed sheep seeking Thee with anxious reasoning without, whilst Thou wast within me . . . I went around the squares and streets of the city of this world, and I found Thee not, because in vain I sought without for Thee who wast within myself.

St. Augustine, *Confessions*

THE MACMILLAN COMPANY
NEW YORK · BOSTON · CHICAGO
DALLAS · ATLANTA · SAN FRANCISCO

MACMILLAN AND CO., LIMITED
LONDON · BOMBAY · CALCUTTA
MADRAS · MELBOURNE

**THE MACMILLAN COMPANY
OF CANADA, LIMITED**
TORONTO

THE UNIVERSITY OF NOTRE DAME ATOM SMASHER

Scientists are discovering through the use of this instrument the tremendous power which the Author of nature has locked within the invisible atom. Their discoveries afford us a glimpse of the order and arrangement of the constellations within the submicroscopic domain and thus reveal a speck of dust to be a world teeming with marvel and with mystery.

PRINTED IN THE UNITED STATES OF AMERICA
BY THE VAIL-BALLOU PRESS, INC., BINGHAMTON, N. Y.

TRUTHS MEN LIVE B

A Philosophy of Religion and Life

BY JOHN A. O'BRIEN, Ph.D., LL.D

THE UNIVERSITY OF NOTRE DAME

THE MACMILLAN COMPANY · *New York*

1947

PREFACE

AFTER winning a war against tyranny we turn toward planning the world we want to build. Now we see the urgent need to learn what the possibilities of life are so that we may choose the best. Basic to choosing our great goal lie such questions as, is there a God interested in us and to whom we are responsible? Are we indeed free to choose our own actions? Are we living for our own lifetime only, or for eternity?

Fascism teaches responsibility to the state. Communism, in its current political form, insists that one's duty is to his social group, in particular to the proletariat. A Christian's supreme obligation is to his God, which is best fulfilled by service for his fellows whose welfare is dear to their Creator.

There are strong reasons for believing that following this Christian doctrine will result in the most stable and satisfying life of men and nations. But in an age of science, we must first ask, what is the evidence? Does the Christian doctrine of a Fatherly God, His divine Son, and an opportunity to live forever fit with what we know of the world around us? Nothing is more important than finding a firm answer to these questions that will set us on the correct path toward choosing the goals of life.

The deeper one penetrates into the secrets of nature, the clearer becomes his awareness of law, order and purposiveness evident in all that happens. The constancy of the laws of nature give a unity to all truth and make our world a cosmos rather than a chaos. By learning these laws one can learn more about the Supreme Mind, about God Himself, that in which we live and move and have our being.

Father O'Brien has faced these problems fairly. He brings out the pregnant truth that in the study of nature we learn more of what man is and what God is. The problems with which he deals are age-old, and in discussing them he has used the collected wisdom of the ages. He is aware, however, of the distinctive attitudes of an age of science. He reinforces belief in God and in the spiritual nature of man with the findings of modern science and philosophy. His book will thus give new strength to multitudes of men and women upset by the confusions and uncertainties of the day. There is here a welcome light that can lead the humble seeker toward a satisfying philosophy of life.

ARTHUR H. COMPTON
Chancellor of Washington University

INTRODUCTION

THIS volume undertakes to present the truths which give meaning and purpose, substance and value, to human life. The conception underlying the entire discussion is that man does not live by bread alone but by truth. Without the latter, his vision fades and his footsteps falter. The truths placed before mankind by the Founder of the Christian faith and the truths thought out by the seers and sages, the philosophers and the scientists, constitute man's true heritage. This book seeks to present that precious spiritual and intellectual legacy of truth which alone makes man free. In so doing, it serves as a guide to right and noble living.

The knowledge of those truths is the supreme need of mankind today. For in those living truths will be found the solvent for the ills which afflict the individual as well as the nations of the world. Until these truths become worked as a leaven into the lives of the peoples of every land, all plans for enduring peace and happiness will be but dust and ashes.

The work is designed furthermore to meet an urgent and widespread human need, namely, to answer the questions in the forefront of the contemporary mind. They are the basic questions which underlie all religious faith: Is there a God? How can I find Him? Does religion really matter? What is its origin? Is it necessary as a foundation for public and private morality? What is the soul? Is the will free? What is the basis of human worth? Is there an afterlife? What is the authority of Jesus and of His revelation? Are the Gospels reliable, historic channels of that revelation? What is the distinctive message of Jesus to mankind?

These questions are not new. They are of perennial interest. The world-wide unrest and unsettlement, brought about by the global war, have given them, however, a new and a peculiar urgence. Unless they are effectively answered, the individual will have no solid foundation upon which to rear the superstructure of his religious faith—so important for wholesome living.

The aim of the author is to answer these questions in the light of the findings of modern research in philosophy, history, scripture, and science. For that purpose the findings in these fields have been presented with meticulous care and their bearing upon traditional concepts of religious faith has been made clear.

It would be folly to deny the far-reaching repercussions of the findings of modern scientific research upon various phases of theistic thought. Evolution is a case in point. If religious faith is to be durable, it must satisfy not only the hunger of the heart but also the stern demands of the intellect. The human personality cannot be dichotomized into emotional hungers and intellectual cravings without disaster ultimately to both mind and heart. The harmonization of religious faith with modern science must be effected with no compromise of intelligence or of intellectual honesty. Throughout all the discussion of religious faith and scientific discoveries, the author has not been unmindful of the warning of Erasmus, "To identify the new learning with heresy is to make orthodoxy synonymous with ignorance."

The harmonization of the truths of religion and of science is not only possible but flows as an evident necessity from the fundamental unity of all truth. God is the author of the truths of Biblical revelation and of the truths of science. He is likewise the author of the human mind by which both sets of truth are known. The truths of science and the truths of philosophy can no more contradict the truths of religion than can God contradict Himself. All truths stream from the same fountainhead and, when properly understood, must harmonize therefore with one another.

This is the thesis that underlies the treatment of every problem in this book. Our method accordingly is not that of subtle dialectics or of sterile controversy, but of constructive exposition. Truth is its own defense. It stands in no need of the smokescreen of partisan appeals to emotions or prejudices. To be believed, truth needs but to be seen. Our efforts have been simply to make clear the winsome face of truth. The ideal held up before the reader is that of the blending of knowledge with holiness, to make one both a scholar and a saint.

While the volume will be of profound interest to all university and college students, it will be of no less appeal to the general reader who wishes to have a faith that will find reënforcement, not opposition, from the progressive discoveries of modern science and historical research. Because it is written in simple non-technical language, the work brings within the ken of the masses the findings of the laboratory and the fruits of philosophic research.

To those who are groping in uncertainty, the volume will open up a sure and a safe path to the feet of God. To those who have faith in God, the volume will deepen that faith by providing a solid intellectual foundation. To all who read it with an open mind, it will bring new vistas of truth. It embodies the results of more than thirty years of study and research in the crucial and all-important field of the philosophy of religion.

The work will prove a source of help and inspiration, we hope, to every family in America. The author sends this book on its mission of light and healing to the people of the English-speaking world, with the humble prayer that it may bring courage and strength to every reader. To the students and faculty members of the University of Illinois, Oxford University, and of the University of Notre Dame, who by question or by answer have aided in the writing of this volume, the author expresses his abiding gratitude. If it makes God and His Christ better known and better loved by all who read it, the author will be more than repaid for the labor of a lifetime.

For reading the manuscript, in whole or in part, and for helpful suggestions, the writer expresses his gratitude to his colleagues, Rev. Dr. Eugene P. Burke, C.S.C., Rev. Dr. Thomas J. Brennan, C.S.C., Prof. Daniel C. O'Grady, Prof. William F. Roemer, as well as to Rev. Leo A. Arnoult, O.P. and Rev. William O'Beirne, O.P. of St. Mary's College, Notre Dame. It is a pleasure for the author to acknowledge the valuable suggestions of Rev. Cuthbert Lattey, S.J. of Oxford University and of Canon Henry de Dorlodot of Louvain; and the counsel, aid and encouragement generously given by his old colleague, Rev. Dr. William J. Bergin, C.S.V., in bringing this work of many years to completion.

JOHN A. O'BRIEN

CONTENTS

PART 1

GOD

His Existence and Nature

Today there is but one religious dogma in debate:
What do you mean by God? And in this respect,
today is like all our yesterdays.

PROFESSOR ALFRED WHITEHEAD,
Harvard University

The foundation upon which all religious faith rests is God. Without a Supreme Being all religion would be a delusion and a snare. There can be no intelligent discussion of religion until the existence of God has been clearly and definitely established. Accordingly in Part I all the important lines of evidence bearing on the existence of a Deity are presented. Some proofs will appeal with especial force to certain minds, while other proofs will attract other intellects. The evidence, streaming from so many different sources, is so overwhelming, however, as to carry conviction to every open mind.

Having demonstrated by reason the existence of God, we then discuss His nature and attributes. He is omnipotent, omniscient, eternal, infinite. While the human mind cannot exhaust the infinite nature of God, it can get a working knowledge of Him from Jesus, the untarnished mirror of the Most High. The reality of our religion rests ultimately upon our knowledge of God, our Beginning and our End. Nothing is more important therefore than the knowledge of God. To know Him is to love Him, and to serve Him is to reign.

CHAPTER I

THE HEAVENS SHOW FORTH

The heavens show forth the glory of God, and the firmament declareth the work of his hands.—*Psalm* 18:2.

Is THERE a God? How can I be sure? Where can I find Him? Do I have to make an act of faith to believe in God? Is it possible to prove the existence of a Supreme Ruler of the universe by logical reasoning? These are questions which are uppermost in the minds of many people today. They are of perennial interest. They have been with us since the race began and they will be with us until the end.

These are the questions of supreme importance which present themselves anew to each generation. Upon the success which the individual achieves in answering them correctly hinge consequences which jut beyond this life into eternity. "Today," observes Professor Whitehead of Harvard, "there is but one religious dogma in debate: What do you mean by God? And in this respect," he adds, "today is like all our yesterdays."

Immanuel Kant expressed the conviction that in all philosophy there are but three great problems, namely, the existence of God, the freedom of the will, and the immortality of the human soul. It is not difficult, however, to show that of these three, God's existence is the central problem and the other two are but its corollaries. In fact, they cannot be treated adequately or intelligently except in the light

3

of the answer reached concerning the existence of a Supreme Intelligence.

The most important knowledge in the world, therefore, is the knowledge of God. Uncertainty about God renders people miserable and unhappy. It makes them less sure of themselves, of the purpose of life and of human destiny. With wistful eyes and groping hands millions of people to-day are searching for something to steady them, for a firm hold on God.

In *The Adventures of the Black Girl in Her Search for God*, George Bernard Shaw pictures his central character in her African homeland accosting a young white man wearing a Greek tunic.

"Excuse me, *baas*," said the black girl. "You have knowing eyes. I am in search of God. Can you direct me?"

"Do not trouble about that," said the young man. "Take the world as it comes; for beyond it there is nothing. All roads end at the grave, which is the gate of nothingness; and in the shadow of nothingness everything is vanity. Take my advice and seek no further than the end of your nose. You will always know that there is something beyond that; and in that knowledge you will be hopeful and happy."

"My mind ranges further," said the black girl. "It is not right to shut one's eyes. I desire knowledge of God more than happiness or hope. God is my knowledge and my hope." [1]

The black girl may be viewed as the symbol of all humanity, of the learned and of the unlearned, in their search for God who alone gives meaning to life. She symbolizes, too, mankind's refusal to shut their eyes and to look no farther than their nose. The theme song of humanity's quest for meaning and purpose amidst the confusions of our day is sounded in the black girl's memorable cry, so simple and yet

[1] *The Adventures of the Black Girl in Her Search for God*, p. 14.

so pregnant with the cry of humanity in every age: "I desire knowledge of God more than happiness or hope. God is my knowledge and my hope."

God—The Meaning of the Universe

What do we mean by God? God is not a mere dream, not an hypothesis, nor the projection of our hopes and aspirations upon the frail canvas of illusion. He is the meaning of the universe and the hope of humanity. He gives a cosmic value to the ideals of truth, justice and righteousness, which point like slanting arrows of light to the Source from which they emanate. "To know God," said Dante, "is to learn how to make our lives eternal."

Long before Dante, St. John proclaimed the important truth almost lost in the contemporary fog: "This is eternal life: That they may know thee, the only true God, and Jesus Christ whom thou hast sent." [2] Back before the dawn of the Christian era, the author of the book of *Wisdom* declared: "To know thee is perfect justice; and to know thy justice and thy power is the root of immortality." [3] Like a cloud by day and a pillar of fire by night runs this mighty truth through the pages of the Old and of the New Testament.

It is our birthright, our priceless heritage. If the birthright be sold for a mess of pottage, and the heritage be lost in the confusion of our day, there is no power on earth that can rescue man from his Babylonian captivity or relieve the nostalgia and loneliness of his exile.

God is the Supreme Ruler of the universe. He is the omniscient Mind who thought out the myriad laws of nature and the omnipotent Power who flung the uncounted planets, stars and galaxies out into the vastness of immeasurable space. He is the Architect not only of the stupendous universe but also

[2] *John* 17:3
[3] *Wisdom* 15:3

of the heart and mind and soul of man. "In Him," as St. Paul says, "we live and move and have our being." [4] He created the universe, and He sustains it by His infinite power. He created man in His image and likeness, and endowed him with understanding and free-will. God is infinitely powerful and infinitely wise. There is not a sparrow which falls to the ground that escapes His all encompassing vision. He is a Being whose center is everywhere and whose circumference is nowhere. "The measure of him," Sophar reminds Job, "is longer than the earth, and broader than the sea." [5] "God's body is truth," said Plato, "and light, His shadow." He is the Alpha and the Omega, the beginning and the end of all things. He is our heavenly Father, in whom truth, justice, mercy, and love abound in their fulness.

An Appeal to Reason

What is the evidence of the existence of such a Supreme Being? In presenting this manifold evidence, we shall appeal not to the authority of the Bible or of the Church but to the court of human reason. If occasionally we quote a writer of the Scriptures or a prelate of the Church, we shall do so not as an inspired or infallible spokesman, but as a witness whose testimony we lay before the bar of human reason.

In our presentation we shall assume agreement upon the validity of but two primary principles: the ability of the human mind to know, and the law or principle of causality. These need not, and in fact cannot, be demonstrated because they are self-evident and shine by their own light.

Thus Kant's investigation of the trustworthiness of the human mind to know, as undertaken in his *Critique of Pure Reason*, was foredoomed to failure, regardless of the conclusion he would reach. If he arrived at the negative conclusion,

---

[4] *Acts* 17:28
[5] *Job* 11:9

as he did, that conclusion was of no consequence because the instrument by which he reached that conclusion was human reason itself. If he arrived at an affirmative answer, that too would have been meaningless, because the instrument used in reaching such a conclusion would be reason, which was ostensibly the object of investigation. This would be to assume the validity of reason and would constitute therefore a begging of the question. The simple fact is that we must start with the validity of these two primary principles, which underlie all philosophic and scientific investigation. To deny them is to close the door to all discussion and to plunge into the hopeless sea of universal scepticism.

We shall not ask the reader if he be Protestant, Jew, Catholic, or non-believer. We ask only that he examine the evidence with an open mind and that he observe the laws of logical reasoning. In this way he will allow the evidence to write the verdict on his own mind and heart. From this spirit of open-mindedness and good will, wherein the inquirer seeks honestly and earnestly to see the evidence and to feel the weight of its uncushioned impact upon his mind, he will derive the largest fruit. We hope, therefore, that our presentation will prove helpful to all earnest seekers for the truth, of whatever religious faith or philosophic creed they may be.

For thirty years we have been engaged in the presentation of this subject to the upper class students in universities, where technical philosophic language is customary. Here we shall endeavor to preserve the vigor of reasoning, but shall dispense with technical terms. Our aim will be to make every fact and every line of reasoning clear to all people of intelligence, whether they have a university background or not.

The evidence of the existence of a Supreme Being comes from many fields, from the world of inorganic matter, from the vegetal and animal worlds, and from the world of human life. While all of it is valid and cogent, experience has shown us that different kinds of evidence make appeals of varying degrees of impressiveness to different individuals. We shall draw the evidence, therefore, from many sources to carry conviction to every reader and to show, furthermore, how the whole field of nature, from a speck of dust and a blade of grass, to the farthest star, echoes the Source from which it comes and bears the unmistakable imprint of the hand of God upon it. As every shell along the seashore, when placed to the ear, gives an echo of the mighty deep from which it came, so every particle of matter in the universe from a grain of sand and an eagle flying high in the skies to the throbbing heart of man, when hearkened to attentively, gives an echo of that infinite Power from whose creative womb it has come.

Evidence of Design

We shall start with the presentation of the evidence which we have found to make the widest appeal—the evidence of order and law in nature. This is commonly called the proof from design. In philosophy, it is known as the teleological argument, that is, the argument built around the evidence of ends or purposes in the organization of nature and in the operations of its laws.

Thus when Robinson Crusoe perceived a footprint on the island of Juan Fernandez, he rightly concluded that it had been made by a man. The clear imprint of the sole of the foot and the five toes was enough to convince him that it had been made, not by a bird or an elephant, or by the wind and the rain playing with the sand, but only by a man.

If a person walking along a seashore comes suddenly upon a watch, he will conclude that there must be a watchmaker. Why? Because as he looks at the mechanism of the watch, with its springs, its cogwheels, its hour hand and its minute hand, with its crystal and its face, with the movement of the minute hand so coördinated that it travels precisely twelve times faster than the hour hand, he knows that this could not have happened by accident or by blind chance. The adaptation of parts and the coördination of movements reflect unmistakably the work of a thinking agent who arranged the whole to achieve a definite, previsioned end. There is blinding evidence here of plan, purpose, order and design, which leaves him in no uncertainty.

Suppose you were to say to such a person: There is no evidence of a thinking agent behind that bit of mechanism. Those parts are simply an aggregation of bits of metal and glass, and were blown together by the winds of chance. Earth, sea, wind, sun, sky, air and the blind forces of nature explain the making of that watch. Would he not conclude that you were either joking or that you were a lunatic? Would he not say: Surely you cannot expect an intelligent person to believe so wild a fairy tale. Even a child of six would scorn such an explanation as an insult to his intelligence. There is woven into that watch an artistry of power and intelligence which convinces me that nothing on this planet could account for that watch except a human being who has mastered the craft of the watchmaker.

A World Clock

Let us now glance at the marvelous universe in which our earth is as a tiny speck. The whole is arranged with wonderful order and design. Our earth rotates on its axis once in twenty-four hours, bringing to us night and day. The earth revolves around the sun once in the course of a year, bringing to us with unfailing regularity the four seasons of the year. This planet of ours, with its great cities teeming with millions of inhabitants, with its lofty skyscrapers, with its vast emporiums of trade and commerce, with its mountains, rivers and valleys, is shooting through space at the startling velocity of 68,400 miles per hour. Yet so smoothly does it move, that it disturbs not a babe in its cradle, nor brings a tremor to the wings of the bee nestling on the frail petals of an autumn rose.

This fact was brought home to the writer as he was traveling in an airplane from Rome to Budapest. Here was as fine a passenger plane as the engineering genius of man has been able to build. Sailing through the air at the rate of 150 miles an hour, with music from Vienna echoing softly from its radio, it would seem to represent the ultimate in skillful organization and in design. Yet how slow, clumsy and jolting was it in comparison with the airplane of the earth which sails through space 456 times faster and with such smoothness that its passengers are unaware that it is even moving!

The stars move in their appointed orbits with a regularity and a precision which shames the most accurate chronometer made by human hands. The most accurate watch or clock made by horologists will falter by some seconds each week in the exact measurement of time, and will have to be corrected by the clock of the stars as caught by the United States Naval Observatory at Annapolis. Here then are order, plan, purpose and design which cry out not less imperiously than the watch found at the seashore for an intelligent and adequate cause.

Inescapable then is the simple conclusion: As the watch implies a watchmaker, so the universe implies a God. As the watch demands adequate cause in the form of an intelligent horologist, so the universe, vastly greater in size, complexity of organization, and adjustment of parts, demands an adequate cause in the form of a Being of vastly greater power and intelligence. This is the Being whom we call by the venerable name of God.

St. Thomas Aquinas gives the classic statement of the argument, which we have just presented and illustrated, in the following words: "We observe that some things which are without understanding, such as natural bodies, operate for an end (as appears from the fact that always or more frequently they operate in the same way to arrive at what is best): whence it is clear that they attain this end not by chance but by intention. Now, these things which do not possess understanding, operate for a purpose only in so far as they are directed by a being endowed with intelligence: just as an arrow is directed by the archer. Therefore, there is an intelligent Being, by whom all the things of nature are directed to their end. And this Being we call God." [6]

"The Fool Hath Said . . ."

If you wish to get a more vivid picture of the numerous galaxies of stars which dot our skies at night with pin points of light than is likely to be gained from textbooks, visit the Planetarium in Chicago or in New York. There you will see the technical skill of our architects and engineers harnessed to the skill of the astronomers in depicting for us the heavenly bodies which swing with order and precision in their appointed orbits through the immeasurable vastness of stellar space. The lights in the building are extinguished. Then on the ceiling, which is so shaped as to represent the dome of the heavens, thousands of pin points of light appear to show us the number, the place, and the distance of the stars that stud our northern sky. These are only inches or fractions of inches apart, but they represent millions of miles. The lights appear as pin points, but they represent heavenly bodies whose size would dwarf our earth. It is a marvelous work of scientific skill and engineering genius, which provokes the admiration of the stream of visitors.

What would you think of the person who, after viewing this depiction of the wonders of the sky, should say: This

[6] *Summa Th.* L, q. 2, a. 2

Planetarium does not imply any intelligent architect or designer. It is the work of chance. It is a pile of bricks, mortar, cement, steel, electric wires, fuses, wood, paint thrown together by chance.

Would you not find it difficult to restrain your indignation at so obvious an expression of utter nonsense? Would you not say: The arrangement of the seats, the fashioning of the ceiling, the contriving of the lights to represent the galaxy of stars in the heavens, are blinding evidence of plan and design of a high order. Only a fool could say that is the work of chance.

If you would be justified in saying that, as you would be indeed, would you not be justified in expressing an even more severe condemnation of the folly of the person who would assert that the vast universe, of which the Planetarium was a fragmentary picture, was itself the result of chance? Would you not feel more clearly than ever the truth of the words of the Psalmist: "The fool hath said in his heart: There is no God." [7]

The great astronomer, Kirchner, had a friend who experienced doubts about the existence of God. Knowing that a simple illustration would be more effective than a long argument, Kirchner made a globe and placed it in his study. When his friend called to see him, he noticed the new globe, and asked:

"Who made this globe?"

"Why," replied Kirchner, "it made itself."

His friend laughed heartily at the joke. Whereupon, Kirchner said:

"You laugh at that as absurd, and rightly so. But it would be a thousand times easier to believe that this little globe made itself than that the large one on which we live made itself."

[7] *Psal.* 13:1

Immensity of the Cosmos

A perception of the immensity of the universe, as disclosed by the findings of astronomers in the last few decades, will serve to increase our wonder and deepen our reverence before the infinite might and power of the Supreme Being who hurled the millions of worlds out into the midst of space. It will serve likewise to put richer content into the words *omnipotent* and *omniscient*, which were becoming anaemic in the nineteenth century. It will show that the ancient prophets and psalmists spoke wisely when they spoke of God as all powerful and all wise.

In the past, we have been accustomed to think of our solar system as involving great distances and great masses. Thus the sun is 94 million miles from the earth. The planet Jupiter has a diameter of 88,640 miles, and could accommodate within itself 1400 bodies of the size of the earth. But now we learn that Jupiter and even our sun are but specks in comparison with other celestial bodies. The nearest star is Proxima Centauri, 25 billion miles away. Indeed, the distances are so great that they cannot well be understood in terms of miles.

Accordingly, astronomers have invented a new measure called a *light year*, to make the distance intelligible. Light travels at the rate of 186,000 miles per second. A light year is the distance traveled by light during that period—6 billion miles. Light from the moon reaches the earth in 1½ minutes and from the sun in 8 minutes. But light from the star, Betelgeux, takes over 100 years to reach the earth. It has a diameter of 273,000,000 miles or three times the distance of the sun from the earth. Betelgeux, however, is small in comparison with some of the giant stars in Nubecula Minor, which have diameters of over 1,000,000,000 miles. There are many stars such as the Cephids, which are more than 60,000 times as luminous as our sun.

Moreover, the number of stars and solar systems floating about in the regions of interstellar space seems to be almost unlimited. The millions and billions of stars in the Milky Way are but a tiny fragment of the myriad worlds coursing through space. The most powerful photographic cameras are continually catching glimpses of new galaxies of stars beyond the outermost rim of the previously charted stellar universe. Professor Shapley of the Harvard Observatory has recently reported "island universes" of stars, far outside the main sidereal system. These globular clusters are over a million light years distant. In other words, they are so far distant that light traveling at the rate of 186,000 miles per second would take more than a million years to reach our earth.

For all that astronomers have been able to discover, this may be but the nearest fringe, the vestibule of a universe that stretches out with its planets, suns, and stars into immeasurable space. Truly does the mind reel and stagger under the weight of such stupendous distances, such unimaginable sizes and such baffling complexity of galaxies of worlds seemingly without number.

Solar System—A Grain of Sand

"Such is the aspect," says Flammarion, "grand, splendid and sublime, of the universe which flies through space before the dazzled and stupefied gaze of the terrestrial astronomer, born today to die tomorrow on a globule lost in the infinite night." "The spirit of man," cries Richter, "acheth with this infinity." Similar was the sentiment expressed by Pascal: "The silence of these infinite spaces frightens me." The status of our earth in the stellar system is, then, that of a dwarf planet revolving about a dwarf star. It is but as a speck of dust floating in the reaches of illimitable space.

The eminent English astronomer, Sir James H. Jeans, helps

kan and Arthur Compton, I thought it would be interesting to get the reactions of laymen and others, untutored in this field, to their startling discoveries.

"Do you think the particles of that pipe you are smoking are stationary or are in motion?" I asked of a cultured student of English literature, Joseph Whitney, who was seated in my room at Campion Hall, Oxford University.

Joe looked carefully at his meerschaum pipe and after rubbing his finger carefully over the stem and the bowl, said: "I think the particles of the pipe are entirely stationary, but the particles of smoke issuing from it are in motion."

"Well," I replied, "get ready for a shock. The particles composing that pipe are electrons and protons, and the electrons are constantly moving around the protons. That much I will tell you. But now try to guess how many times per second those electrons are revolving around their protons."

"Perhaps, if they hurry," answered Joe, "they'll get around a dozen times or so."

"Now, Joe," I said, "brace yourself for the shock of your life. Those electrons in your pipe are shooting around their atomic orbits more than a *thousand million million* times per second."

"I don't believe it," blurted out Joe. "It sounds crazy to me. Sounds like Gertrude Stein talking physics. Or perhaps," he added with a touch of irony, "some of your physicists have been reading James Joyce's *Finnegan's Wake* or Lewis Carroll's *Alice in Wonderland*, and are trying to outdo them."

Well, Joseph Whitney, looking at his meerschaum pipe and feeling it with his finger, and finding it still and motionless may not believe it. And maybe millions of others may not believe it. But physicists ask us to believe it as an established fact of science. Such distinguished scientists as Millikan, Pupin, Eddington, Jeans and Compton tell us that a whole new subatomic world of marvelous mystery has been discovered. The atom has been broken up into proton and electrons. The whole concept of matter has been revolutionized. Instead of matter consisting of hard, inert pellets, as the man in the street still imagines, science has shown these infinitesimal constituents of matter to be in a state of tremendous activity.

The atom is viewed as a small solar system. Around its central nucleus of positive electricity called a proton, the electrons revolve as the planets revolve about the sun. The movements, however, apparently follow no fixed path or orbit. While the atom is so small as to be invisible to the naked eye, science has measured the speed of these electrons and tells us that they move in an orbit of less than one-millionth of an inch in diameter, faster than an airplane or a bullet from a revolver. Thus the average electron revolves around its central nucleus several thousand million million times every second, with a velocity of hundreds of miles a second. This amazing orbital speed which is greater than that of the planets or even of the stars, is achieved in spite of the infinitesimally small chamber in which it is imprisoned—namely less than one-millionth of an inch in diameter.

Man—As Science Sees Him

Indeed the whole conception of matter has been revolutionized by the discoveries of nuclear physics. Instead of a stone wall, for instance, being a solid mass with no holes or gaps between the particles, it is now declared by physicists to be full of such openings and to bear a closer resemblance to what we might call a wire fence. So all matter, even the hardest metals, is permeated by gaping holes which occupy a vastly greater amount of the space than the particles of matter which are in a constant state of lightning-like velocity.

"How much do you weigh?" I asked Milt Piepul, one of

our largest students here at Notre Dame, and a power full-back on the football team.

"Two hundred and twenty pounds," he answered.

"How tall are you?"

"Six feet, two inches."

"Now if you were all put compactly together, so that all the empty spaces in your body and in your head—I mean no disparagement," I added quickly as the students snickered—"were eliminated, how large would you be?"

"I don't believe there are any appreciable empty places in my body," replied Milt, "and I know there are none in my head. But if I were pressed tightly together, perhaps I might be squeezed down to five feet ten inches or so."

"Well, prepare yourself for a shock," I warned. "You would be about the size of a speck of dust, so tiny as to be invisible to the naked eye."

The students roared with laughter at such a seemingly incredible and even ridiculous statement.

Milt's reaction was identical with that of my young friend at Oxford.

"I don't believe it," said Milt. "I'm from Missouri," he added, "and you'll have to show me."

"Don't take my word for it," I said. "But read the statement of one of the most distinguished physicists in England, Arthur S. Eddington, of the University of Cambridge. Read the very first page of his epochal book, *The Nature of the Physical Universe*." [1]

I handed him the open book.

Science Speaks

Milt read:

"When we compare the universe as it is now supposed to

[1] Macmillan, N.Y., 1929

be with the universe as we had originally preconceived it, the most arresting change is not the rearrangement of space and time by Einstein but the dissolution of all that we regard as most solid into tiny specks floating in void. That gives an abrupt jar to those who think that things are more or less what they seem. The revelation by modern physics of the void within the atom is more disturbing than the revelation by astronomy of the immense void of interstellar space. The atom is as porous as the solar system. If we eliminated all the unfilled space in a man's body and collected his protons and electrons into one mass, *the man would be reduced to a speck just visible with a magnifying glass.*"

Science asks us to believe as literal facts statements which no amount of reasoning could have induced the previous generation to accept. What a world of almost infinite potentialities are locked up in a small particle of matter, awaiting a skillful hand to release them from their thralldom! Consider the energy stored up in a piece of coal smaller than a pea. Jeans states it as a scientific fact that if all the atomic energy locked up in so tiny a piece of coal could be released, it would be sufficient to take the *Mauretania*, a very large passenger vessel, across the Atlantic and back again! "If the energy in a single pound of coal," he says, "could be completely utilized, it would be sufficient to keep the whole British nation going for a fortnight, domestic fires, factories, trains, power stations, ships and all." [2]

In the light of these discoveries of modern physics, a speck of dust and a grain of sand become teeming worlds of marvel and of mystery. In a speck of dust so small as to be beyond our naked vision are more particles than there are inhabitants upon our planet. They are moving in their atomic orbits, so silently as to be inaudible, with a velocity which bewilders

[2] Jeans, *The Universe Around Us*, Macmillan, N.Y., 1929, p. 181

our imagination. Science with its huge cyclotron, or atom crusher, is able occasionally to split an atom. Science has not been able as yet, however, to penetrate deep enough into the depths of the atom to ferret out the network of laws which stretch from the heart of an atom to the galaxy of the farthest stars. These laws hold the whole vast universe together and support the stars in their courses, much as milady's clothesline holds securely the whole family washing flapping in the summer breeze.

As far as science has been able to peer into the depth of an atom, it has found an amazing network of law. Indeed, the working out of the molecular arrangement in a grain of sand calls for a knowledge of a higher mathematics which few humans possess. The researches of Jeans into the ultimate constituents of elements lead him to think of a speck of dust as a long series of algebraic symbols. Will any human ever learn enough mathematics to decipher fully the algebraic formulae written on the heart of a speck of dust or on a grain of sand? Only time can tell. But if we do, it is reasonably certain that such discoveries will only open the door to a still vaster world of marvels and of mysteries, as all the scientific discoveries of the past have done.

"Put Off Thy Shoes"

Thus Dr. George L. Clark, Professor of X-ray Chemistry at the University of Illinois and a world authority in that field, threw upon the screen an x-ray picture of a particle of soot. I can still remember the expressions of wonderment and awe which came spontaneously from my students as they perceived the beauty and symmetry of the molecular arrangements therein disclosed. Like flakes of snow on a window pane tracing out geometric figures of remarkable

symmetry and wonderful diversity, so these figures stood revealed like frozen pieces of glorious architecture. Indeed
within a speck of soot which an individual will flip disdain-
fully from his white kid glove, there is a perfection of symmetry in the arrangement of the molecules and an embodi-
ment of mathematical precision which would make the Taj
Mahal of India or St. Peter's Cathedral in Rome seem like
child's play in comparison.

That is why the scientist who has peered even a little way
into the unfathomed and mysterious depths of a particle of
matter, will stand with reverent eyes and uncovered head before a particle of dust or a grain of sand. Like Moses standing
before the burning bush, he too hears the voice which says:
"Put off thy shoes from thy feet, for the place whereon thou
standest is holy ground." [3] To him there is no common clay.
For every particle of matter is aglow with miracle and with
mystery, singing a refrain in homage to that infinite Power
from whose creative hands it came.

In the past, the appeal has been to the star-studded sky as
evidence of a Supreme Being. That appeal grows stronger
with each advance of astronomy which deepens our reverence and fills us with awe as we gaze upon the wonders of
the firmament. Not less impressive or awe-inspiring is the evidence of a Supreme Intelligence in the galaxies, solar systems,
and island universes floating about in the mysterious depths
of a speck of dust. In the whirling depths of a grain of sand
there appear to be more particles than there are comets,
planets, and stars in all the heavens. In the algebraic flecked
sky of a speck of dust there may be more geometric symbols
and mathematical formulae than can ever be written in all our
books. Truly, indeed, the world of the infinitesimally small
is not less wonderful than the world of the infinitely large.

[3] *Exod.* 3:5

Nor does it speak less cogently nor less eloquently of a Supreme Ruler of the universe. "In all the vast and the minute," as the poet, Cowper, says, "we see the unambiguous footsteps of the God who gives its luster to the insect's wings and wheels His throne upon the rolling worlds."

CHAPTER III

THE TESTIMONY OF LIFE

If I have made a single contribution to biology which I
feel confident is permanent, it is the profession that living Nature is purposive.—HENRY FAIRFIELD OSBORN

THUS far we have been presenting the evidence of God's existence from the order and design in the world. Our illustrations have been taken solely from the inorganic world. More
impressive and wonderful still, however, is the evidence of
plan in the world of life. Here we come to a higher category
of being, a category where matter exemplifies the reign not
only of physical law, but also of biological law. In other
words, matter bursts through into a higher realm where it
grows not by accretion, but by intussusception, that is, by
taking lifeless external matter and changing it into its own
living protoplasm. It lifts matter from the lifeless inorganic
world into the living organic world. It solves the riddle which
from time immemorial has baffled the mind of man. It has
found the mysterious bridge which spans the chasm which
has forever barred man's own efforts to carry lifeless matter
over into the domain of life.

How did matter first find that bridge? How does it continue to find it, when it eludes the high-powered microscopes
in the hands of our most penetrating scientists? "What incredible concatenation of circumstances," asks Bruce Bliven,

"brought the first cell into being among the atoms of such substances as hydrogen and oxygen?" [1] No wonder it was that the scores of scientists, whom he interviewed, listed it as among the most baffling of all the mysteries of science.

In the plant world, the process by which the chlorophyll in a blade of grass utilizes the sunlight to break up the carbon dioxide in the air, retaining the carbon for its own plasm, and giving back the free oxygen to the air is called photosynthesis. After learning the correct label for this process, most students hurry along, we fear, without ever pausing to consider the teleological significance of this action. Yet in that elementary action of all vegetal life, an action we meet at the very threshold of our study of biology, there is a teeming world of miracle and mystery.

Photosynthesis Explains What?

The term, photosynthesis, formed by joining the two Greek words, *photos*, meaning light, and *synthesis*, meaning put together, merely indicates that the sun has had something to do with the putting together process. It throws no single ray of light, however, upon the essential problem: How does the chlorophyll use the sun's rays to perform the complex chemical operation, whereby an inorganic element is transmuted into living matter? What is the technique which the molecules of chlorophyll have worked out—a technique which the greatest scientists in the world are unable to discover or to duplicate? What is the principle which guides the molecules in the subtle technique of bridging the gulf between the world of inanimate matter and the world of life, which has thus far baffled the greatest chemists in the world with all their stores of knowledge accumulated from a thousand laboratories? If the action is merely one of chemical at-

[1] *The New Republic*, November 17, 1941

traction, why does it not take place when light falls on the chlorophyll of a blade of grass torn from its roots?

Let us push this investigation a step further. For implications of profound significance are still to be traced out. I took a blade of grass to a distinguished biochemist at a great university, and I said:

"Analyze this for me and tell me all the elements of which this is composed."

He broke it up in his laboratory and after analyzing its contents, he replied:

"Carbon, nitrogen, hydrogen, oxygen, iron, chlorine, phosphorus, sodium, potassium and silicon."

"All right, now," I continued, "put these lifeless inorganic elements back together again in such a way that they will perform the process of photosynthesis, the rudimentary action of all vegetal life."

"Oh, that's impossible. Neither I nor all the chemists in the world, together with all our wonderful laboratory equipment, can do such a thing."

"Why can't you? Aren't you and your colleagues intelligent?"

"Yes. At least we think we are," he added with a smile.

"But aren't the elements, carbon, hydrogen, nitrogen and the other elements which compose a blade of grass, unintelligent?"

"Yes."

"Why then can't you, with all your intelligence and with the accumulated experience of all the chemists who ever lived, do what these unintelligent chemical elements do with despatch, with unfailing regularity, and with unerring accuracy?"

"Oh," he replied, "there's some principle which guides them in the performance of that complicated biochemical action."

"Some principle? What do you mean by that?"

"Oh, some Power, some Intelligence, call the principle what you will."

The proper name for that Power is, I think, the Author of nature, the Ruler of the universe, the Supreme Intelligence who has infused into all the particles of matter in the universe, whether they be inorganic or organic, the laws which guide them in their operations from the whirling of electrons and protons in a speck of dust and in a blade of grass to the movements of the stars in the galaxies floating at the rim of the universe.

"One Step Further"

"Professor," I continued, "I would like to push our investigation one step further."

"You admit that there is some principle or power or intelligence which guides the unintelligent elements in a blade of grass in the solving of the mystery of transmuting lifeless matter into living matter. From your study of nature, are you led to believe that the principle works arbitrarily, or does it follow the path of a definite law?"

"From the investigations which scientists have conducted in all the fields of nature, we are persuaded that every operation in nature follows definite laws. Nothing happens by accident or by blind chance."

"But do not laws indicate the necessity of a lawmaker? Can you have a law without a legislator? If you stand on a busy intersection and you see cars scurrying rapidly along a highway and all coming to a stop when the traffic light flashes red, and then all starting again when the light flashes green, don't you conclude that there is a law which so ordains them to act?"

"Yes," replied the scientist. "A law implies a lawmaker.

But here you are getting outside the field of science into that of the philosopher. A scientist sticks to matter and energy and the laws of their operations."

"True, indeed," I said. "But how many are the scientists who do not observe the limitations which you so correctly indicate, and who rush in to pontificate in the fields of philosophy and theology, for which they are utterly untrained."

An Inescapable Conclusion

Please note that all the data for our conclusion are drawn from science, namely, that such unintelligent elements as carbon, nitrogen and hydrogen in a blade of grass solve unerringly and with despatch the complicated biochemical operation of changing lifeless, inorganic matter into living protoplasm. This is an operation which transcends the ability of our most brilliant chemists to duplicate. Therefore, we are compelled by the laws of logic to say that there is manifested therein the working of a Power, an Intelligence, a Lawmaker which far transcends the genius of man. Whether we are just ordinary laymen, or scientists, or philosophers, we are driven to that inescapable conclusion by the ruthless force of the laws of logic.

For this is simply to say, what every scientist and philosopher and, in fact, every intelligent person admits, that every effect must have an adequate and proportionate cause. Obviously, it could not be carbon, nor hydrogen, nor the other chemical elements which are themselves utterly unintelligent. Therefore, the complicated operations they perform in solving a problem which transcends the genius of man to duplicate, indicate the existence of an adequate Cause of surpassing Power and of transcending Intelligence—a mighty Lawmaker who holds the whole vast universe, from a blade of grass to the farthest nebula, subject to the reign of His all-embracing network of law. Such a Supreme Ruler of the universe is essentially what we mean by God.

It is to be noted that this line of reasoning proves the Ruler of the universe to be a Being of vast power and intelligence. Strictly speaking, however, it does not prove Him to be of infinite power and of infinite intelligence. This cannot be done by any of the evidence of design, law and order in the universe. For these are all of a finite character. We can show only by metaphysical proofs that the Supreme Ruler of the universe must be a Being of infinite power and of infinite intelligence. This we shall do later on.

For the present, let us point out that the existence of a Being of vast power and intelligence is evidenced from the network of laws which control the functioning of the electrons and protons in a speck of dust, as well as from those which guide the particles of matter in a blade of grass in the biochemical operation of photosynthesis. Those who look, therefore, with understanding eyes upon a grain of sand or a blade of grass, see mirrored therein flashes of the power and of the wisdom of the Most High. The subtle and mysterious laws which the electrons obey in solving problems which transcend our puny intelligence may be said to be the objectified thought of the Great Naturalist and the algebraic formulae of the Divine Mathematician, whom mankind calls by the venerable name of God. As Wordsworth has well said:

> To me the meanest flower that blows can give
> Thoughts that do often lie too deep for tears.

Joyce Kilmer expresses the conclusion that is forced upon every thoughtful person who peers deeply into the wonders of nature, in the memorable lines:

> Poems are made by fools like me,
> But only God can make a tree.

Tennyson likewise perceived that the whole universe rests upon the all-encompassing network of the laws of God. If we could look deeply enough into the mysterious and unfathomed network of law in any single object in all creation, we would see God and understand man, nature, and God. Tennyson gave admirable expression to this mighty truth when, in passing through the woods, he beheld a flower bursting out in the crevice of a wall, which he thus apostrophised:

> Flower in the crannied wall,
> I pluck you out of the crannies,
> I hold you here, root and all, in my hand,
> Little flower—but if I could understand
> What you are, root and all, and all in all,
> I should know what God and man is.

Scientist, poet, philosopher and theologian can make those words their own. The great scientist, Robert Andrews Millikan, expressed this same thought when he described his researches into the nature of the cosmic ray high up in the stratosphere of the sky as "the finger printing of God." [2]

[2] *The Literary Digest*, Jan. 24, 1931, p. 27

CHAPTER IV

A FEATHER SPEAKS

What then is the selective or directive power which extracts from the blood at every point where required the
exact constituents to form here bone-cells, there muscle-
cells, there again feather-cells, each of which possesses
such totally different properties?
—ALFRED RUSSELL WALLACE, *The World of Life*

THUS far, we have presented evidence of God's existence
from the order and design in the universe. As instances of
such design we first considered the universe as a whole and
then focused our attention upon its smallest part—an atom
of matter. Coming then into the world of life, we turned our
attention to the process which met us at the threshold—the
process of photosynthesis in a blade of grass.

Let us now consider the coördination and adaptation involved in an object with which we are all familiar—a feather.
This is regarded by scientists as one of the most perfect structures in the world. For its complete evolution it is estimated
that approximately a million years were required. In a single
pinion from an eagle's wing there are nearly a million different parts. There are the barbules which give the feather its
essential character both as an organ of flight and as a covering
preserving the heat of the body. But the barbules are themselves highly specialized structures with definite shapes and
surface-texture, attaching each one to its next lateral barbule,
and then by a kind of loose hook-and-eye formation, to those

of the succeeding barb. Each barbule is built up of many thousands of cells, varying considerably in form and powers of cohesion, in order to give the exact strength, elasticity and continuity to the whole web.

"The whole," says Professor J. Arthur Thompson, "is a sail that strikes the wind, firmly and yet elastically, not letting the air through the web and yet not getting broken. It enormously increases the bird's power of rowing in the air, and yet how little it adds to the weight. As long as it is growing, it is fed; when the constitutionally ordained limit is reached, it stops growing and yet does not die too quickly. When it dies, it is moulted off and a new one takes its place, often just in time for the migratory journey, when frayed feathers might be dangerously ineffective. And this is not nearly all, for the feather is difficult to wet, it forms part of an admirable non-conducting robe conserving the precious animal heat, and it is often so colored that it gives its possessor a garment of invisibility. And this is not all, for we may admire the neat way in which the feathers are adjusted when the wing is raised for the next stroke, so that energy is economized just as in rowing. And even the fallen feather may form part of the best of quilts for keeping the young ones snug within the nest." [1]

In order to secure a deeper insight into the coördination of processes and the adaptation of means necessary to attain the finished structure of a feather, it is necessary to penetrate beyond the end products and try to peer into the problem of the forces guiding the many thousands of cells in the devising of the million different parts of a feather. The writer recalls no one who has sought to show the implications of the growth of a single feather with greater penetration than Alfred Russell Wallace, the great English scientist, in his monumental

[1] J. A. Thompson, *Science and Religion,* Chas. Scribner's Sons, N.Y., pp. 132-133

work, *The World of Life*. Because he penetrates beyond the surface of external adjustments, and comes to grips with the problem of the directive principle guiding the infinitesimally small particles constituting the protoplasm of a cell, which is the crux of the whole problem of purpose in living nature, it will be worthwhile to quote him somewhat extensively.

Directing Power—Where?

"Now," he points out," each feather 'grows' as we say, out of the skin, each one from a small group of cells, which must be formed and nourished by the blood, and is reproduced each year to replace that which falls away at moulting time. But the same blood supplies material for every other part of the body—builds up and renews the muscles, the bones, the viscera, the skin, the nerves, the brain. What, then, is the *selective* or *directing* power which extracts from the blood at every point where required the exact constituents to form here bone-cells, there muscle-cells, there again feather-cells, each of which possesses such totally distinct properties? And when these cells, or rather, perhaps, the complex molecules of which each kind of cell is formed, are separated at its special point, what is the *constructive* power which welds them together, as it were, in one place into solid bone, in another into the extremely light, strong, elastic material of the feather —the most unique and marvelous product of life?

"Yet again, what is the nature of the power which determines that every separate feather shall always 'grow' into its exact shape? For no two feathers of the twenty or more which form each wing, or those of the tail, or even of the thousands on the whole body, are exactly alike (except as regards the pairs on opposite sides of the body), and many of these are modified in the strangest way for special purposes. Again, what *directive* agency determines the distribution of the coloring matter (also conveyed by the blood) so that each feather shall take its exact share in the production of the whole pattern and coloring of the bird, which is immensely varied, yet always symmetrical as a whole, and has always a purpose, either of concealment, or recognition, or sexual attraction in its proper time and place?"

Wallace then proceeds to stress the point, to which we have already called attention, namely, the failure of nearly all scientific writers to penetrate beyond the enumeration of the various steps which occur to raise the question of what is the principle directing the series of complex operations. "Now," he continues, "in none of the volumes on the physiology of animals that I have consulted can I find any attempt whatever to grapple with this fundamental question of the *directive* power that, in every case, first secretes, or as it were, creates, out of the protoplasm of the blood, special molecules adapted for the production of each material—bone, muscle, nerve, skin, hair, feather, etc. etc.,—carries these molecules to the exact part of the body where and when they are required, and brings into play the complex forces that alone can build up with great rapidity so strangely complex a structure as a feather adapted for flight. Of course, the difficulties of conceiving how this has been and is being done before our eyes is nearly as great in the case of any other specialized part of the animal body; but the case of the feathers of the bird is unique in many ways, and has the advantage of being wholly external, and of being familiar to everyone. It is also easily accessible for examination either in the living bird or in the detached feather, which latter offers wonderful material for microscopic examination and study.

"To myself, not all that has been written about the *properties* of protoplasm or the *innate forces* of the cell, neither the physiological units of Herbert Spencer, the pangenesis hypothesis of Darwin, nor the continuity of the germ-plasm of Weismann, throw the least glimmer of light on this great problem. Each of them, especially the last, help us to realize to a slight extent the nature and laws of heredity, but leave the great problem of the nature of the *forces* at work in growth and reproduction as mysterious as ever. Modern physiologists have given us a vast body of information on the structure of the cell, on the extreme complexity of the processes which take place in the fertilized ovum, and on the exact nature of the successive changes up to the stage of maturity. But of the *forces* at work, and the power which *guides* these forces in building up the whole organ, we find no enlightenment." [2]

It is refreshing to see a great scientist like Wallace state so frankly the real problem involved in all the adaptations of living organisms. It is the problem of searching into the nature of that vital principle which guides the elements through the network of coördinations necessary to effect the adjustment in the structure of the external organ. Wallace's frank recognition of the essential problem and his attempt at least to grapple with it are in pleasant contrast to the superficial manner in which so many biologists have glossed over the matter, either ignoring it altogether or using euphemistic phrases which apparently explain. When these phrases are scrutinized, however, it will be found that they leave the essential problem of the principle, which steers the forces and guides the movements of the infinitesimal molecules within the cells in the deft performance of their appointed tasks, completely untouched.

The Mystery of the Molecules

The writer has presented somewhat extensively the details of the formation of a single feather, as set forth by one of the

[2] Alfred R. Wallace, *The World of Life,* Moffat, Yard & Co., New York, 1911, pp. 318, 319

greatest biologists of all time, simply that the reader may see
for himself the almost unbelievable complexity of the maneuvers and the marvelous precision with which they are ex-
ecuted. The achievement of the principle directing the movements of the billions of molecules in the building of a feather
far transcends the genius and the power of man. Man can
build such majestic structures of architecture as the Rheims
Cathedral and the Empire State Building of New York City.
He is impotent, however, to plumb the mystery of the molecules in building a feather that falls from a sparrow's wing.
With all the tools in his laboratory he is unable to reproduce
the architectural achievement of the mysterious principle hidden within the depths of the living cell.

Let us pause here to inquire if the vital process above described can be explained by any of the findings of chemistry
which has made such remarkable progress in the study of organic matter. Hertwig reflects the conviction of the outstanding scientists when he declares that the work of the investi-
gator of the problems of distinctly vital activity begins where
that of the chemist ends. "Over the growth," he says, "of the
chemical molecules is placed the growth of the cell and over
this again the growth of plants and animals with their unions
of millions and millions of different cells. Chemical knowledge as it exists at present has nothing to do with that new
world of organized substances in which the manifestations of
life are first made obvious." [3]

Physics is equally incompetent to explain the intimate nature of vital activity. The results of the research of physicists
during the last quarter of a century serve but to confirm the
conclusion reached by the great Lord Kelvin after a lifetime
of painstaking investigation into the properties of matter:
"The only contribution of dynamics to theoretical biology is
absolute negation of automatic commencement or automatic

[3] *Allegemeine Biologie*, 2te ed., s. 19

maintenance of life." [4] In other words, while the operations of the cell doubtless obey the laws of physics and chemistry, there still remains a unique principle which guides the work of the millions of the protons and electrons of its constituent elements, but remains unfathomed and inexplicable in the light of the present knowledge of the physical sciences.

The Search For a Directive Principle

The efforts to discover the nature of this principle, to catalogue it, and to plumb the depths of its mysterious being has constituted one of the most fascinating and alluring problems in the history of human thought. Far back in the time of the ancient Greeks, we find Aristotle wrestling with this problem, calling the principle vivifying matter and directing it in its functioning, an *entelechy* which today still looms up so impressively in our language after the lapse of twenty-three centuries. We find in the writings of the ancient Stoic philosophers frequent references to this principle as the *logoi spermatikoi*. St. Augustine and the early Christian philosophers, seeking to discover the principle which guided *materia prima* to higher stages in the evolutionary process, termed it the *ratio seminalis*.

Hegel speaks of a "plastic instinct," an unconscious purposive activity, *bewusstlose Zweckthatigkeit*, which "acts without consciousness with a view to an end." Blumenback refers to this directive principle as the *Bildungstrieb* or the nisus *formativus*. Johann Mueller styles it simply "organic force"; Cudworth calls it "plastic nature"; Virchow labels it "inner necessity"; Nageli has a longer word for it in *Vervollkommungsprinzip* or "tendency to progressive development." In his *Geschichte des Materialismus*,[5] F. A. Lange

---

[4] *Properties of Matter*, p. 415
[5] P. 581

speaks of "the mystical domination of the part by the whole," apparently having in mind the principle which General J. C. Smuts has popularized under the label "holism."

Hans Driesch returns to the *entelechy* of Aristotle, describing it as "an agent *sui generis,* non-material and non-spatial, but acting 'into' space, so to speak." In the philosophy of Henri Bergson, it becomes the *evolution creatrice,* while Robinet terms it *idée generatrice.* Among the neo-vitalists, it is frequently referred to as the *élan vital* or "vital principle." One recognizes the same principle in the works of the botanist, Reinke, under the term "steersmen of the energies," in the writings of Moore as "biotic force." It is to be identified with the "constellations of energy" of Weismann, and with the "biophors" or "determinants" of recent writers in biology.

The very fact that it has cropped out under so many different names in the writings of all men in all ages and races, who have thought deeply of the problem of life and who have endeavored to probe its innermost essence, points unmistakably to the reality of such a principle or Power—call it what you will—which is the guiding genius in all vital activity. The literature on the subject shows the impossibility of even coming to close grips with the problem of the distinctive nature of life without postulating some such principle as has appeared under so many different labels.

Even when the effort is made to explain vital activity exclusively in terms of physical and chemical forces, the writers use such terms as "biotic force," "steersmen of the energies," "coördinations of matter" which, in a surreptitious and unconscious manner, steal in the very element they openly profess to exclude. For unless these terms imply a directive principle, coördinating the movements of the protons and electrons of living matter to the attainment of the distinctive operations of life, they are absolutely meaningless. It is a vague form of apotheosis by which men attribute to matter properties and attributes which endue it with a form of intelligence and purposive action while they deny the same to any principle or extraphysical element behind the phenomenon of life.

Nature's "Quarterback"

In seeking to make clear to undergraduate students the meaning of a directive principle in nature's operations, the writer has found the following analogy helpful.

"The football team is playing a crucial game," I said, "executing forward passes, line bucks and sweeping end runs, with each player trying desperately to take out an opponent from the play.

"A visiting foreigner," I continued, "is watching the game. He doesn't understand much about football, but seeing the marvelous teamwork, the skillful coördination of the line with the backs, all adapted to enable the ball carrier to advance farther into the opponent's territory, he inquires:

" 'What is it that guides these eleven players in coöperating so harmoniously, enabling them to work as a single unit? What is the guiding or directive principle behind all these complicated and tricky formations?' "

I called on one of the students to answer.

"Professor," he said, "I wish all questions in our class were as easy. The answer is: the quarterback. He calls the signals, directs the play, chooses the strategy; and, in accordance with the signals he calls, every player does his particular job."

"Then, for the sake of clearness," I added, "we can call the directive principle guiding the activities of the atoms in a blade of grass or in a feather, *nature's quarterback.*"

"Ah!" he said. "Now I see."

A Supreme Intelligence Required

If the universally accepted principle of logic be true, that one may ascertain something of the nature of a being from its activities, then we are obliged to say from a study of distinctly vital activity that somewhere in the universe there is a Supreme Intelligence, since His laws are written indelibly into the network of the marvelous coördination of activities and the dovetailing of complex physical and chemical forces which conspire to effect the phenomenon of life, even in the lowest unit of organized protoplasm in a microscopic amoeba. If the process of building a feather, previously described, does not imply coördination, arrangements of parts to attain a definite end, then we confess to a complete failure to understand the meaning of these words. If the harmonious coördination of millions of protons and electrons in a single protoplasmic cell, all working toward the production of another cell to serve a somewhat different purpose, does not imply purpose and plan, then such do not exist anywhere in the universe. If the purpose and plan do not imply intelligence, then the laws of human reasoning do not reflect the realities of the external universe and the structure of the human mind is so constitutionally defective as to preclude all possibility of attaining truth of any kind—which would spell universal scepticism for mankind.

It is to be carefully noted that the validity of this reasoning does not in any way hinge upon the presence of an extra-physical element in the vital process. Neither would its validity be impaired if scientists should discover the secret of this vital process and succeed in reproducing in their laboratories the complex maneuvers which the molecules spontaneously go through in the vast laboratory of nature. Nor does its validity depend upon the continued unamenability of the distinctive phenomena of life to explanation in terms of merely physical and chemical forces. For the operation of these complex forces would require laws, and the deft coördination of the laws of physics one with another, and the dovetailing of these laws in turn with those of a chemical nature in such a way as to achieve a common and predetermined end, as, for example, the production of two perfectly similar amoebas where but one existed before, would still constitute supreme evidence of order and purpose and therefore of an Intelligence somewhere behind the functioning of the complicated network of physical and chemical laws.

Trace back the links in the chain of instrumental, physical and chemical causes, and at the end of the sequence, the human mind always discovers a Cause to which it is necessary to assign intelligence on the basis of its purposive activity.

"Let the chain of secondary causes be ever so long," as Lavington has pointed out, "the first link is always in God's hand." For a Being who has fashioned the laws of nature and who directs by His all-encompassing power the movements of the protons and electrons within the nucleus of the living cell, as well as the movements of the stars in their appointed orbits, is substantially what we mean by God. Recognizing God's power manifested in every particle of matter, animate or inanimate, Theodore Parker aptly declared: "The universe, broad and deep and high, is a handful of dust which God enchants. His is the mysterious magic which possesses— not protoplasm, merely, but—the world." [6]

When visiting the famous Cathedral of St. Paul in London, the writer saw down in the crypt, the tomb of the architect, Sir Christopher Wren, who had conceived and planned and directed its construction. Upon a tablet near the tomb was inscribed the significant epitaph: "*Si monumentum requiris circumspice.*"—If you require a monument, look around you.—Those are words which might well be inscribed upon

---

[6] Lloyd Morgan, *Interpretation of Nature,* p. 77

every particle of dust, upon every grain of sand, upon every living cell as well as upon the whole vast universe. For the immeasurable world and everything in it are monuments to the wisdom and power of the Supreme Being who is both their Architect and their Creator.

Cowper gives a poetical expression of this mighty truth in the lines: [7]

> God moves in a mysterious way
> His wonders to perform;
> He plants His footsteps in the sea
> And rides upon the storm.

[7] *Light Shining Out of Darkness*

CHAPTER V

A BEE TAKES THE WITNESS STAND

For so work the honey-bees,
Creatures that by a rule in nature teach
The act of order to a peopled kingdom.
They have a king and officers of sorts,
Where some, like magistrates, correct at home.
Others, like merchants, venture, trade abroad,
Others like soldiers, armed in their stings,
Make boot upon the summer's velvet buds,
Which pillage they with merry march bring home.
SHAKESPEARE, *Henry V*, Act 1, Scene 2

WE MIGHT rest our case here, confident that the evidence thus far presented points clearly and unmistakably to a Supreme Being, in whose intelligence and power we can find the only rational explanation for the marvelous order and design evident throughout the universe, from a blade of grass to the uttermost star. We would like, however, to drive this fact of God's existence so deeply into the minds of our readers, that God's presence in the universe will be as palpable as the chairs whereon they sit, and as luminous as the sun in a noon-day sky. Accordingly, we shall present the evidence of design in the field of animal instinct.

Anyone who has watched a bird build its nest, has witnessed an interesting display of plan, purpose and design, which is organized into the instinctive actions of animals. Take a robin which for the first time builds a nest in which to hatch her young. How does she know that a nest is nec-

45

essary? Where did she learn the art of building one? What a skillful piece of work it is to build out of such flimsy material as grass and straw a nest which will remain securely in its perch despite the storms and winds which menace it.

What prompts a hen to remain like a prisoner on her eggs for twenty-one days, scarcely leaving them for food or drink? Instinct, we answer glibly. But who fashioned it and twined it into the nervous system of the hen, so that it does the deed as naturally and as spontaneously as it gobbles up a grain of corn from the ground? This is a question seldom, if ever, raised by the scientist. It is inescapable, however, to anyone who seeks to penetrate beyond the *method* of acting to the *principle* directing that activity, and to push that inquiry beyond the network of physical causes to the First Cause.

Let us take the case of the bee. Insects which have a highly organized community life, such as bees, wasps, and ants, need the most complex pattern of instinct if their polity is to survive. Individual members must render the most diverse types of services, working for the common welfare of the society rather than for the individual's own profit. While still young, the worker bee begins the series of acts which it will do all the rest of its life. It leaves the hive, flies about in search of flowers, goes through the complicated process of extracting nectar from them, and after traveling many miles, finds its way alone back to its hive. Maraldi states that he has seen bees return to the hive, loaded with large balls of wax, the same day they were born. Their instinct told them their first task was to build their cells.

A Problem in Mathematics

Now let us consider the problem which the wax-worker bee must solve if her cell is to give a maximum of strength and capacity with a minimum of material. To calculate this form, mathematicians must propose to themselves the following problem: "To find the construction of a hexagonal prism terminated by a pyramid composed of three equal and similar rhombs, such that the solid may be made of the least quantity of materials." This was the manner in which the French naturalist, Reaumur, presented it to the noted mathematician, König. This problem resolves itself into another, namely, what should be the angles of the rhombs that cut the hexagonal prism, so as to form with it the figure of least possible surface. After prolonged work upon the problem, König calculated the angles at 109° 26′ and 70° 34′. The bees had reached a different answer and had formed the angles at 109° 28′ and 70° 32′.

Which party was right—the bees or the mathematician? Further calculation showed that the trifling error was on the part of the mathematician, or rather in the table of logarithms which he used. The bees had bested the noted mathematician, solving the problem with perfect precision. The instance is a noted one. It throws into clear relief the immediate spontaneous manner in which instinct solves for them with marvelous precision a problem over which reason often halts and stumbles and which it fails to solve with accuracy.

The mathematical deftness of the working bee does not end with the solution of this complicated problem. It must penetrate farther. The bee must have the power of striking perfect circles from centers, the distance of which from each other must be accurately adjusted, and the center of the circle drawn on one side of the comb must be equi-distant from the centers of the three adjacent circles on the other side. This is a problem which man, even though equipped with compass and rule, would not find easy. Yet the bee goes to work and solves it with unerring despatch. How does it do it? Through instinct, we answer. We do not solve this problem, however, by covering it with the name, instinct, any more than we solve the problem of determining how a blade of grass converts lifeless inorganic matter into living matter, by covering the mysterious process with the word, photosynthesis. In both cases, the labels cover not only the hidden processes but also our ignorance of what really occurs within those processes.

Many stop here and fail to raise the relevant questions: What is instinct? What Power or Intelligence created the instinct and placed it in the nervous system of the bee? Since the bee is not endowed with the faculty of reasoning, it obviously cannot have reasoned out for itself the mathematical and geometric answers to the problems indicated. Therefore, the problems must have been solved by an Intelligence equal to the difficulties involved, and that solution was woven into the nervous system of the bee to guide it in its life activity. Here again we are driven to the conclusion that the marvelous functioning of instinct within the animal kingdom, solving difficult and complex problems with ease and despatch, bespeaks the work of a Supreme Intelligence whose laws are as operative in the world of life as in the realm of inorganic matter.

CHAPTER VI

AN OVUM SPEAKS FOR THE RECORD

O child! O new-born denizen
Of life's great city! on thy head
The glory of the morn is shed,
Like a celestial benison!
Here at the portal dost thou stand,
And with thy little hand
Thou openest the mysterious gate
Into the future's undiscovered land.
LONGFELLOW, *To A Child*

IMPRESSIVE as is the evidence of order, design and law in the realm of inorganic matter, and in the domains of vegetal and of animal life, it is overwhelming in the world of human life. Here the argument from design sounds its most forceful and eloquent note. "The proper study of mankind," rightly observed Pope, "is man." For, as the Jungfrau and the Matterhorn tower majestically up above the plains and the lowly foothills, so the body and the mind of man tower up above all the other objects in the universe.

We shall consider two phases of man—his beginning as a single fecundated ovum, scarcely visible to the naked eye, and his maturity, as a full-orbed human personality. The operation which for many years has seemed to the writer to be the most marvelous and awe-inspiring achievement known to man, aside from the domain of conscious thought, is that by which a single cell builds itself into a full-blossomed hu-

49

man being. In comparison with this, the achievements of our engineers in building Boulder Dam and in erecting the 102-story Empire State Building, the accomplishments of our astro-physicists in peering into the mystery of the atom and in plumbing constellations millions of light years away, and the feats of our chemists in developing synthetic rubber and in forging ladies' sheer hose from corn stalks, are but as children's play.

Let us look for a moment at this microscopic speck of protoplasm and see what wonders it performs. A female cell, called an ovum, is secreted and starts down the Fallopian tubes. It is unable to advance a single step in its journey to maturity, however, unless it is united with a male cell, or spermatozoon. Once fecundated, however, it begins its majestic upward march. Here then are two distinct cells, each coming from a different parent. Each has no previous knowledge of the other's existence. Yet each is unable to do anything until one is merged with the other. Locked up within the chromosomes of each cell are the physical and psychological characteristics of the parent from which it comes, and of the forebears of that parent as well.

When these two cells unite to make one, you have a blending of these two cargoes of physical and psychical qualities. Buried deep down in the mysterious depth of the chromosomes are such psychical attributes as those which constitute the aptitude of a musician, an artist, a poet, a scientist. How are such psychological traits carried in suitcases of threads of chromatin, we ask in wonderment. But let us pass on to its achievements. That single fecundated cell then proceeds to play the roles of physicist, chemist, sculptor and architect —and to play them like an actor who has long rehearsed his lines. Out of the blood in the mother's womb it proceeds to fashion such divergent structures, of different physical and chemical elements, as bones, muscle, sinews, nerves, cartilage, skin, blood, hairs, and teeth. This truly is a bewildering performance—one which makes the achievement of the alchemist of old in changing the baser metals into the more precious ones, appear simple in comparison.

Different Antennae—Why?

Let us concentrate, however, on one of its achievements— that of building nerve cells. There in the darkness of the mother's womb, whither neither light nor color has ever penetrated, the fecundated ovum, developing into the embryo, takes the common material and transforms it into nerve cells which will respond later on only to light and color. How does it do this? How does it know that there exist light and color? It has had no experience of either. Then, out of that same material, it fabricates there in the silence of the womb other nerve cells which will respond later on only to stimuli of sound. Others it builds into nerve cells which are adapted only to stimuli of temperature. These respective types of nerve cells it places in their appropriate places in the developing embryo—in the end organs with corresponding centers in the brain. How does that fecundated ovum, without hands or tools of any kind, build finely spun nerve cells with different kinds of antennae, the details of whose architecture even the trained eye of the neurologist, armed with a high-powered microscope, is unable to trace? How does that speck of protoplasm build a heart and gear it into an elaborate musculature that will keep it pumping blood through the body all the days of a life stretching perhaps close onto a century? How does it fabricate eyes, which make the finest camera seem rudimentary and awkward in comparison? How does it fashion ears which make our dictaphones seem like crude and unwieldy contraptions? How does it achieve that miracle of miracles, that mystery of mysteries, the crowning achievement in the biological world—the brain of man?

These are questions which have never been answered. In all probability they will never be answered this side of eternity. They are questions, however, which should be raised to indicate the breath-taking and awe-inspiring achievements of a speck of protoplasm. If all the chemists, physicists, physicians, sculptors and scientists in the world could do any one of the numerous feats which that unicellular organism performs, we would herald the dawn of a new day in science. The fact is that science's coarse thumb and finger cannot plumb the depths of the functioning of a single living cell, much less duplicate its miracles. Since that speck of protoplasm, a fertilized ovum, has neither hands, feet nor tools to use, nor brain to guide it in its complex and mysterious operations, we are compelled to say that its actions bespeak the work of a Supreme Intelligence whose network of laws guides the movements of its molecules from a tiny cell to the journey's end—a full-blossomed human being.

CHAPTER VII

THE HUMAN BODY AFFIRMS

What a piece of work is man! how noble in reason! how
infinite in faculty! in form and moving how express and
admirable! in action how like an angel! in apprehension
how like a god! the beauty of the world! the paragon of
animals!—*Hamlet*, Act II, Scene 2

No TREATMENT of the problem of purpose in nature would
be at all complete, if it did not at least refer to that marvel of
intricate organization, the human body, reaching its climactic
expression in the cerebral cortex. If the structure and functioning of a unicellular organism, such as an amoeba, manifest
a complexity that baffles the ingenuity of scientists to unravel,
how much more bewildering is the complexity of the human
organism with its billions of parts functioning as a unified
whole? The most delicate and complex machine ever devised by human hands appears as a child's toy in comparison
with the human body, self-repairing and self-reproducing.

It is refreshing to see so eminent a scientist as Professor
Thompson state in so straightforward a manner the conclusion that would seem to flow implicitly from the marvelous
design exemplified in the structure of the human organism.
"Man," he says, "is fearfully and wonderfully made. We
never fail to be impressed with an intricate mechanical de-
vice, such as a linotype printing-machine, a loom, a calculat-
ing-machine; and we praise the maker. Why are we not more
generous in our admiration of a living creature, which is more

than any machine? Why are we not more inclined to do homage to the Prime Mover, who made things make themselves?

"We are confronted, then, with the intricacy of life. We have twenty-five trillions of red blood corpuscles and four billions of white blood corpuscles, and each is a living unit of great complexity. The microscopic capillaries, which Harvey inferred and Malpighi demonstrated, connecting the end of the arteries with the beginnings of the veins, are so numerous that if those of our body were placed end to end they would stretch across the Atlantic; and a drop of blood, if we could suppose it to retain its individuality, has a journey of about a mile a day. The nerve-cells of our cerebral cortex, the seat of the higher intellectual processes, weigh no more than half an ounce, yet there are nine thousand, two hundred millions of them, between five and six times the number of people living on the earth. And each cell is a complex intricate living unit often like a busy telephonic exchange, receiving calls and bringing one part of the body into communication with another.

"How glibly we say 'a single cell'; but a cell is a little world in itself. The living matter is in a colloidal state: that is to say, it shows a motley multitude of jostling particles and immiscible droplets suspended in a fluid, and divided somehow into eddies so that diverse chemical processes can go on at the same time side by side. In the cell-substance there are, in many cases, strands and rods and other definitely formed bodies, which are of at least three different kinds and bear many different names—as long as the things themselves are minute—such as mitochondria, chromidia, and Golgi's apparatus. In many animal cells there are two minute central corpuscles, or centrosomes, which play an important part as weavers at the loom when the cell is going to divide into two. In the center of the cell-substance, or cytoplasm—a whirlpool of eddies, with its diverse flotsam—there floats the nucleus, a little world in itself. Inside its membrane, through which materials are ever permeating out and in, there are the readily stainable chromosomes, usually definite in number for each species. Thus the number for man is probably forty-eight. But each of these rodlets, or chromosomes, is built up of microsomes, like beads on a string. Our heads begin to reel —body, organs, tissues, cells, nucleus, chromosomes, micro-somes, and beyond that, though we cannot see, there are smaller units still." [1]

Is there any possible escape from the conclusion that the amazing complexity of the human body with its 9,200,000,-000 nerve cells delicately intertwined in the cerebral cortex weighing only half an ounce, manifests plan and purpose in its arrangement and demands, therefore, the attribute of in-telligence in its Cause? Such is the conclusion that is dictated not only by the common sense of the generality of mankind, but also by the disciplined reasoning powers of a high order of intellect. Any effort to escape from such a conclusion would lead to the negation of the most basic laws of human reasoning and to a chaos in the universe that would be deep and hopeless.

An insight into the marvelous organization of the universe and the operation of its laws, such as we have sought to afford in the instances cited, reveals nature as a vast mirror, reflect-ing the power and intelligence of a Supreme Mind. Glimpses of the workings of that Mind, and of the divine plan may be had by the person who painstakingly endeavors to decipher the story written in mysterious hieroglyphics across the face of nature. If the story be read aright, nature herself supplies the answer to some of the deepest questionings of the human mind. It was this truth which Carlyle perceived when he said: "We speak of the volume of Nature and truly a volume it is—

[1] J. A. Thompson, *op. cit.*, pp. 120–122

whose author and writer is God. To read it—dost thou—does man so much as know the alphabet thereof? With its words, sentences and grand descriptive pages, poetical and philosophical, spread out through our solar systems, it is a volume written in celestial hieroglyphs, in the true sacred writing of which even the prophets are happy when they can read a line here or a line there." The lines which we have been able to decipher, however, tell a uniform story of plan, order, and design. Purposiveness written into the mosaic of nature is the universal Esperanto by which mind discerns the work of mind and loses the sense of its cosmic loneliness in the realization of the abiding omnipresence of Intelligence throughout the universe.

Mirrors Divine Lawmaker

The ceaseless research conducted by medical science into the structure and functioning of the human body, resulting in continued new discoveries of secrets previously hidden from our eyes, far from lessening the admiration of scientists, increases it with every new discovery. It is only when the work is that of a magician that our admiration is dissipated on learning of the deception, tricks, and legerdemain by which the end was achieved. But no student familiar with the profoundly realistic methods of nature has ever accused her of being a charlatan.

The fact that the technique employed by living matter to bridge the gulf separating it from inanimate matter has thus far surpassed the capacity of the human mind to discover or comprehend, tends to heighten the impression of awe we experience for the power and intelligence which first tied these forces of nature together in so remarkable a union, and then endowed them with the fecundity of offspring disclosed in the hieroglyphics of the evolutionary story. Yet if the human mind should ultimately succeed in fathoming the depths of the present mystery of life, may it not truthfully be said that while perhaps some of the feeling of awe would disappear with the discovery, the intellectual admiration would only be deepened by the revelation of new marvels of delicate coördination of forces and synchronization of movements on the part of the billions of infinitesimally small protons and electrons which course about in a cell of protoplasm as stars traverse the regions of almost infinite space? Then, too, this additional achievement of the human mind would mirror forth more strikingly than ever the intelligence of that ultimate cause which fashioned the nature of its complex organization and formed the laws for the processes of thought.

After having premised these interpretations of the implications of such a discovery, the writer hastens to agree with all careful students of the subject that life today remains as baffling a mystery as it ever was. All efforts to explain it in terms of mechanisms and physico-chemical forces fail abysmally to account for the principle directing its activities. Mechanisms and physico-chemical forces there doubtless are. But that "something else," that entelechy which eludes the scales, escapes from the test tube, and hides from the microscope, remains about as mysterious as in the days when Aristotle, the ancient Stagirite, sought for it in vain amid the plants and flowers on the Grecian hillsides.

This, however, we can say with certainty: The mysterious process of life reflects the work of a Supreme Mind, a Divine Lawmaker, whose thought is mirrored in the laws which guide the movements of every proton and electron in every particle of matter, living or non-living, in the universe.

The Mind Testifies

In our last illustration we considered man, first in his beginning as a unicellular organism and then as a fully developed organism. We saw how plan is written in every lineament of its structure, and purpose in every movement of the organism and of all its parts. Our attention has been riveted, however, upon merely the physical aspects. The intellectual is far more wonderful. When we reach the mind of man, we reach the pinnacle of all creation. It is the apex in the pyramid of values to be found in the universe. It is this which constitutes the dignity of man as a moral personality and makes him a being of surpassing worth.

It is in the processes of thinking, especially in abstract thinking, wherein the mind reaches the concept of what Plato calls "universals," such as truth, justice, right, stripped of all material notes or attributes, that we find the supreme evidence of plan, purpose and design. While the material universe, as disclosed to us by modern astronomy, is indeed marvelous in its order and staggering in its immensity, still more marvelous is the mind of man which no scale can measure, because it transcends the properties of matter and reaches into the world of spirit. How wonderful, indeed, is the mind of man which measures the girth of Betelgeux and weighs stars a million light years from our planet! There is the supreme evidence of design, and the crowning argument of God's existence.

Man is a microcosm, a small universe, in which are found the properties of the material world, of the vegetal and of the animal kingdoms, and of the spiritual world. He is a walking argument of God's existence, a moving advertisement of God's power, an articulate herald of God's intelligence. As man is the crowning work of God, so we affirm man is the supreme argument and the blinding evidence of God's existence. Well might we alter the famous syllogism of Descartes, "I think. Therefore, I am," to read: "I think. Therefore, God exists." For only in God do we find a suitable Cause for the mysterious power of human reason. Among all the objects in the visible universe, the mind of man sounds the loudest and the most eloquent note, proclaiming the existence of a Supreme Being, an Omniscient Mind, and an Infinite God, who is, in the words of St. Paul, "the Alpha and the Omega, the beginning and the end of all things."

With this, we conclude our presentation of evidence of plan, order, and design in the universe, demonstrating the existence of a Supreme Designer and an Infinite Lawmaker. In concluding, we thus summarize the line of reasoning running all through this discussion: The universe as a whole and all its parts are arranged with marvelous order and design. Now this order must be effected either by matter itself or by a cause outside of matter. Order, however, is the suitable arrangement of parts into a harmonious whole and requires intelligence. But matter itself is unintelligent. Therefore, the existence of order and design in the world demands the existence of an Intelligent Cause to produce it. But such an Intelligent Cause, external to the universe, and yet directing by His power and His all-encompassing laws the movement of every particle of matter in the universe, is what we mean by God. Therefore, God exists.

CHAPTER VIII

THE ORIGIN OF LIFE DEMANDS

Life, like a dome of many colored glass,
Stains the white radiance of Eternity.
SHELLEY, *Adonais*

A PROOF of God's existence may be drawn from the universally accepted findings of two different sciences. First, the science of biology affirms, as one of its most basic generalizations, that life comes only from pre-existing life. Since the historic experiments of Pasteur, the old theory of spontaneous generation has been universally discredited. "Under no circumstances whatever," declares the eminent botanist, Reinke, "can chemical and mechanical forces produce a living being."[1] J. W. N. Sullivan, recognized by scientists as a competent reporter of their work, states: "So far as science has gone at present, a mechanical explanation of life, has not been even approached."[2] Not less forceful are the words of Tyndall: "I affirm that no shred of trustworthy experimental testimony exists to prove that life in our day has ever appeared independently of antecedent life."[3]

Now the science of geology assures us that there was a time when the earth was a molten mass, so exceedingly hot that no form of life could possibly have existed thereon. The fossil remains of life first appear in the strata which were de-

[1] *Die Welt als Tat*, p. 315
[2] *Science: A New Outline*, p. 196
[3] Quoted by F. J. Koch, *A Manual of Apologetics*, p. 19

posited when more temperate conditions prevailed. In the igneous rocks the paleontologist can find no trace of living organisms. Science affirms likewise that life has been found on no other planet in the universe. Therefore, life must have been produced or created by a Living Cause, external to this universe. But such a living, supramundane Being is substantially what we mean by God. Therefore, God exists.

Here then is a demonstration which should appeal to all those who want to have their philosophical conclusions based upon the findings of science. This conclusion follows with inescapable necessity from the universally accepted findings of biology and geology. Nor can its validity be impaired by asserting that in previous epochs life sprang spontaneously from inorganic matter. There is not a shred of scientific evidence to support that hypothesis, and it is thoroughly unscientific to forge hypotheses unsupported by a scintilla of evidence.

The whole tendency of scientific thought is to affirm the constancy, the invariability and the universality of nature's laws. Furthermore, even if we grant the hypothesis that life emerged in past eons from inorganic matter, even though that be unsupported by a shred of evidence, we would still be forced to raise the query: What caused it to emerge from lifeless matter? Since blind chance or fortuity is ruled out by all reputable scientists, we are back again at our previous conclusion that life could have been originally produced only by a Living Cause, which is merely another name for what we mean by God.

CHAPTER IX

THE VOICE OF CONSCIENCE

There is a true law, right reason, consonant to nature, coextensive with the race of man, unchanging and eternal.—CICERO, *De Republica*

THE experience of all men and the literature of all races bear witness to the voice of conscience. Man is conscious of an inner voice that commands and forbids, that reproves and commends, that admonishes and entreats. No matter how hardened a criminal a man may be, he still hears echoes of that voice which he has persistently ignored. If his mind is not deranged, he cannot get beyond the range of that internal monitor. More potent than all the brass-buttoned policemen in the land is the restraining power of conscience. It warns the individual that evil must not be done, even though his deed would go undetected by an officer of the law. It takes ethical principles out of the abstract and applies them to the concrete tasks of life.

We define conscience as the practical judgment of reason concerning the rightness or wrongness of an act here and now to be performed. It is distinct from purely speculative judgments on ethical principles, and it is distinct from judgments in literary, scientific or artistic fields. It concerns the moral order, and relates to acts which we propose to perform. The conscience of all men tells them that good is to be done, evil is to be avoided.

While individuals, through faulty training, may err in the application of this universal moral principle to concrete cases, they still pay homage to the validity of that principle when they endeavor honestly to apply it. Hence, we say, they are in good faith. By this we mean that they are not acting wilfully contrary to the light as they see it, and hence are not culpable in the eyes of God or conscience.

They must endeavor, of course, to make their subjective perception of the moral order conform to the objective reality. This is the basic purpose of the science of ethics. To reach that goal, as every teacher of ethics knows, is a long haul. For man does not settle questions of right and wrong as easily as men differentiate sweet things from bitter simply by tasting them. "There is no authentic copy of the moral law," points out Joseph Rickaby, S.J., "printed, framed, and hung up by the hand of Nature, in the inner sanctuary of every human heart." [1] Just as man must study the principles of mechanics to construct a bridge, and the laws of health to promote his physical well-being, so he must study the principles of ethics and the art of applying them to changing conditions of life in order to make his subjective judgments mirror the eternal law of the Divine Lawgiver.

Basis of Argument

Hence we do not base our argument for God's existence upon the untenable assumption that conscience is a mystical faculty in the mind, independent of reason, as many writers seem to depict it, nor upon the equally untenable assumption that every pronouncement of conscience is an infallible echoing of the voice of God. We base it upon the fact that there is a moral order in the universe, mirrored in the stern commands of conscience to do what is right and to avoid what is wrong.

That sense of moral obligation is found in all the race, from the budding of reason to hoary old age. It sounds its com-

[1] *Moral Philosophy*, p. 145

mands in the ear of the peasant grubbing in the fields and penetrates through the stone walls of the royal mansion to echo its stern edict in the ear of the king. It is not confined to any degree of civilization, to any geographical area, or to any tribe or race of men. It is absolutely universal. Therefore, it reflects a universal moral order. But this moral order can be produced only by a great Moral Power whose nature is goodness and holiness. Otherwise, the effect would transcend the cause, and thus violate the basic law of logic that every effect must have an adequate cause. Therefore, God, the author of the universal moral order, exists.

While the sense of moral obligation is universal, the eyes of its perception can be sharpened by appropriate education, especially by ethical training. Ready obedience to the dictates of conscience makes one more sensitive to its whisperings, while disobedience blunts our moral sensitivity and renders us callous and neglectful. Even a lifetime of vice, however, does not completely stifle the dim whisperings of conscience.

St. Paul reflected this truth of the spiritual life when he said: "But the sensual man does not perceive the things that are of the Spirit of God, for it is foolishness to him, and he cannot understand, because it is examined spiritually." [2] The more one listens, the more clearly does he hear the delicate whisperings of conscience. "It never frightened a Puritan," observes Phillips Brooks, "when you bade him stand still and listen to the speech of God. His closet and his church were full of the reverberations of the awful, gracious, beautiful voice for which he listened." [3] If one is to recognize the voice of God, he must acquaint himself with God. This is a truth to which Cowper has given a noble expression: [4]

[2] 1 *Cor.* 2:14
[3] *The Seriousness of Life*, in a volume of his *Sermons*
[4] *The Task*, Bk. V

Acquaint thyself with God, if thou would'st taste
His works. Admitted once to his embrace,
Thou shalt perceive that thou wast blind before:
Thine eye shall be instructed; and thine heart
Made pure shall relish with divine delight
Till then unfelt, what hands divine have wrought.

This argument grows in force when we advert to the sanctions with which the ordinances of conscience are implemented. They are not like so many laws on our statute books, "dead letter laws," with no teeth to enforce them. They are not like the pious pronouncements of the League of Nations, with no world sheriff to put them into execution. The Author of the moral order and its ordinances, as apprehended by conscience, has implemented them with both subjective and objective sanctions.

Subjective Sanctions

The subjective sanctions are in the form of the approval of conscience for obeying the moral law, and of rebuke and remorse for having violated it. Is there any person in the world who has not felt at some time the joyous accolade of an approving conscience and the ceaseless scourging of a rebuking one? It is one of the most universal of all human experiences. This automatic response of conscience, acting independently of the praise or blame of others, steeling the martyr to face death with a smile, or scourging the tyrant on his gilded throne, has impressed such diverse minds as Pascal, Fenelon, Bossuet, Butler, Cardinal Newman and Kant as among the clearest of all the evidences of God's existence.

"There are two things which fill me with perennial delight," said Kant, "the starry heavens above my head and the moral law within my breast." Butler thus pays tribute to the supremacy of conscience: "Were its might equal to its right, it would rule the world."

The unconditional absolute, "Thou oughtest," spurning contemptuously the usual litany of *ifs* and *ands* and *buts* with which the weak-willed voluptuary vainly seeks to wheedle an unwarranted dispensation from conscience's stern command, gripped the minds of Kant and Newman with an unmistakable fascination, and spoke most forcefully and most eloquently to them of the Divine Ethician, the echo of whose thunder they detected in the still small voice whispering within their inner ear. Conscience cannot be cajoled. It cannot be bribed. It cannot be coerced. It cannot be silenced. It can be disobeyed. For man is a free agent. But it cannot be disobeyed with impunity. The thunder of its condemnation, the gnawings of its remorse, the stabbing of its outraged authority, are among the most vivid facts in human experience and among the strongest accents in all literature. Sometimes they shine most luminously when the effort is made to conceal them and echo most loudly when the effort is made to silence or deny them. Thus they reflect something of the magisterial dignity, the calm majesty and the transcendental qualities of the judgments of the Divine Ethician. Just as a shell picked up by the seaside and placed to the ear carries an echo of the mighty ocean from which it came, so conscience carries an echo of that mighty moral Power from whose creative hands it too has come.

The Categorical Imperative

To appreciate fully the cogency of this argument, it is necessary to penetrate to an understanding of the unique character of the commands of conscience. It is an unconditional, absolute mandate. Kant styled it in a fine phrase "the categorical imperative." The judgments of the speculative intellect are usually hedged around with conditions. Thus it may issue decisions decreeing: "Do this, if you want to get rich." "Do this, if you want to be popular." "Do this, if you want to be elected to office." They are dovetailed with conditions which the individual may accept or decline with impunity.

Not so, however, the commands of conscience. Once the conscience has decided that a proposed act is wrong, it thunders an unqualified prohibition: "Under no circumstances must you do this bad act. Neither the promise of riches, nor the assurance of popularity, nor the avoidance of the dungeon or of death itself will justify your doing this vicious deed. Even though the heavens fall, you must not do it." In conformity with that stern and unconditional ultimatum, heroes, saints, and martyrs in all ages have hurled defiance at cannon, sword and firing squad, and have faced death with a smile. It is in the categorical and unconditional character of the commands of conscience that one perceives with unmistakable clarity an echo of that universal moral order whose Author and Underwriter is God.

A Double Function

A careful investigation of the working of conscience discloses that it performs a double function. First it passes judgment upon the goodness or badness of a proposed act, then it issues a command that the act should or should not be performed. The first may be called the judgment. The latter may be termed the command. Because of bad uprearing, faulty moral training and other factors, the judgment may at times be wrong. But the command of conscience to do what the intellect apprehends as good and to avoid what it apprehends as bad is always to be obeyed. It is the immediate and proximate norm of conduct, as the mind of God is the ultimate and eternal norm.

In following the voice of conscience, one is always blameless in the sight of God. It is in this latter act of conscience, in its ruling that duty is to be done at all costs, and evil is to be avoided even though the heavens fall and the pillars of the universe collapse, and in the unswerving invariability of that ruling, that one perceives with great clarity a mirroring of the moral order of the universe, and detects with unfailing certainty an echo of the mandates of the Divine Ethician— the infinitely holy Author of the moral law.

The distinction we have made here is, we venture to assert, of vital importance to all who would understand how conscience bears witness to God. The failure to distinguish carefully between these two different operations of conscience, puts writers in the embarrassing position of asserting that conscience is the voice of God when it is demonstrable that the judicial act of conscience is clearly wrong and cannot be, therefore, the voice of God. It is only in the secondary act of conscience, *the command*, that we find an unfaltering and unerring invariability. The secondary act of conscience is the stern mandate that what is apprehended as good is to be done and what is apprehended as evil is to be avoided even at the cost of life itself. It is only in this latter decree that one can say there is reflected the voice of God.

It is in this secondary act of conscience that we discern most clearly the evidence of a Divine Ethician. Herein conscience bears witness to God. For not only does it issue its command with unbroken invariability to do the good and to avoid the evil, but it also implements its mandates, as we have pointed out, with appropriate sanctions. It not only commands, but it buttresses its mandates with the promise of joy and exultation upon the fulfillment of duty, and threatens the individual with inner castigation and gnawing remorse if he fail to do his duty.

It is in the quiet peace, joy and exultation of an approving conscience, and in the acute distress and biting remorse of a rebuking conscience that the face of God shines forth. Indeed many writers find in this phase of conscience the clearest testimony to God. It is upon this aspect of conscience that Cardinal Newman dwells at length, and with force and eloquence, in *The Grammar of Assent:* "No fear is felt," he writes, "by anyone who recognizes that his conduct has not been beautiful, though he may be mortified at himself, if perhaps he has thereby forfeited some advantage; but if he has been betrayed into any act of immorality, he has a lively sense of responsibility and guilt, though the act be no offense against society—of distress and apprehension, even though it may be of present service to him—of compunction and regret, though in itself it be most pleasurable—of confusion of face though it may have no witnesses. These various perturbations of mind, which are characteristic of a bad conscience, and may be very considerable self-reproach, poignant shame, haunting remorse, chill dismay at the prospect of the future —and their contraries when the conscience is good, as real though less forcible, self-approval, inward peace, lightness of heart, and the like—constitute a generic difference between conscience and our other intellectual senses." [5] It is in these subjective sanctions of conscience, it is to be noted, that Cardinal Newman finds the grounds for a *generic difference* between the operations of conscience and of the speculative intellect.

The cogency of this argument was recognized by the writers of classical antiquity. Many of them affirm the existence of a law, rooted in the very nature of man, immutable by any human power and universal in its binding force. No ruler, however absolute his sway, they declare, has the power of veto over the verdict of this inner court which derives its authority from God Himself. Lactantius has preserved for

[5] P. 105

us a passage from Cicero's lost work, *De Republica,* which will vie with the writings of any of our moderns in insight on this point. It runs as follows: "There is a true law, right reason, consonant to nature, coextensive with the race of man, unchanging and eternal. . . . It is not allowed us to make any alteration in that law: we may not take away any least portion of it: nor can we repeal it as a whole. Neither senate nor people have power to release us from our obligation in its regard. We need not search for some one to explain or interpret it. We shall not find one law at Rome, another at Athens: one now, another hereafter; but that law, one, everlasting and immutable, is binding on all races and at all times: and there is one common Master and Lord of all, God. He it is who drew up this law, determined its provisions, and promulgated it." [6]

Punishes and Rewards

Probably no secular writer has depicted with greater vividness the power of conscience to reward and to punish than has Shakespeare. After Cardinal Wolsey had fallen from the King's grace and had been stripped of all his honors, he bids "Farewell! a long farewell to all my greatness," and turns to the God he had neglected for the favor of his sovereign. In the sorrow for his misplaced loyalty and in the rededication of his services to the God who will not leave him naked to his enemies, Wolsey finds the whisperings of an approving conscience which bring him a quiet joy never felt when his security hinged upon the approval of his whimsical king. To Cromwell's question, "How does your Grace?" Wolsey replies in words vibrant with the experience of all humanity:

Why, well:
Never so truly happy, my good Cromwell.

[6] Cited in Lactantius, *Inst. Div.,* B.i, C. viii

> I know myself now; and I feel within me
> A peace above all earthly dignities,
> A still and quiet conscience.

Contrast this quiet joy with the thousand tongues which plague King Richard III for his butcheries, and sear his restless mind with the ceaseless cry of guilt:

> My conscience hath a thousand several tongues,
> And every tongue brings in a several tale,
> And every tale condemns me for a villain,
> Perjury, perjury, in the highest degree:
> Murder, stern murder, in the dir'st degree;
> All several sins, all us'd in each degree.
> Throng to the bar, crying all, "Guilty! guilty!"

The Bible abounds with passages descriptive of the power of conscience to reward and to punish, to mete out happiness or misery. Thus vividly does the author of the *Book of Proverbs* enumerate the blessings which flow from an approving conscience:

Then shalt thou walk confidently in thy way, and thy foot shall not stumble:

If thou sleep, thou shalt not fear: thou shalt rest, and thy sleep shall be sweet.

Be not afraid of sudden fear, nor of the power of the wicked falling upon thee.

For the Lord will be at thy side, and will keep thy foot that thou be not taken.

The evils which overwhelm the man who sins against the light of his own conscience are thus depicted with a great power of imagery in the mighty drama of *Job:*

"The wicked man is proud all his days, and the number of the years of his tyranny is uncertain. The sound of dread is always in his ears: and when there is peace, he always suspecteth treason. He believeth not that he may return from darkness to light, looking round about for the sword on every side. When he moveth himself to seek bread, he knoweth that the day of darkness is ready at his hand. Tribulation shall terrify him, and distress shall surround him, as a king that is prepared for the battle. For he hath stretched out his hand against God, and hath strengthened himself against the Almighty."

After the murder of his brother, Abel, Cain hid himself from the Almighty. But his conscience found him and avenged the murder, as conscience, regardless of the fallible ministrations of human officers, always does. It is the tribunal wherein God holds court with the human soul. His verdicts are written in shining glory or seared in scarlet letters upon the human mind. As Stanton A. Coblentz puts it,

> Man is himself the judgment-book: his deeds
> Leave a clear verdict, in a light or scar
> On his own mind, which flowers, droops or bleeds.
> For we are blessed or cursed by what we are.

Fidelity to conscience is one of the favorite themes of the New Testament. Its approval is to be sought at the cost of every pain and hardship. Its reprimand unleashes upon man a train of miseries far worse than the fury of the elements—the pensive music of a world out of tune. St. Paul traces his joy to the approving voice of conscience, a voice which echoes its refrain through all the books of the New Testament: "For our glory is this, the testimony of our conscience, that in simplicity of heart and sincerity of God, and not in carnal wisdom, but in the grace of God, we have conversed in this world."

Objective Sanctions

In addition to the subjective sanctions, the joy of an approving conscience and the remorse of a reproaching one, there are objective ones as well. These are external to the individual and are rooted in the moral order of the universe. Aside entirely from the rewards or punishments of one's own conscience, honesty is the best policy and brings the most fruit. The testimony of ten thousand convicts languishing in prison cells echoes the one refrain: "Crime does not pay." Here and there, a culprit may violate the laws of man and God, and escape for a time the lariat of the law. Sooner or later, however, it will close in on him and drag him from his hiding place. The long record of human history shows that the moral order of the universe is friendly to moral and spiritual values but is hostile to cruelty, vice and injustice. Truth, justice, mercy, love are self-authenticating. Tyranny, cruelty, injustice, hate are self-defeating.

The wages of sin are misery and death. The wages of virtue are happiness and life. It is true, however, that the wages of virtue are not always paid at five o'clock on Saturday afternoon. Their payment may be long postponed because of circumstances. Their ultimate delivery, however, is as certain as the dawning of day after the darkness of the night. The tyrant may burn the saint, the sage, and the hero at the martyr's stake, but the moral order of the universe cannot be frustrated by man. It stretches out into the long tomorrow to place the crown of victory upon all those who strive, even unto death, to obey

> The written and unchanging laws of heaven
> They are not of today or yesterday,
> But ever live and no one knows their birthtide.[7]

The marvelous organization of the world of matter and of life reveals to us the wisdom and the power of God, while the universal moral order, reflected in the voice of conscience, with its mighty sanctions for the autonomous enforcement

[7] *Antigone*, 454–456

of its commands, discloses to us His ineffable holiness. The direction of every proton and electron in the cells of a blade of grass, guiding them in the complex and baffling process of photosynthesis, would seem to have its counterpart in the intimate stirrings of conscience and in the aspirations that rise from the secret depths of the human soul and find their answering echoes in the heart of God. Thus we see that the world, as W. R. Inge has pointed out, "is a hymn sung by the creative Logos to the glory of God the Father. Its objects, so far as we can discern, are the manifestation of the nature of God under His three attributes of Wisdom, Beauty and Goodness." [8]

[8] "Confessio Fidei" in *Outspoken Essays*, p. 20

CHAPTER X

UNIVERSAL BELIEF OF MANKIND

Father of all! in ev'ry age,
In ev'ry clime adored,
By saint, by savage, and by sage,
Jehovah, Jove, or Lord!
POPE, *Universal Prayer*

HUMAN reason is fundamentally a trustworthy faculty. It is
the means by which we discriminate between truth and error.
It is the basic tool by which we have ferreted out the laws of
nature, discovered her sources of energy, and harnessed them
to do our bidding. It is the fundamental means by which we
have achieved our mastery of nature and reached our present
state of civilization. To impugn the reliability of man's intellect would mean, therefore, the repudiation of the findings
of modern science in which we take such glory and such
pride. You might as well ask a modern to deny his own existence as to deny either the verified discoveries of modern
science or the trustworthiness of the intellect by which those
truths were ascertained.

Now it is a fact abundantly established by historians and
anthropologists that mankind in all ages, in all countries and
in all stages of civilization has believed in the existence of a
Supreme Being. No matter whether the race or tribe was
civilized or uncivilized, whether it was in communication
with other races or whether it was isolated in the darkness
of an African jungle, we find the clear and unmistakable evi-

dence of the belief in a Ruler of the universe. True, individuals who doubted or denied the existence of such an Infinite Power can be found here and there. These are the exceptions, however, which prove the rule.

They are, moreover, so infinitesimally small in comparison with the overwhelming majority of mankind that they do not affect the moral unanimity of the judgment of the human race. Mankind in all ages has affirmed the existence of a Supreme Being. Can such a deep, universal conviction of the race be an illusion? If "fifty thousand Frenchmen can't be wrong," can all the race be wrong? If we have been endowed with reason to ascertain the truth, can the functioning of that reason in all mankind have served but to lead them to a gigantic conspiracy against the truth?

Could it have served but to mislead them in answering the most important question which the human mind is called upon to answer? To answer in the affirmative is to impugn the trustworthiness of the intellect to know the truth. It is to plunge the race into universal scepticism. But the facts discovered in science, the truths of philosophy, pounded out on the anvil of free discussion, and the general experience of mankind that our intellect is a light and not a darkness, preclude such a conclusion. Therefore, we are obliged to regard as valid the argument for God's existence that is drawn from the universal consent of mankind.

No Exceptions

Now let us look at the scope and sweep of that belief. In the light of the investigations of the past half century into the religious belief of primitive peoples, we can now confidently assert that no race has been found without a belief in a Supreme Being. Travelers have from time to time reported certain tribes to be devoid of such a belief. Closer investigation, however, by experts familiar with their language, and capable of penetrating the veil with which such beliefs are sometimes concealed from strangers, have invariably disclosed belief in a Supreme Power or Deity.

This question, formerly a subject of warm dispute, has now been relegated, as the competent authority, F. B. Jevons, writes, "to the limbo of dead controversies." [1] The findings of research workers approaching the problem from widely different points of view, such as Professor Tylor, Max Muller, Ratzel, de Quatrefages, Tiele, Waitz, Gerland, Peschel and, the greatest of them all, Father Wilhelm Schmidt of Vienna, are in agreement that no race, no matter how primitive, has been found without religious beliefs and practices. While many superstitious elements, such as animism, fetishism, totemism and magic, may be found in them, at the core of their religion will be found the belief in a Supreme Ruler of the universe.

As to the manner in which the different branches of the race first acquired the idea of God, we express no opinion. The long period of darkness, which preceded recorded history, and which has been penetrated only by a few pin-points of light, suggests to us the wisdom of suspending judgment on the various theories proposed in answer to this question. [2]

Idea of God

It is to be noted that an idea of God may exist, and be worthy of that name, even though it be inadequate and faulty. Thus mankind has always believed in the existence of the sun. Yet what strange conceptions of its nature have existed among the peoples of the past? What odd notions about it are to be found today not only among uncivilized

[1] *Introduction to the History of Religion*, p. 7
[2] Cf. W. Schmidt, *Origin and Growth of Religion* and G. H. Joyce, S.J., *Principles of Natural Theology*, p. 181

tribes but among highly civilized nations as well? Stop any
ten people passing you on the street in an American city, and
ask them how the sun gives heat and light to a planet 96,000,-
000 miles away. In all probability not a single one will come
within speaking distance of the scientific explanation of the
molecular action which enables the sun to send us its beneficent rays. How different are the popular conceptions from
the views held by astrophysicists. How greatly do they differ
even among themselves. Yet, would anyone be justified in
saying that the peoples of the world do not have in consequence a real idea of the sun? Not at all. A real idea of that
luminous body exists in the minds of all people, even though
they may not understand everything about its nature and its
operations. So it is with their conceptions of God.

It is not necessary that God be conceived as omnipotent,
omniscient or as Creator. It is sufficient that He be regarded
as the Supreme Being, to whom man owes homage and reverence. Much confusion and error may exist in regard to the
attributes of the Deity, and in regard to the manner of paying honor and homage, without invalidating a conception as
containing a true idea of the existence of a Supreme Being.
Plato and Socrates believed in the eternity of matter, and
held some erroneous notions about some of the attributes of
the Deity. Yet no informed person would deny that they
reached an exalted conception of God.

So, likewise, primitive peoples may possess a true idea of
the Deity, even though they have no notion of the universality of His providence or of the infinitude of His knowledge
and power. Nor is this conclusion in any way impaired by
the many superstitions, beliefs, and even revolting practices
which may be interwoven into their conception of the Deity
and into their crude efforts to acknowledge His sovereign
dominion over life and death. There have been, and there

still are, certain savage tribes which have been arrested in their development and have been subjected to long periods of degeneration.

It seems inevitable that their religious practices should be affected and colored by the deforming and degenerating conditions under which they lived—that myth and magic should spread like a fungus over their religious practices. "There are two currents," observes A. Lang, "the religious and the mythical, flowing together through religion. The former current, religious, even among very low savages, is pure from the magical, ghost-propitiating habit. The latter current, mythological, is full of magic, mummery and scandalous legend. Sometimes the latter stream quite pollutes the former, sometimes they flow side by side, perfectly distinguishable, as in Aztec ethical piety, compared with the bloody Aztec ritualism." [3]

The attention of travelers and of anthropologists has at times been so attracted by the gross superstitions and unusual rites which too frequently overlay the religion of primitives, that they have occasionally failed to penetrate to the central core—the belief in a Supreme Being who was to be reverenced and propitiated. Closer and more scientific investigation has invariably disclosed such a central belief. The results of recent investigations are aptly summed up in Hastings' *Encyclopedia of Religion and Ethics* as follows: [4] "Increasing research into the mental habits of the least advanced races of mankind now living tends to demonstrate that side by side with the most foolish, tedious, and often repulsive myths, there is almost invariably a high if vague conception of a good Being who is the Maker of all things, the undying Guardian of the moral life of man."

[3] *Making of Religion*, 2nd ed., p. 183
[4] *Article on Creation*

Testimony of Civilized Races

Coming now to the civilized races of the ancient world, we find the evidence of their belief in a Supreme Being so impressive as to be beyond all dispute. It is woven into their art and civilization and is found inscribed upon their monuments and tombs. Indeed, in visiting the Museum in Cairo, Egypt, wherein were exhibited the numerous objects excavated from the tomb of Tutankhamen, carrying us back to the dawn of civilization along the Nile, the writer was especially impressed with the numerous objects pointing to a belief in a Supreme Being.

Among the Babylonians the supreme deity was Marduk. Among the Romans, Jupiter was supreme; while among the Greeks, Zeus held the highest place. In the early Chinese writings, Shank Ti is represented as supreme. In the Iranian religion, Ahuramazda is the name given to the Supreme Being, while in the Vedic religion, the same deity is known as Varuna. In Egypt, the chief deity differed with the district, each locality representing its own god as supreme.

The universality of the belief in a Supreme Being among the ancient civilizations is authentically mirrored in the writings of Herodotus and Plutarch among the historians, of Aristotle, Plato, Cicero and Seneca among the philosophers, and of Homer, Hesiod, Virgil and Ovid among the poets. "If you traverse the earth," observes Plutarch, "you may find cities without walls, or literature, or laws, or fixed habitations, or coin. But a city destitute of temples and gods—a city that employeth not prayers and oracles, that offereth not sacrifice to obtain blessings and avert evil, no one has ever seen, or ever shall see." [5]

Similar is the testimony of Plato: "The earth, the sun and stars, and the universe itself, and the charming variety of the

[5] *Contra Coloten.*, C. XXXI

seasons, demonstrate the existence of a Divinity. Moreover, the barbarous nations unite with the Greeks in proclaiming this truth." Again he asserts: "No man has persisted from youth to old age in the opinion that there are no gods." [6]

Aristotle, "the master of those who know," sums up the case thus succinctly: "According to the avowal of the whole human race, God is the Cause and Principle of things." [7]

How weighty was this argument from universal belief to the ancient world is thus stated by Seneca: "We are accustomed to attach great importance to the universal belief of mankind. It is accepted by us as a convincing argument. That there are gods we infer from the sentiment engrafted in the human mind; nor has any nation ever been found, so far beyond the pale of law and civilization as to deny their existence." [8]

The following inscription on one of the most ancient monuments of the Egyptians bears eloquent witness to their belief in God:

Sovereign of life, health, and strength, Chief of the gods
We worship Thy Spirit who alone hast made us;
We whom Thou hast made, thank Thee, that Thou hast given
    us birth;
We give to Thee praises for Thy mercy towards us. [9]

We conclude our list of witnesses with the testimony of one of the foremost scientists of our day, Robert Andrews Millikan. Because of his wide acquaintance with the scientists and scholars in many fields, he is in a position to testify concerning contemporary thought on this subject. "I have never known," he declares, "a thinking man who did not believe in God. . . . Everyone who reflects at all believes, in one way

[6] *De Legibus*, Lib. XI
[7] *Metaphysics*, II, 11, 820
[8] *Epis.*, CXVII
[9] See Hoare's *Religion of the Ancient Egyptians*

or another, in God. . . . To me it is unthinkable that a real atheist should exist at all. . . . It seems to be as obvious as breathing that every man who is sufficiently in his senses to recognize his own inability to comprehend the problem of existence, to understand whence he came and whither he is going, must in the very admission of that ignorance and finiteness recognize the existence of a something, a Power, and Being in whom and because of whom he himself 'lives and moves and has his being.' That power, that something, that existence, we call God." [10]

To sum up: We have shown that the belief in a Supreme Being has existed among all races and all lands and in all ages and that it exists in the same universal manner among the peoples of the world today. But a belief so universal that it cannot be attributed to one nation or to a set of circumstances must be rooted in the realities of the objective world. Otherwise, the faculty of intellect, by which we discern truth from error, would be deceiving us and working a gigantic hoax upon all mankind. But such a conclusion would impair the validity of all knowledge and would plunge us into universal scepticism from which there could be no escape. Therefore, we are compelled to conclude that the belief of all mankind in a Supreme Being reflects the fundamental validity of the human mind to perceive truth and mirrors authentically the existence and the objective reality of God. Careful study of this line of reasoning will show that it is not a mere superficial attempt to determine truth by counting noses, but is based upon the fundamental validity of the human mind to know, and upon the recorded facts of human history. It is a valid and irrefutable proof of God's existence.

[10] World's Work, April, 1926, pp. 665, 666

CHAPTER XI

THE METAPHYSICAL ARGUMENT

Let the chain of second causes be ever so long, the first
link is always in God's hand.—GEORGE LAVINGTON

WE COME now to considerations of a metaphysical character
which demonstrate the existence of an infinitely perfect Being. While many persons are apt to be somewhat frightened
at the prospect of reasoning along metaphysical lines, and
to regard themselves as incapable of following the logic of
the argument, there can be no gainsaying that the arguments
from metaphysics are among the most valid and indestructible
of all the proofs of God's existence. They call, however, for
rigorous thinking and sustained attention. They are not so
popular as the arguments already presented. We would not
use the metaphysical argument in discussing the subject with
the untutored man-in-the-street.

After much debating with ourselves, we have decided to
present one of the metaphysical proofs. We have reached this
decision for three reasons. Firstly, there will be many of our
readers with philosophical training, to whom this line of reasoning will appeal with a finality and a conclusiveness more
categorical and absolute than in the other lines of evidence.
Secondly, we think that the person who carefully follows
the line of reasoning, even though he have no technical philosophic training, can appreciate its cogency.

Thirdly, we think that the presentation of the evidence of
God's existence would be lacking in that full, rounded bal-

ance at which we aim, and would be sadly incomplete, if we did not give our readers at least a glimpse into the serene stratosphere of thought wherein Plato and Aristotle, Augustine and Thomas Aquinas, and the mightiest intellects of the race, perceived the indestructible and inescapable evidence of the Absolute, the Eternal, and the Infinite Being whom we call God.

There are four historic metaphysical arguments. They are: (1) The cosmological argument—God as the First Cause; (2) the argument from contingency—God as Necessary Being; (3) the argument from motion—God as the Prime Mover; (4) the henological argument—God as the One and the Perfect. When we say they are metaphysical proofs, we mean that they flow directly from the primary principles of reason so that it is impossible to reject them without calling into question the validity of human reason itself. Moreover, our proof is drawn not from the working of physical law in the universe, nor from the nature of man as a moral agent, but simply from the nature of finite being as such. Any visible object in the universe is a finite being, and is capable of furnishing us with all the data for the reasoning which leads us at last to the one Necessary Being—God.

Argument from Contingency

We will present the argument from contingency. This is closely related to the cosmological argument, which is sometimes called the argument from efficient causation, and may indeed be more accurately described as the same proof viewed under a new aspect. Running through all the metaphysical arguments and through all the other arguments already presented, is the thread of causality. The principle that every effect must have an appropriate cause may be said to constitute the spinal column of all scientific reasoning and of all philosophic thinking as well. It is fundamental in all the lines of our reasoning concerning the existence of God.

Having taught this subject matter to university students for some thirty years, we are quite familiar with those aspects which present too abstract and lack-lustre a countenance to the student, and so we shall present illustrations which would not be necessary for professional philosophers. With a view of making the presentation as interesting and as effective as possible we shall throw it into the form of a discussion which we had with a university student of sceptical tendencies.

"Is it true, Herbert, that you have had some doubts about the existence of God?"

"Yes, too true. They have bitten into me, and they are unsettling me about many things. For, if I'm not sure about God, how can I be sure about the meaning of life or the end for which I should be striving?"

"You are quite logical, Herbert. Doubt about God is likely to paralyze your striving for altruism and nobility of life and make you grovelingly egocentric. Why die for an ideal, if there is no Power that sustains and underwrites that ideal, and will ultimately reward your self-sacrifice? Would I surprise you, however, if I were to tell you that everything in the universe proclaims the existence of God—not excepting your very act of doubting Him?"

"Do you mean that you can deduce the existence of God from the fact that I *doubt* His existence?"

"Yes, paradoxical as it may seem, that is precisely what I mean."

"Well, go ahead. But you'll surprise me all the more if you succeed in proving God's existence from such a strange starting point."

Be Logical

"All right. All I ask is that you be rigorously logical and that you admit whatever is logically implied in your premises."

"That's fair enough."

"In acknowledging that you doubt, you must admit all that is essential to doubt. By the essence of anything is meant that without which it could not exist. For example, the essence of water is H_2O. Whoever, therefore, admits the existence of water, *ipso facto*, or by that very act, admits the chemical compound, H_2O. To admit water and to deny H_2O is indeed an absurd procedure. Similarly, a circle is a figure in which every point of its circumference is equi-distant from its center. No one can admit the one and deny the other without involving himself in obvious absurdity. One cannot, therefore, admit the existence of anything and deny its essence without manifest contradiction. Is this clear so far, Herbert?"

"Crystal clear so far. Certainly no one could quarrel with anything you have said thus far. Go on."

"Splendid. Let me apply this now. If, as you admit, one cannot admit the existence of anything and deny its essence, then one cannot doubt the existence of God without admitting whatever is essential to this doubt. What then is essential to doubt? We may say at once that intelligence is essential to doubt or denial. One without intelligence can no more doubt or deny than he can believe or affirm. Whoever doubts the existence of God must, therefore, affirm the intelligence without which doubt or denial is impossible. Do you agree?"

Where Does This Get Us?

"Perfectly. What you say so far is beyond all question. But where does this get us?"

"I'll show you presently. For the same principle which you acknowledged in regard to doubt applies with equal rigor to intelligence. Having admitted intelligence, one must admit whatever is essential to intelligence under penalty of denying what has been affirmed. We now ask what is essential to intelligence? The answer is not far to seek. The intelligible is essential to intelligence. By intelligence we understand the power or faculty by which we know. Quite obviously, to know necessarily implies something to be known. If one knows at all, he must know something. He cannot know nothing. Knowledge, therefore, implies two things, the intelligent subject which knows, and the intelligible object which is known. Suppress either of these and you suppress the possibility of knowing. Whoever, therefore, doubts the existence of God, must admit the intelligible. Don't you agree, Herbert?"

"Certainly. But I'm still waiting for you to prove that God really exists."

"One step at a time, Herbert, and we are coming to that by single steps which are so clear that you will never fail to see the why of each step we take. Now the intelligible must be something or being. It cannot be nothing because nothing is unintelligible. Therefore, something or being is affirmed in the very act of doubt. But the something or being thus affirmed must be either contingent or necessary being."

Contingent Being Means What?

"But what do you mean by contingent being?"

"By contingent being, Herbert, is meant that which derives its existence from another. It can neither exist nor be intelligible without that upon which it depends. No matter how far we may be disposed to extend a series of contingent beings, even if, by impossible hypothesis, it were unto infinity, no one of them singly and no series of them can either exist or be intelligible without the being upon which they depend and without which they cannot exist."

An Infinite Series?

"But," interjected Herbert, his face lighting up, as though he saw a way of escape from the iron chain being forged around him, "why can't you account for your series of contingent beings by stretching the series out to infinity?"

"Well, Herbert, that assumption has been made by those who thus sought to escape from the being upon whom the series depends. Now while I do not really believe that the series either is or can be infinite, I am willing, for the sake of the argument, to grant your assumption. It will not long deflect us from the inevitable conclusion. For the point we are here making is that even though an infinite series of contingent beings were admitted, you have not decreased, but rather increased, the necessity of a being, on which they depend."

"Would you please illustrate this?"

"Yes, Herbert, gladly. An idiot is not a reasonable being. If you multiplied the number of idiots to a million, or to an infinite series, would they ever suffice to constitute one reasonable thing?"

"Of course not."

"Well, it would be as logical to suppose that an infinite series of idiots would constitute a reasonable being, as to suppose that an infinite series of contingent beings would constitute an uncontingent or necessary being."

"Capital. I'm beginning to see. The illustration helps mightily."

"Well, then, Herbert, here's another. Each link in a suspended chain is kept from falling only because it hangs on another. Now, if you stretch the chain to any length whatsoever, will that escape the need of some support to keep it from falling?"

"Obviously not. It would make it fall all the faster unless the support were proportionately strengthened."

Infinite Series—No Escape

"Right you are, Herbert. Yet it would be as logical to assume that by the mere expedient of multiplying the links in a suspended chain you could keep it from falling, as it would be to assume that by multiplying the series of contingent beings you could ever escape the necessity of coming ultimately to the uncontingent being upon whom the whole series, be it infinite or not, depends."

"Who said that reasoning along metaphysical lines was difficult to understand? Those illustrations make it so clear that even a child could understand the point you make."

"Thanks, Herbert. As this point is crucial, I shall clinch it once and for all with still another illustration. For if one clearly perceives that no manner of multiplying the number of contingent beings will ever yield a being of an altogether different nature, an uncontingent being, he will have no difficulty in grasping this entire metaphysical argument demonstrating clearly and unmistakably the existence of a necessary uncaused Being, which is the metaphysical description of God."

"Well, I'm eager for the third illustration. What is it?"

"Suppose you have a clock with five wheels driven by a spring. It is evident that the movement of the wheels is de-

pendent upon the spring, and is neither possible nor intelligent without that spring. Suppose now that you multiply the
wheels by a million, or by any number you please, or raise
the number to the n-th power, the movement of the wheels
would be neither possible nor intelligible unless the strength
of the spring were increased correspondingly. If, therefore,
it were possible to raise the number of wheels to infinity, it
would require an infinite force to set them in motion. Must
we not conclude then that an infinite series of contingent or
dependent beings, if such were possible, would demand an infinite, necessary being without which they could neither exist
nor be intelligible?"

"I don't see how anyone," said Herbert with enthusiasm,
"can escape from that conclusion. I see now that the breast-
works I threw up in the form of an assumption of an infinite
series of contingent beings has completely crumbled under
your reasoning, lit up by illustrations which allowed no vestige of obscurity to remain."

Necessary Being

"You'll make me blush, Herbert, if you're not more mod-
est in your praise. I hasten to assure you that the line of reasoning is not original with me, but has been forged out by
some of the most profound thinkers of the race. Now, let me
continue. From the existence of contingent being, or from
any such series of contingent beings, we are compelled, as
we have already seen, to demand the existence of a necessary
being which is dependent upon no other, which has the reason
of its being in itself, whose non-existence is therefore inconceivable, because that would be self-contradictory."

"Here then in brief," resumes Herbert, "are the links in
the chain of our reasoning so far: One cannot doubt the existence of God without affirming intelligence. But intelligence

necessarily implies the intelligible or being. Now being is either contingent or necessary. Contingent being, however, can neither exist nor be intelligible without necessary being. Therefore, it follows with all the inexorable force of logical necessity that whoever doubts the existence of God must implicitly affirm necessary being. But tell me now just how you get from necessary being to God. I'm anxious to see how you will get to God."

"That's the next step. We get to God by tracing out the inescapable, logical implications of necessary being. I call them inescapable because no man can escape what is logically contained in his affirmations and negations without abdicating his reason. The first conclusion which forces itself upon us is that necessary being is eternal. What is not eternal had a beginning. What had a beginning must have had some cause which brought it into existence. It cannot be the cause of its own existence. What does not exist cannot be a cause. Therefore, a being which is not eternal must owe its existence to some other being which is prior to it. But it is a simple contradiction in terms to say that a necessary being owes its existence to another being, for that would make it contingent, not necessary. Since, therefore, every being which is not eternal is contingent, we are compelled to conclude that the necessary being is eternal."

How Establish Infinite?

"Yes," said Herbert, "that conclusion follows logically enough. But isn't God also infinite? How do you establish that?"

"By a similar process of reasoning we are forced to conclude that the necessary being is infinite. It cannot be finite or limited. Whatever is limited must be limited either by itself or by another. But the necessary being can be limited in neither way. Therefore, it cannot be limited at all. It cannot be limited by itself. For to limit is to act. But action necessarily presupposes existence. What does not exist cannot act. Therefore, the existence of the necessary being is presupposed before any self-limiting action is possible or conceivable.

"Neither can the necessary being be limited by another. If, by impossible hypothesis, the necessary being should be limited by another, then unmistakably it would depend upon that other to make it what it is—a finite being. But a being which depends upon another is a contingent being, not a necessary being. Therefore, the necessary being cannot be limited by another. But beyond all shadow of doubt, a being which is limited neither by itself nor by another is not limited at all, and is infinite. Therefore, the necessary being is infinite. The same conclusion may be reached by other equally valid lines of reasoning, but the argument already advanced is sufficient to establish the point on a thoroughly demonstrative basis."

How Establish Infinitely Perfect?

"Yes, I see," said Herbert. "You have demonstrated that the necessary being, which is the metaphysician's name for God, is eternal and infinite. But isn't God all perfect? How do you establish that?"

"If the necessary being is infinite, then it must be perfect. It cannot be imperfect, because imperfection necessarily implies limitation of being. But limitation is so incompatible with the idea of the infinite that they are mutually contradictory and exclusive. Consequently, by its very nature, the infinite is and must be perfect. Since, as we have already shown, the necessary being is infinite, it follows at once that the necessary being is perfect."

"The links in your chain of reasoning are closing in around me. You have established the existence of a Being, necessary, eternal, infinite and perfect. But one more line remains to be forged. How can you prove that there can be only one such infinitely perfect Being, or only one God?"

"If the necessary being is infinitely perfect, then it must follow that it is one. For only one being is or can be infinitely perfect. If it be supposed that two infinitely perfect beings exist, then there must be something by which they are distinguished one from the other. Otherwise, they would be identical and therefore one, not two. Now that by which they are distinguished must be either a perfection or an imperfection. It cannot be an imperfection because that would contradict that which is supposed—an infinitely perfect being.

"For the same reason, the characteristic which distinguishes the one from the other cannot be a perfection. If one is distinguished from another by a perfection, then one must have a perfection which the other has not. It is manifestly impossible to suppose that the infinitely perfect is wanting in any perfection. Therefore, two infinitely perfect beings are impossible because such a concept is self-contradictory. The infinitely perfect being consequently can only be one. We arrive then, at last, at the existence of one necessary, eternal, infinite, perfect Being, which is what the metaphysician means by God."

"Well, for the life of me," said Herbert, "I do not see a single step you have taken in all this logical Odyssey which did not follow from the premises. It gives me a new and deeper respect for the marvelous faculty of reason which is able to trace a path from the analysis of any finite or contingent object in the world, such as a man, a rose, or a grain of sand, to the infinite Being from whose creative power the whole universe has come. It shows me that the marvels which scientists have achieved in the domain of matter have their counterpart in the wonderful structures of logical reasoning which philosophers have established in the realm of thought. They are not less worthy of our homage and respect."

Inexhaustible Being of God

"Thanks, Herbert. It has been a real pleasure. You deserve more credit for whatever has been achieved than you imagine. For an open mind and a willingness to recognize a point when one is made, are two of the greatest sources of stimulation which can be given to any teacher. Then, too, remember that this great edifice of logical thought, erected over the span of centuries, embodies the cumulative work of a mighty host of the most penetrating thinkers of the race. We acknowledge that the description given by the metaphysician, like that given by the scientist, the mathematician, the naturalist, the poet, is inadequate to mirror in halting, finite words the inexhaustible being of God. The description is accurate, however, as far as it goes.[1]

"Moreover, it gives us a clear and distinct idea of God because it enables us to distinguish God from every other being whatsoever. God, and God alone, can or does possess the attributes which have been enumerated. Furthermore, whatever other perfections can exist or be conceived must be ascribed to God, since He is an infinitely perfect being. Since, therefore, power, wisdom, mercy, justice, goodness, truth and beauty are perfections, they must all be found in God— the one, eternal, infinitely perfect Being in the universe."

[1] The author is indebted to his old colleague, Dr. W. J. Bergin, C.S.V., for many valuable suggestions in the formulation of this argument.

CHAPTER XII

CHRIST MANIFESTS GOD

*Thou art a true speaker, and teachest the way of God in
truth.—Matthew 22:16*

So MUCH then for the proofs of God's existence, fashioned
by human reason from the data of science and philosophy.
That they are convincing, we think, no one, who has followed this discussion with an open mind, can doubt.
Throughout the entire discussion, we have appealed to no
external authority, such as the Bible or the Church, but have
directed our appeal exclusively to the tribunal of human
reason. We frankly admit, however, that the knowledge of
God gained by the unaided intellect is meager, sketchy, and
without the richness which is supplied by divine revelation.
Where reason ends, revelation begins. Consequently it is the
part of wisdom to supplement our knowledge of God with
the penetrating insights and the richness of the revelation of
God supplied by the Bible.

Indeed, the best picture we can ever acquire of God is that
afforded us by the person of Jesus Christ, the untarnished
mirror of the Most High. "No one has at any time seen
God," declares St. John. "The only-begotten Son, who is
in the bosom of the Father, he has revealed him." [1] Uniting
in Himself the nature of man and the nature of God, Christ
gives us a better and a truer picture of God than can be

[1] *John* 1:18

95

found in the writings of all the philosophers, theologians, prophets and mystics since time began. God stands revealed to us in the character of Him who cleanses the lepers, heals the sick, restores sight to the blind, forgives the woman taken in adultery, washes the feet of His disciples, and sheds His blood for the redemption of mankind.

See Him as He walks over the dusty roadsides of Judea and Galilee and says to His disciples: "Learn of me, for I am meek and humble of heart." It was His ministry of mercy and love that inspired His disciple, St. John, to give the noblest definition of God ever uttered, when he said simply: "God is love." "If any one love me," said Christ, "he will keep my word, and my Father will love him, and we will come to him and make our abode with him."

God then is infinite Beauty, Truth, Goodness, Mercy, Love. It is this vision of God which has inspired the noblest enterprises of Christianity, built hospitals, orphanages, homes for the friendless, and has prompted man to find in the service of the poor and the lowly his title to nobility. When Christians have allowed this vision of a God of love to fade, and to be replaced by a God of vengeance, cruelty and wrath, they have stained the pages of history with some of the worst crimes in its long annals. It was this false picture which prompted John Calvin to burn his theological opponent, Michael Servetus, which caused the fanatics to kindle the fagots under Joan of Arc at Rouen, which stirred Torquemada to torture the heretics in Spain.

Rufus Jones tells of a little child who was being put to bed by his mother. After she had given him her good-night kiss, she turned out the light and started for the door. Suddenly the little child realized the loneliness and the darkness which he would be enduring.

"Am I to be left all alone, and in the dark, too?" he asked anxiously.

"Yes, my dear," replied the mother, "but you know you have God with you all the time."

"Yes, I know God is here," said the child, "but I want someone who has a face."

Such, too, is the anxious, wistful cry of all humanity. "We know in the abstract," observes Rufus Jones, "that God is Mind and Spirit and that He is near us, but we want to have a more vivid sense of His reality and His presence in our world, and above all, we want to *see* Him and to discover Him as a real Person with an actual Life and Character. It is *that* that Christ does for us. It is in Him that the Face is seen and the personal character is revealed." [2]

A Pure Heart

To know God, mere intellectual groping is not enough. More helpful in seeing God than intellectual subtlety is a pure heart and a clean conscience. When Ignatius, Bishop of Antioch, was being led to martyrdom, a Roman soldier asked him leeringly: "Who is this Christian God of yours?" Gazing into his sensual, brutal face, Ignatius replied: "You shall know him when you are worthy of him."

The person who suffers persecution for justice's sake, who sacrifices for truth, who hungers for righteousness, who lives a godly life, penetrates to the deepest understanding of God. Virtue is more important than knowledge in enriching one's vision of God. Live a holy life and God will dwell in you and make Himself known to you. "God's thoughts," observes George Macdonald, "His will, His love, His judgments are all man's home. To think His thoughts, to choose His will, to love His loves, to judge His judgments, and thus to know that He is in us, is to be at home."

When God dwells in the soul of a person, a radiance

[2] *Pathways to the Reality of God*, Macmillan, N.Y., 1931, p. 125

shines in his face, a spiritual resonance in his voice, and peace fills his heart. Nothing in the universe can supply the radiance lost when God is banished from a human life. The experience of humanity the world over verifies the finding of St. Theresa: "Where God is, there is Heaven. Where God is not, there is Hell." Plato too caught a glimmering of this mighty truth when he declared: "To escape from evil we must be made, as far as possible, like God; and this resemblance consists in becoming just, holy, and wise."

God, then, is the answer to the cry of the human soul for happiness. In the partial possession of God in this life, we catch glimmerings of that supreme ecstasy which the soul will experience when it shall be in intimate union with infinite Beauty, Truth, and Love, when the unveiled majesty of the eternal King shall ravish the soul with beauty and still its restless yearning with a love that knows no ending. "Eye hath not seen," says the great Apostle of the Gentiles, "nor hath ear heard, nor hath it entered into the heart of man, the joy that is prepared for those who love and serve Him." A foretaste of that ineffable bliss is experienced by all who walk in the paths of peace and righteousness, who keep always the joy of a good conscience, and who feel the immanence of God in their hearts by the radiance of a love that embraces all mankind.

Such a one can make his own the words which Henry VI addressed to Humphrey, Duke of Gloucester, after relieving him of his office of protector to the king, that he might find in God his sure defense:

> God shall be my hope,
> My stay, my guide, and lantern to my feet.[3]

[3] Shakespeare: *Henry VI*, Second Part, Act 2, Sc. 3

Nothing Ever Happens

While we have studied, with some care, a few objects to decipher thereon the handwriting of the Most High, the fact is that every object in the universe, from a speck of dust, a dandelion, a crawling ant, to the nebula so distant that it floats in the uncharted regions of cosmic space, proclaims the existence of a Supreme Being. Blades of grass are the handwriting of God and flowers are His capital letters. What would you think of the traveler who, standing on Inspiration Point above the Canyon of the Colorado River, gazes at all the beauties of nature spread out in profusion before him, yet sees no beauty. The gorgeous coloring of the mountain rock reflecting the sunsets of a thousand centuries, the vast expanse of grass and wild flowers that stretches like a verdant carpet through the valleys, the mighty ocean of pine and spruce tumbling over the mountain sides, the thousands of vari-colored birds making a symphony of music in the branches, the snow-covered peaks reaching up into the skies, produce no stirring of his imagination, no tug at his sense of awe, reverence and mystery.

Such a person cannot say with Browning: "A spark disturbs my clod." He should, however, utter the prayer of Stevenson: "Stab my spirit wide awake." For all the arguments of philosophers and theologians, written in all the volumes since printing began, seem wraithlike and anaemic in comparison with the blinding evidence which nature pours in upon the eye that is wide awake. Would you not say that such a man, though capable of physical vision, was mentally blind and spiritually dead?

Persons such as he, who look but do not see, are well depicted in the character of Otternschlag in Vicki Baum's *Grand Hotel*. Comedy, romance, tragedy are crammed into the scenes being enacted in the different rooms of that hotel. Just the night before, Kringelein, living on borrowed time and out for a last fling, commits suicide. Baron von Gaigern, caught pilfering in the room of the magnate, Preysing, is murdered. In the midst of all the alarums vexing the brow of the hotel manager, Senf, he learns that his wife is having a baby.

As the casket containing the body of the murdered Baron is being carried out the door, a wedding party with their peals of gleeful laughter drive up to the entrance. Lewis Stone, playing the role of Otternschlag, blasé, tired of life, and blind to all the colorful and moving drama being enacted before his very eyes, gazes upon the departing hearse and the disembarking bridal party with unseeing eyes, and flecking the ashes from his cigarette, remarks in a bored manner: "People come; people go. Nothing ever happens."

Such is he who gazes at all the marvelous beauties of nature, at all the blinding evidence of plan, order and design written in the handwriting of the Most High upon every particle of dust, upon every leaf of the tree, upon every flower and upon every star, and yet says: "I see no fingerprint of God, no evidence of a Supreme Designer." It was of a person of this blind and stupid type, of whom the Psalmist spoke: "The fool hath said in his heart: There is no God." The thousands of intervening years have produced, we think, no better characterization. For everyone who has eyes to see can say with the Psalmist: "The heavens show forth the glory of God, and the firmament declareth the work of His hands."

CHAPTER XIII

THE NATURE OF GOD

This is Eternal Life: that they may know Thee, the only true God.—John 17:3

FROM His footprints upon the earth and His handwriting upon the illuminated manuscript of the skies we have come to the knowledge of the Supreme Architect of the universe, almighty God. By a rigorous process of metaphysical reasoning, we have demonstrated that God is a Being infinitely perfect. The personality of the God-man, Jesus Christ, takes these qualities of perfection out of the blue of the skies and renders them incarnate before our very eyes. When we read of the mercy, tenderness, humility, compassion and love of Christ, Who with His dying breath utters a prayer for the pardon of His crucifiers, our hearts, like those of the Apostles who walked with Him to Emmaus, burn within us.

The homage of our minds and the love of our hearts go out to the divine Master who is the perfect Model for all mankind. In the measure in which we approximate His goodness and His love, do we rise in perfection. All who wish to know God and to grow into His image and likeness will do well, therefore, to study the character and the life of Christ as revealed to us in the Gospels.

We can further supplement that knowledge by availing ourselves of the revelation contained in the other books of the Bible. We can do this with logical propriety now, for we have already established the fact of God's existence from reason, science and philosophy. Because the picture which these latter give us, however, is somewhat blurred and wraith-like due to the limitations of the human mind, it is well for us to fill in that outline with the revelations which the inspired writers of the Old and of the New Testament give us.

The increased insight thus achieved will make God a more potent influence in our lives. He will become for us in very sooth the beginning and the end of all our striving. Our love will mount with our knowledge, and our loyalty with our love.

Language Falters

We begin our task by pointing out how feeble and inadequate is human language to express the inexhaustible riches and the infinite perfections of God. Words are but slender and fragile bridges upon which we carry from mind to mind the light cargo of human thought. Try to place upon them a heavier burden and they collapse. They are like footbridges made of trellised vines, scarcely able to support a single traveler together with his knapsack for the day's journey. Burden him with the equipment and provisions for a journey into a far country and you find that the trellised bridge groans and reels and is unable to support the added weight. So the language even of the inspired writers groans and staggers and is unable to bear fully the burden of divine revelation.

Perceiving this, the writer of Ecclesiasticus says significantly: "We shall say much, and yet shall want words"; but struggling bravely under his burden, he continues, "the sum of our words is: He is all."

Our difficulty is further increased by the finite character of the human mind in seeking to grapple with the infinite. For God is infinite in all His perfections. Thus does He outstrip in all directions the reaches of our limited understanding.

It is related that St. Augustine was walking along the shore, trying to comprehend the infinite nature of God. A little boy was digging a hole in the sand. Then filling his little pail with water from the sea, he poured it into the hole.

"What are you trying to do, my child?" inquired the saint.

"I'm trying to empty the ocean into this hole," replied the child.

"You can't do that. The ocean is much too big to be put into such a tiny hole."

"Neither can you with a finite mind comprehend the infinite," answered the child, who was thus revealed as an angel sent by God to teach St. Augustine this fundamental truth. Whether the incident be legendary or not, the lesson it teaches is authentic and all-important.

While we can attain only a fragmentary knowledge of God, even that fragment is of supreme importance and practical value. The least knowledge of the highest things, observed Aristotle thousands of years ago, far transcends in value the most detailed knowledge of the lowest things. God is the highest in the scale of value. He is the *Summum Bonum*, the highest good, the supreme truth, infinite beauty, unutterable love. Even a partial knowledge of Him is the pearl that passeth all price. Realizing then the inadequacy of language and the limitations of the human mind, we begin humbly and reverently to try to peer even a little way into the infinite perfections of God.

The Infinitude of God

God is revealed to us as a spirit, all-wise, all-powerful, eternal and omnipresent. "God is a Spirit," says our Lord, "and they that adore Him, must adore Him in spirit and in truth." God is a *simple* Spirit. By this we mean that His divine nature is not composed of parts and in it are no unrealized potentialities. For only that which is material has parts, and God is immaterial. Furthermore there is no combination of being and attributes, such as exist in creatures. The divine nature is one and the same with its attributes. Thus God *is* what He *has*, i.e., He *is* life, beauty, goodness, love. In man these qualities exist in a fragmentary and partial manner. In God they exist in their plenitude.

The infinitude of God surpasses the finite understanding of man. "The things that are of God," says St. Paul, "no man knoweth, but the Spirit of God." [1] "We know in part," the Apostle tells us, "and we prophesy in part." [2] "It is impossible," declared St. Augustine, "thoroughly to grasp and comprehend God, for couldst thou comprehend Him, He would not be God." [3]

Since the mind of man is incapable of comprehending fully God's infinity, it is likewise incapable of devising a name to express His greatness. Hence God is said to be *ineffable*. Whatever name be used for God is inadequate, since it designates only one aspect of His divine being. The most sacred and significant name used by the ancient Hebrews is Jahve, meaning being. Something of the eternal being of God is reflected in the answer given to Moses who asked God to tell him His name. "*I am who am*," replied God. "Thou shalt say to the children of Israel: He who is hath sent me to you." [4] Unlike our existence, which is a series of consecutive states, God's is a perpetual *now*. "Before Abraham was made, I am." [5]

[1] 2 *Cor.* 2:11
[2] 1 *Cor.* 13:9
[3] *Serm.* 41, de V.D.
[4] *Exod.* 3:14
[5] *John* 8:58

Time and Eternity—What?

What is time? What is eternity? These are both difficult questions. Philosophers have long struggled to ascertain the essential nature of time. Yet probably none of them would claim to have penetrated to the core of its being. We get some inkling of its nature when we think of it as a way to measure motion. Thus the measure of the earth's motion on its axis around the sun is the universally accepted time we use as a measure for every other motion. This motion is comparatively stable. It is continuous and, like all motion, successive.

Hence we divide it up into days, months, years and into hours, minutes, seconds and fractions of a second. It is these latter measures of motion which our watches indicate with their hour, minute and second hands. While the astronomer encounters many motions far faster than that of the earth, he measures them in terms of the earth's motions.

Were it not for motion, we would have no idea of time. A man, sound asleep, is unconscious of the passing of time. On the other hand, a person tossing sleeplessly on his bed, hears the clock strike every quarter and wonders why the seconds move with feet of lead. How interminable does a minute seem to a basketball team struggling to protect a narrow lead, while the opponents have possession of the ball. They are acutely conscious of the slow passing of the time because they are acutely conscious of every movement of their opponents, fraught, as it is, with danger to them.

Let us scrutinize now more closely the relation between time and motion. Here is a football player who has broken loose for a long run, speeding with the ball from the fifty-yard mark down toward the goal line. He is now at the twenty-five yard mark. The motion of his legs that *has* carried him there no longer exists. The motion that *will* carry him to the goal does not yet exist. What does exist? Only the motion that occurs on that twenty-five yard line, speeding him from there to a point one step ahead.

So it is with time. The past exists no more. The future is not yet born. All the reality of time, philosophers tell us, is found in the present moment, the "flowing now," the present instant that bridges the past and the future. The fundamental reason why this is so is because change cannot take place in an instant. Like the feet of the football player, moving one after the other toward the goal, change has parts which come one after the other in regular succession.

This succession of steps, characteristic of time and of human life, does not apply to God, to Whom the whole of existence is the eternal present. Hence eternity is defined by Boethius as "the simultaneously whole and perfect possession of interminable life." More briefly it has been described as the "*now* standing," in contrast to the "*now* flowing" which is the nature of time.[6] Man achieves a measure of perfection through a succession of actions, living his life piecemeal, second by second. God, however, has always possessed the complete perfection of His infinite Being. Eternity is not something external to God, whereby we measure His duration. It is inherent in the nature of an infinitely perfect Being.

Not only is God eternal, without beginning and without end, but He is also *immutable*. By this we mean that the infinitely perfect Being undergoes no change. For any change involves either increase or diminution which would be impossible in a Being possessing every perfection in its fulness. "With God," says St. James, "there is no change nor shadow of alteration."[7]

[6] The statement of Boethius, which has become a classic, is: *Nunc fluens facit tempus; nunc stans facit aeternitatem.* It is a model of conciseness and brevity.
[7] James 1:17

God is likewise *immense* or immeasurable. By this we mean that He has no limitations in space. God does not merely exist in the universe and with it, but also beyond and above it. This is the truth which Solomon expressed at the dedication of the Temple: "If heaven and the heaven of heavens cannot contain Thee, how much less this house which I have built!" [8]

The attributes of God's being or existence are then *eternity*, *immutability*, *immensity*, and *ubiquity*. In reality these perfections are identical with the divine essence. The limitations of our human intelligence, however, prevent us from understanding how these attributes or qualities constitute in God a unified essence. Yielding to that limitation we undertake to consider these attributes separately. We have already *discussed* the first three.

We come now to a consideration of God's ubiquity or omnipresence. As this consideration is, we think, of enormous practical importance and furnishes strong motives for rectitude of conduct in all the changing circumstances of human life, we propose to treat it at some length.

God is *omnipresent*. By this we mean that He is everywhere, in heaven, on earth, and in every place. God is present everywhere in three ways: by His essence, by His knowledge, and by His superintending power.

Present by His Essence

God must be present wherever His action is because He is a being of such infinite perfection that His substance and His action are one and the same. God's action extends throughout the universe, governing the fall of the raindrop and the swing of the farthest star. As the wind is present with the ship which it propels, so God is present with every

[8] 3 *Kings* 8:27

creature, holding it in existence by His conserving power. The relation of a mover to motion, of fire to heat, is not more intimate than God's relation to everything that exists. Well does St. Luke declare: "In Him we live and move and have our being." [9] Just as our soul permeates our whole body, so does God pervade the entire vast universe.

Herein we perceive an essential difference between a human architect and the divine Architect. When an edifice is completed, it stands without the aid of the builder. The works of God, however, continue to lean upon Him for support. Unable to subsist without Him, they depend upon Him as much for their conservation as they did for their creation. As a glass bulb, held in my upraised hand, would, if I withdraw my hand, fall helplessly to the floor and break into fragments, so every creature brought into being by the creative power of God would, if He withdrew His conserving power, fall into the abyss of nothingness.

Look up at the star-studded sky and realize that God is there. Look through the telescope into the vastness of interstellar space until you discern stars so dim in the far distance that they eluded your naked eyes, and realize that God is there. Descend with the diver into the ocean depths and there too you will find God. Peer with the eyes of science into the mysterious depths of a molecule of matter, and amidst the whirling of protons and electrons in their unplumbed orbits, you will find God. In the sublime words of Isaias, "Thus saith the Lord: Heaven is my throne, and the earth my footstool." [10]

While God fills all space, He is circumscribed by none. He is not dismembered nor divided. He is not partly here and partly there, but entire everywhere throughout the universe. "He is higher," says Job, "than heaven. He is deeper

[9] *Acts* 17:28
[10] *Isaias* 66:1

than hell. The measure of Him is longer than the earth, and broader than the sea." [11]

What a source of comfort and of strength is it for us to realize that God is present always and everywhere. Nature abhors a vacuum and the human heart dreads loneliness. It shrinks from the thought of being imprisoned in a solitary cell of matter, with no mind to know its hunger, and no heart to beat in unison with its throbbing. God is the answer to the cry of every heart for companionship and life and love. For God is present with us wherever we go. If we mount on the wings of an airplane high into the fleecy sky, God is there. If our labor takes us down into the inky blackness of a mine to dig coal from the bowels of the earth, God is there. He envelops the chair upon which we sit. He dwells within our throbbing heart. He interpenetrates our very being with His Divine Presence more completely than water penetrates a sponge. He envelops us more thoroughly than the waters of the sea its finny denizens, more intimately than the air surrounds the bird in its flight. The Apostle crowds this spacious truth into brief compass when he says: "In Him we live and move and have our being."

Present by His Knowledge

God is present with us not only by His essence, but also by His omniscient intelligence which extends to the movement of the farthest star, to the fall of every leaf from its tree, and to the stirring of every living creature. Since God is infinitely perfect, He must possess omniscience—all knowledge. If there were anything which God did not know, no matter how small or how hidden, His knowledge would be only finite. But God is infinite in every respect, in His power, in His righteousness, and in His knowledge.

[11] *Job* 11:8, 9

We can get some glimmering of how God can be present by His knowledge from our own experience in listening to the radio. When we tune in to a symphony concert, and secure from the broadcaster a vivid picture of the opera hall, the musicians, the audience and then listen to the music, we feel that we are present. We know all that is occurring there. We hear the great melodies of music from their gentle beginnings to their soaring and roaring climaxes. So too when we listen to a speech, a drama, a baseball game, we have such detailed knowledge, simultaneous with the event being broadcast, that we feel we are present.

Indeed, listening to a radio while undergoing an exciting experience elsewhere gives one the sensation of enjoying the power of bilocation—of being in two different places at the same time. This was the writer's experience in flying in a plane traveling 150 miles an hour over the English Channel. Down below were throngs of ships looking like large splinters on a glassy surface, with the English coast just appearing on the horizon. With the plane soaring through the heavens at tremendous speed, battling head winds and gusts of storm, suddenly the pilot slipped over my ears the head-phone of a radio.

In came the soft melodious voice of a concert singer from the Opera House in Vienna. It was so clear that I felt as though I were present in that audience. Here I was with the shores of France fading and the green fields of England coming into my view, while the scene in the Vienna Opera House was equally vivid and clear. Thus did I seem to be present at both places, in spite of their distance, through the knowledge that was coming through my different senses of sight and hearing. If man with his limited knowledge can thus achieve a sense of being present simultaneously in different places, how much more easily can an infinite God,

Who knows the smallest detail of every happening, achieve through such knowledge a presence throughout the universe.

The Eternal Present

The past, the present, and the future are all spread out before God, like a vast panorama. He sees them all, as it were, in one view. Strictly speaking, there is no past or future to God. He lives in the eternal present. The division of time into successive moments of duration is necessitated by the finite character of the human mind. But God's eternal knowledge, evident from His infinity, excludes successive moments, excludes past and future. For succession necessarily involves a loss and a gain, the abandoning of one moment's experience for that of the next succeeding moment. But the infinite can experience no increase or diminution, no loss or gain.

As every aspect of the infinite surpasses the capacity of man's finite mind thoroughly to understand, so God's infinite and eternal knowledge stretches beyond man's complete comprehension. An illustration or two, however, will help. The explorer, climbing up the stately Jungfrau, sees one side of the mountain at a time. As he crosses over to a different side he perceives new contours, new vistas of its massive bulk, towering up into the Swiss skies. If he were, however, in an airplane poised high above it, he could with a single glance perceive the snow-crowned summit, and all its sides stretching down to the lower earth. The mighty vista he is able to secure from his exceptional vantage point helps us to get at least a glimmering of the all-embracing vision of God.

Let us take another illustration. Two great football teams, unbeaten and untied, meet to decide the question of supremacy. Battling with fury, desperation and abandon, they send alternate fevers of hope and chills of fear, thrills of joy and pangs of dismay, into the vast crowd of spectators. For about two hours they hold the spectators breathless and spell-bound. The battle is filmed.

Now suppose that instead of a few feet of the film being thrown on the screen, all of it were thrown simultaneously on a tremendously wide screen. If our vision were adequate, we would see the final play simultaneously with the opening kick-off. This will help us to see how an infinite and omniscient God perceives all things, not in a succession of moments but in a single eternal *now*. It is well to keep in mind God's reply to Moses: "*I am who am.*" Thus did God bring out the sublime truth that with Him there is no succession of time, that He lives and sees and knows in the eternal present.

God's Knowledge and Human Freedom

Consequently it is inaccurate and misleading to speak of God's *foreknowledge*. God does not foreknow. He knows. Difficulties which are based upon the use of such a misleading term fall to the ground when we remove this incorrect term when referring to the eternal and infinite knowledge of God. True, the term may be employed in discussing the matter in a popular manner with people untrained in metaphysical reasoning. Care should be taken, however, to point out that it is merely an accommodation to our customary way of speaking and to the limitations of our finite mind and that any difficulties arising from such usage are merely verbal difficulties, and do not flow from the operations of the divine powers or attributes when properly stated.

Such a difficulty is the one raised in connection with God's knowledge and the free actions of man. If one speaks of God *foreknowing* the actions of man, the implication may be unwittingly conveyed that such actions are foreordained and necessary and that free will plays no part. The difficulty collapses, however, when we remove the misleading term, *foreknow*, and point out that God does not foreknow. He knows. Thus God's knowledge may be viewed as a mirror of the free actions of man.

As I look out of my window, I see students playing tennis. They are playing because they want to play. My knowledge of their actions is not the cause, but the result of the exercise of their free will in the manner described. So may God's knowledge of all the actions of humanity be said to be.

This is the solution given by some of the greatest Christian thinkers to the objection of infidels. "Things do not happen," declared Origen back in the third century, "because God foresees them in the distant future; but because they will happen, God knows them before they happen." Similar is the observation of St. Jerome in the fifth century: "Not because God knows that something will happen, must it therefore happen. But God, knowing the future, foresees it, because it is to happen." [12] We cannot point out too often that what we call past and future stand before God as the eternal present.

If you ask us how God knows all things in the perpetual now, we answer: We don't know. God is infinite, and no finite mind can comprehend the infinite. Otherwise it would not be finite. Our inability thoroughly to understand *how* God knows presents no difficulty to our acceptance of the *fact* of God's infinite and eternal knowledge. We do not know *how* a blade of grass grows, yet we experience no difficulty in accepting the fact that it does grow. If we meet

[12] *Christian Apologetics*, Devivier-Sasia, vol. I, p. 84 f., J. Wagner, N.Y., 1924

with mysteries wherever our eyes fall upon finite things, why should we not be prepared to meet with mysteries when we are dealing with the infinite?

Practical Implications

Our reverence and awe are deepened when we reflect upon the all-embracing knowledge and the infinite wisdom of God. "He telleth the number of the stars," says the Psalmist, "and calleth them all by their names." [13] There is not a star whirling its lonely way in the outermost stretch of cosmic space, not a bird winging its way across the trackless sky, not a blade of grass in the verdant carpets of the Western prairies, not a fish in the ocean's depths, not an insect burrowing its way in the bowels of the earth, not a grain of sand on the sea-shore, not an electron whirling in the unplumbed depths of a tiny atom, that escapes the all-seeing eye of God. Even "the very hairs of your head," says St. Matthew, "are all numbered." [14]

How impossible it is to hide our thoughts or our deeds from the all-seeing eye of God. We may escape detection from the eyes of neighbors, and even from the prying eyes of officers of the law. But the deeds done in secret are as the pages of an open book to the eyes of God. "Shall a man lie hid in secret places and I not see him, saith the Lord." [15] Similarly says St. Paul: "There is no creature invisible in His sight; but all things are naked and open to His eyes." [16] "The eyes of the Lord," says the author of the book of Proverbs, "in every place behold good and evil." [17]

The utter futility of trying to escape from the all-encom-

[13] Psal. 146:4
[14] Mat. 10:30
[15] Jer. 23:24
[16] Heb. 4:13
[17] Proverbs 15:3

passing vision of God is told with moving eloquence by the Royal Prophet: "Lord, Thou hast known my sitting down and my rising up. Thou hast understood my thoughts afar off, my path and my line thou hast searched out. And thou hast foreseen all my ways. . . . Behold, O, Lord, thou hast known all things, the last and those of old . . . thy knowledge is become wonderful to me; it is high, and I cannot reach to it. Whither shall I go from thy Spirit? or whither shall I flee from thy face? If I ascend into heaven, thou art present. If I take my wings in the morning and dwell in the uttermost part of the sea, even there also shall thy hand lead me, and thy right hand shall hold me." [18]

Every law-maker as well as every student of human behavior realizes the importance of establishing proper *sanctions*, in the form of rewards and penalties, to secure the observance of laws. Without such teeth to enforce them, laws are scarcely worth the paper they are written on. What a magnificent sanction for the observance of the moral law is found in the fact that not merely a minor official but the Supreme Legislator Himself perceives every observance as well as every violation, and will mete out reward or punishment according to one's deserts. Here is a sanction which is worth more than all the skilled operatives in the F.B.I. and more than all the brass-buttoned policemen in all our cities.

This is the sanction which the inspired author of *Ecclesiasticus* brings out so clearly. He pictures the sinner saying to himself: "Who seeth me? Darkness compasseth me about, and the walls cover me, and no man seeth me: whom do I fear? The Most High will not remember my sins. And he understandeth not that His eye seeth all things, . . . and he knoweth not that the eyes of the Lord are far brighter than the sun, beholding round about all the ways of men and the bottom of the deep, and looking into the hearts of men,

[18] *Psal.* 138:1–10

into the most hidden parts. For all things were known to the Lord God before they were created: so also after they were perfected, He beholdeth all things." [19] The person tempted to sin would do well to reflect upon these words of the sacred writer. For surely the inclination to violate an ordinance of the Most High will speedily vanish if one realizes that the eyes of God are upon him and His hands are already fashioning the sinner's deserts.

Present by His Power

God is present everywhere not only by His essence, not only by His infinite knowledge, but also by His *superintending power*. Just as the soul pervades the body and is necessary for every movement I make, so God's concurring power is necessary for every move I make, for every word I utter, and for every thought I think. Just as God brought us into existence out of the yawning abyss of nothingness by His creative power, so He sustains us in existence by His conserving power. Were God to withdraw His sustaining hand from us for one instant, we would fall back into the nothingness from which we came. God is as necessary for our life as the air we breathe.

While God is present throughout the whole universe by His essence, knowledge and power, He is present in the chosen members of the human family in a still more intimate manner. The prophet Jeremias tells of this mysterious indwelling of God: [20] "Behold the days shall come, saith the Lord, and I will make a new covenant with the house of Israel and with the house of Juda: not according to the covenant which I made with their fathers. . . . But this shall be the covenant that I shall make with the house of

[19] *Ecclus.* 23:25-29
[20] *Jer.* 31:31-33

Israel: I will give my law in their bowels, and I will write it in their heart: and I will be their God, and they shall be my people."

Present in Intimate Manner

In the tabernacle of every faithful and devout soul God dwells in a particular manner. Attentive indeed are His ears to the prayers of him who communes with Him within this living temple. It is of this divine Presence that St. Paul writes to the Corinthians: "Know ye not that you are the temple of God, and that the Spirit of God dwelleth in you? But if any man violate the temple of God, him shall God destroy. For the temple of God is holy, which you are." [21] With Tennyson can the devout soul say:

> Speak to Him, thou, for He hears, and Spirit
> with Spirit can meet ——
> Closer is He than breathing, and nearer
> than hands and feet.

God is present in an especially intimate manner in the soul that is filled with the love of God. Such a person is fulfilling the great commandment, in which are contained all the laws and the prophets. "If any one love me," said Jesus, "my Father will love him, and we will make our abode with him." [22] It was in this manner that God abode with Abraham, Isaac, and Jacob; with Moses, Josue, and David; with the prophets, Apostles, and martyrs; and with all the holy souls who clung to Him in deeds of righteousness, in prayer, and in acts of love. God and one constitute a majority. When God is with one, he need fear no power in heaven, on earth, or under the earth.

The realization of the intimate presence of God in the

[21] I *Cor.* 3:16
[22] *John* 14:23

souls of those who love and serve Him is a powerful bulwark against temptation and an incentive to strive constantly to make one's soul a more fitting habitation for the Most High. For this reason there are few exercises of the spiritual life more profitable than that of the practice of the presence of God, the constant recollection, even if only subconscious, of the indwelling of our Maker, our best Friend, and our ultimate Judge. When we forget about God, and turn our backs upon Him, then danger stares us in the face.

Creatures can at times take on such a garb of attractiveness that, almost before we realize it, we find our hands stretching out to possess them. The experience of the race, sad and tragic as it is, shows us, however, that they are like Dead Sea apples that crumble at the touch. They do not yield the promised joy but only boredom, nausea and remorse. We shall be spared from learning by the costly method of painful experience, if we remember the all-important fact of God's presence. Thus sin becomes an offense not to a distant Being in the far-off firmament, but an insult to One present within us. Is it likely that an individual will deliberately insult a friend in his very presence?

Cannot Flee from God

Furthermore one cannot flee from God's presence, even if he would. He may separate from His friendship but not from His presence. Even though guilty, He must still face His maker and His Judge. What experience in life is more embarrassing and painful than that of facing a friend with whom you have not kept faith? What gnaws more deeply into the marrow of your being than the agony which comes from the realization that you have shattered the high ideals that he has held of you. The shame you experience is hotter than a red-hot iron, more piercing than a serpent's tooth. How can one escape that bitter humiliation, that cup of gall, if one fails to keep faith with his Lord and Master Who has deigned to make His abode within the individual's heart and soul?

The realization of God's abiding presence is helpful not only in resisting temptation but also in bearing with patience and even with joy the hardships and the pains which life in this valley of the shadow of death inevitably brings. Is it not easier to bear sickness and pain when we know that we are in the presence of friends, doctors and nurses who will not fail to do all in their power to help us? So likewise the consciousness of the presence of our best Friend will not fail to give us strength to carry our burden and to bear our suffering with patience and resignation.

God will not fail to make each moment of pain bear its rich fruition in the ineffable joys of life everlasting. Such tribulation as He permits to fall upon us is but the "shade of His hand outstretched caressingly." In all the vicissitudes of life, in times of joy, temptation, or suffering, the consciousness of the presence of God will not fail to give us the humility, the protection, and the strength of which we stand in need.

We have presented at some length the truth of God's abiding presence throughout the universe and throughout the whole of human life. We have done so because a realization of this important truth is bound to exercise an enormous influence in our lives. "The more we are penetrated with this thought," observes Cardinal Gibbons, "the more perfectly shall we possess interior freedom, indifference to human judgment, and a habitual disposition to rectitude of conduct." [23]

When my students at Notre Dame came to me to say "Good-bye," before being sent to the far-flung battle fronts

[23] Cardinal Gibbons, *Our Christian Heritage*, J. Murphy Co., p. 70

of World War II, I could think of no truth more comforting to propose to them than that of the constant presence of God.

"Remember," I have been accustomed to say, "whether you are sent to the Solomon Islands in the South Pacific, or to the Aleutians in the far North, to Tunisia or to any of the countries of Europe; whether you are assigned to a submarine to prowl in the depths of the sea, or to an airplane to wing your way through the trackless skies, or to be encased in a mighty iron tank to penetrate to areas where no other vehicle could travel, remember that God is with you wherever you go."

It has not always been easy for youth to leave home and friends and native lands to go out to face death in all its hideous forms in the far corners of the world. But what, perhaps more than anything else, nerved them for the difficult task which their country asked of them, was the realization that *God went with them all the way*. It is a truth, as helpful as it is comforting, for old and young. To clasp the outstretched hand of God in all our gropings and wanderings is to find a sure and a safe road.

Omniscience and Omnipotence

Thus far we have presented the principal attributes of God's being or existence. Now for a brief word about those belonging to His knowledge and to His will.

The attributes belonging to God's knowledge are *omniscience* and *wisdom*. By omniscience, we mean that God knows everything perfectly and has known it for all eternity. The past and the future, as we have already pointed out, stand before God as in the living present. God is also all-wise. By this we mean that He knows how to dispose everything so as best to accomplish what He wills. Wisdom in creatures is different from knowledge. Knowledge may consist of mere information. Wisdom is the ability to use that information to the best advantage.

The knowledge then of all that is contained in all the encyclopedias and libraries in the world would not necessarily indicate that such a man is wise. He might not know how to use such encyclopedic knowledge. In God, however, knowledge and wisdom are one with each other and with the divine essence. "How great," says the Psalmist, "are thy works, O Lord! Thou hast made all things in wisdom." [24]

The chief attributes of God's will are *omnipotence, freedom, sanctity, justice, goodness, mercy, patience, fidelity*. By omnipotence, we mean that God can do all things and that nothing is hard or impossible to Him. God can accomplish whatever He wishes by a mere act of His will. "No word," St. Luke tells us, "shall be impossible with God." [25] With God, to will and to perform, constitute one and the same act. This follows from God's infinite perfection which includes boundless power and excludes the imperfections of effort, toil, fatigue and successive partial accomplishment.

Can God make a square circle? Can God make a rock so large that He cannot lift it? These are variations of the old question. What happens when an irresistible force meets an immovable object? The answer is: These all involve contradictions and are therefore devoid of all reality. God can do *anything*, but the contradictions mentioned, and all others like them are *nothing*. Their intrinsic repugnance puts them beyond the sphere of both physical and metaphysical possibility and strips them of all being.

[24] *Psal.* 103:24
[25] *Luke* 1:37

"The Depth of the Riches . . ."

It is not necessary to develop each of the previously mentioned attributes of God's will. They and all the other noble attributes which the human mind can conceive, exist in their fullness, without an alloy of imperfection, in the infinite perfection of God. No catalog could list all His perfections. No litany could sing all His glories. We find ourselves exclaiming with St. Paul: "O the depth of the riches of the wisdom and of the knowledge of God! How incomprehensible are his judgments, and how unsearchable his ways! For who hath known the mind of the Lord? Or who hath been his counsellor? . . . For of him, and by him, and in him are all things: to him be glory forever. Amen." [26]

The formal language of philosophy and theology, while accurate as far as it goes, falters and collapses in the effort to reveal the heights and the depths of the unscaled and unfathomed being of the infinite God. We can secure, however, some feeble concept of the perfections of the Almighty, when we realize that the admirable and lovable qualities found in the noblest of human beings are all found in their plenitude in Him. These qualities can exist in only a limited way in human beings because their containers are limited.

Years ago the writer sat one evening at sunset looking out over the waters of the sea of Galilee along whose shores the divine Master had so often walked with His Apostles. Suddenly my reverie was broken by the arrival of a group of native women. They had come, as their forbears from time immemorial had come, to fill their vessels from the waters of the ancient sea. Then, placing their vessels on their heads, they returned to their homes. They come to a goodly lake, but they go away with such a tiny bit. Not because

[26] *Rom.* 11:33, 34, 36

there is no more water to take, but because that is all their receptacles will contain.

How like a picture of humanity! We come from the illimitable ocean of the being and perfections of the infinite Creator. But we carry away only a few tiny drops of that vast ocean because that is all our finite human nature will bear. What the mighty expanse of the waters of the Pacific is to the thimblefull scooped out by a little child, the immeasurable being of the infinitely perfect God is to the finite being of man. We are a drop of water. He is the mighty sea. We are a grain of sand. He is the vast sea-shore. We are a splinter of time. He is the ageless sequoia. We are a farthing candle. He is the blinding sun.

"His Magnificence Is Wonderful"

The perception of the grandeur, the majesty, and the power of God in contrast with the puniness of man stirred many a prophet of old to reach the heights of eloquence. Listen to Ecclesiasticus as he wrestles with this mighty theme: "What shall we be able to do to glorify him? For the Almighty himself is above all his works. The Lord is terrible, and exceeding great, and his power is admirable. Glorify the Lord as much as ever you can, for he will yet far exceed, and his magnificence is wonderful. Blessing the Lord, exalt him as much as you can: for he is above all praise. When you exalt him put forth all your strength, and be not weary; for you can never go far enough. Who shall see him, and declare him? and who shall magnify him as he is from the beginning? There are many things hidden from us that are greater than these; for we have seen but a few of his works." [27]

[27] *Eccles.* 43:30–37

Similar too are the sentiments uttered by the great prophet of divine unity, Isaias. "Praise ye the Lord, and call upon his name: make his works known among the people: remember that his name is high. Sing ye to the Lord, for he hath done great things: show this forth in all the earth. Rejoice and praise, O thou habitation of Sion: for great is he that is in the midst of thee, the Holy One of Israel." [28]

"The Light of the World"

There is no theme which is so worthy of our reverent consideration as that of God, His nature and attributes. "This," says St. John, "is eternal life: that they may know Thee, the only true God." [29] We avail ourselves of the ripe thought of the greatest philosophers and theologians to peer a little way into the illimitable being of God. We supplement it with the insight of the prophets and inspired writers of the Old and of the New Testament. We lean upon the consideration of all the perfections found in human creatures to try to conceive what the result would be if they were all combined in their fullness in a single personality.

More authentically still do we see God mirrored in the winsome figure of Jesus. He is God incarnate, and reflects the mercy, the compassion, and the love that fill the heart of God. Repeated and devout reading of the Gospels will make the personality of Christ a living influence in our lives and thus make us more Godlike. "Draw near to God," says St. James, "and he will draw near to you." [30] The more earnestly we strive to know God, to serve Him, and to love Him, the more intimately will God dwell in our souls and make His radiant presence known to us.

God is the answer to the cry of every lonely soul for

[28] *Isaias* 12:4-6
[29] *John* 17:3
[30] *James* 4:8

friendship and love. He is the end of our ceaseless quest for life and happiness. He is the end of the rainbow, the Alpha and the Omega, the beginning and the end of all things. He is the light of the world, and they who follow Him do not walk in darkness, but shall have the light of life. He is love unutterable, and the only love that can still our restless hearts. "Our hearts," says St. Augustine, "have been made for Thee, O God, and they shall never rest, until they rest in Thee." The practice of the presence of God fills our heart with a quiet peace and makes our face to shine with a radiance which neither clouds can obscure nor grief banish. For to know God is to love Him, and to serve Him is to reign.

friendship and love. He is the end of our ceaseless quest for life and happiness. He is the end of the number—the Alpha and the Omega, the beginning and the end of all things. He is the light of the world, and they who follow Him, to not walk in darkness, but shall have the light of life. He is love unutterable, and the only love that can still our restless hearts. "Our hearts," says St. Augustine, "have been made for Thee, O God, and they shall never rest until they rest in Thee." The presence of the presence of God fills our heart with a quiet peace and makes our face to shine, with a radiance which neither clouds can obscure nor grief banish. For to know God is to love Him, and to serve Him is to reign.

PART II

RELIGION: MAN'S BOND WITH GOD

Its Origin, Nature and Value

Reason and experience both forbid us to expect that national morality can prevail in exclusion of religious principle.

GEORGE WASHINGTON, *Farewell Address*

Because God exists, man must take cognizance of His existence and render to Him due homage and worship. Hence religion comes into being. Without God, religion would be meaningless. With God, religion becomes the most meaningful and significant act which man can perform. Religion comprises all the relations which bind man to God. Those relations reflect the relations of a creature to his Creator and embody his homage, propitiation, love, gratitude and supplications.

Religion is the basis of the good life, the foundation of morality for the individual and for society. An individual without religion is like a ship without a rudder. Because it puts man in contact with God, the fountain of life and light and love, whence stream inspiration for his mind and strength for his will, religion is man's most precious treasure—the pearl that passeth all price. Rob man of religion and you pauperize and barbarize him. You make him a walking biped who knows not whither he is going.

CHAPTER XIV

THE MEANING OF RELIGION

Religion, pure and undefiled before God and the Father,
is this: to visit the fatherless and widows in their tribulation, and to keep one's self unspotted from this world.
—*James* 1:27

No FORCE in human history has exercised so potent an influence upon the life, thought and civilization of mankind
as has religion. Whether the civilization be rudimentary or
highly advanced, the influence of religion is paramount and
all-pervasive. It puts its imprint upon man's laws, colors his
art, creates the atmosphere for his literature. It shapes his
ethical codes, filters through into his philosophy and embeds
itself in the innermost conscience of the individual and in
the corporate mind of the society in which he lives.

It supplies the answers to man's deepest questionings:
Whence have I come? Whither am I going? What is the
meaning and the purpose of human life? How can I achieve
my ultimate destiny? Thus religion concerns itself with
man's deepest values.

It gives him guidance in his relations with his Creator
and with his fellow man. It enables him to walk safely along
the path of reverence and obedience to his God and of justice and kindliness to his neighbor. When that light is extinguished man gropes about in the darkness, and life becomes a game of blindman's buff. Rob man of his religious

belief, and he sinks to a level one step removed from the beasts of the field. An attack upon God is an attack upon the dignity of man and upon the sacredness of the human personality. This is the truth which has been painted in tragic and flaming colors upon the canvas of the world's history.

Mankind has no stronger bulwark for the protection of his own freedom and dignity than the teachings of religion concerning the essential equality of all men in the eyes of God and of their accountability to Him for their treatment of one another. "What doth the Lord, thy God demand of thee," thundered the prophet Micheas, "but that thou love mercy, do justly, and walk humbly with thy God?" For the right of men and women everywhere to walk humbly and freely with their God, without the club of a dictator over their heads, America has poured out her treasures and her blood in two World Wars.

Importance of Religion

Because religion plays so far-reaching a role in the life of individuals and of nations, it is of paramount importance for every person to understand its real meaning. For how can a person properly appreciate this great treasure if he does not understand what it is? How can he go out to fight and die for something which he does not really understand? Yet, are there not millions of people in our land, to whom religion is not much more than a word, and a confused word at that? To many it conjures up the thought of Sunday school, of preaching, of restrictions and taboos, of denominational rivalry, and of other notions which blur or caricature the real nature of religion.

Accordingly we shall undertake to resent the essential nature of religion, its universality, its reasonableness, its various kinds, its relation to morality, and the values it renders to the individual and to society. Without sacrificing any of the values of scholarship, we shall discuss the subject in popular language, seeking to carry to the general reader the fruits of scientific and philosophic research. We shall treat of religion in its broadest and most universal sense, embracing not only Judaism and Christianity, but the religion of all believers in a Supreme Being. We cherish the hope that the treatment will bring to the citizens of our land not only a better understanding of religion but a deeper appreciation of its powerful assistance in enabling them to live richer, nobler and more godlike lives.

From such increased understanding should result a renaissance of religion in America so that its wholesome influence will envelop every home in our land. Such an effect will, we are confident, be no small contribution to the morale of the American people. More important than that, the revival of religion will enthrone God in the life of the individual, of the family, and of the nation. By making us humble, charitable and obedient to His divine commands, it will merit for us in the stern hour of crisis the divine assistance, without which we cannot succeed, and with which we cannot fail.

Its Root Meaning

What is the meaning of religion? By tracing a word to its root or roots we can secure an insight into its original and basic meaning. The etymology of religion, however, has been a matter of dispute from ancient times. In his *De Natura Deorum*, Cicero derives religion from *relegere*, to treat carefully, saying: "Those who carefully took in hand all things pertaining to the gods were called *religiosi*, from *relegere*." [1] This is the view favored by Max Müller. As religion is an ele-

[1] *Qui omnia, quae ad cultum deorum pertinerent, diligenter retractarent et tamquam religerent, sunt dicti religiosi ex relegendo.* II, 28

mentary notion, however, long antedating the time of complicated ritual presupposed in this explanation, we must look elsewhere for its etymology.

In his *City of God*,[2] St. Augustine derives religion from *religere*, in the sense of recovering. He says: "Having lost God through neglect (*negligentes*), we recover Him (*religentes*) and are drawn to Him." Inasmuch as this explanation implies the notion of Redemption, it is not suited to the primary idea of religion.

Lactantius, a renowned Father of the Church who lived in the late third and early fourth centuries, derives religion from *religare*, to bind. In his *Divinae Institutes*, he writes: "We are tied to God and *bound* to Him (*religati*) by the bond of piety, and it is from this, and not as Cicero holds, from careful consideration (*relegendo*), that religion has received its name." [3] Here we have most likely the true origin of the term, religion. For in its simplest form, religion implies the idea of being bound to God. This same idea is uppermost in the word *religion* in its most specific sense, as applied to the life of poverty, chastity, and obedience, to which individuals bind themselves by vows. Hence, those who are thus bound are called *religious*.

St. Augustine later came to espouse the explanation of Lactantius. "He has certainly seized the broad popular sense of the word," observed Canon Liddon, "when he connects it with the idea of an obligation by which man is bound to an invisible God." [4]

This brief discussion of the root meaning of religion will not be without fruit, if it leaves in the mind of the reader the basic and indisputable truth, conveyed by the term *religion*, that man is bound by the bond of devotion, obedience and

[2] X, 3
[3] *Vinculo pietatis Deo religati sumus, unde ipsa religio nomen accepit, non, ut Cicero interpretatus est, a relegendo.* IV, 28
[4] *Some Elements of Religion*, Lecture I, 19

love to God, the Heavenly Father, to whom he owes his
very existence. Whenever the word *religion* is uttered, let
it remind man of that everlasting and unbreakable bond which
is designed to draw him ever closer in reverence, love and
service to the Father from whom he has come and to whose
all-embracing arms he is destined ultimately to return.

Essence of Religion

"Whatever be the truth about the origin of the name,"
observes St. Thomas Aquinas, "religion as a reality indicates
the relationship of man towards God." This relationship is
the voluntary subjection of the creature to His Creator in
acknowledgment of his complete and abiding dependence
upon Him and of God's absolute and sovereign dominion
over him. This sense of dependence upon God, this keenly
felt need of divine assistance, coupled with the conviction
that he can place himself in friendly and helpful communion
with the deity along with the efforts to do so, constitute the
very essence of religion. At the very heart of religion, then,
lie two ideas: the consciousness of man's need of God, and
the conviction that the appropriate expression of the need for
divine aid can and will be answered.

The felt needs of the individuals vary with the tribes and
societies in which they live, and with their own development. In lower stages of development the solicitude is more
for material welfare than for moral perfection, though
the latter is not neglected. The emphasis would seem, however, to be upon material prosperity and bodily comfort. In
the higher religions the perfection sought in religion becomes increasingly that of moral goodness. In Christianity,
the highest of religions, the individual aims at communion
with God through the achievement of high spiritual perfection.

This entails a participation in the supernatural life of grace as children of God. In the Christian there is a clear perception of God's sovereignty and a consequent recognition of his duty to acknowledge that sovereignty by appropriate acts of praise, adoration, propitiation, and thanksgiving.[5] The crown of such acts of filial homage is the love of God for His own sake, inasmuch as He is the infinitely perfect being, in whom truth, beauty and goodness are realized in their highest possible degree.

A Personal God

From what has been said thus far it is evident that the concept of a deity required for religion is that of a *free personality, possessing intelligence and will*. Where the deity is identified with the earth and the sky, with sticks and stones, as in pantheism, and is thus devoid of all consciousness, religion ceases to exist. For the essential acts of religion, prayer, adoration, propitiation, supplication imply the power to hear and the power to respond. What would be the sense of talking to a rock or a clod of earth?

A deity without personality, and hence without consciousness, is no more capable of awakening the sense of religion in the heart of man than is the all-pervading air or the universal force of gravitation. Hence all attempts to substitute the cosmos or nature—even when written with capitals—for a personal deity are so many arrows aimed at the heart of religion. Man can admire the autumnal coloring of a tree, the fragrance of a rose, the beauty of a sunset. He can no more talk to them, however, than he can to a stick or a stone. Personality, consciousness, intelligence, the power to hear

[5] Hence St. Thomas Aquinas defines religion as "the virtue which prompts man to render to God the worship and reverence which is His by right" (*virtus per quam homines Deo debitum cultum et reverentiam exhibent.*) II–II, Q 81, a. 1

and the power to answer, constitute, then, the core of the concept of a deity required for religious purposes.

Religion is thus seen to be essentially a personal relation. It is the relation of the creature to his Creator, of the subject to his Sovereign, of man to his God. In that relationship man turns with outstretched arms, seeking to clasp the hand reached down from on High. He opens his lips to a listening ear. He pours out the love of his heart to a heart which reciprocates with an overwhelming love. Religion is not a one-directional line. It is not talking to a deaf-mute. Reciprocation is of its very essence. God both listens and replies. Says James Russell Lowell: [6]

> God is not dumb, that he should speak no more;
> If thou hast wanderings in the wilderness
> And find'st not Sinai, 'tis thy soul is poor.

Those who train their ears to catch the answering echoes from the mind and the heart of God hear a message which carries courage and inspiration, and feel a love which fills them with a rapture which transcends all the pleasures of earth and sense. It is this union of the soul with God in perfect love which constitutes the end of all religious striving, a union which is approximated in this life by high moral perfection, and which is achieved in the next life by the soul which experiences a joy which no tongue can describe. "Eye hath not seen," says the Apostle Paul, "nor ear heard, neither hath it entered into the heart of man, what things God hath prepared for them that love him." [7]

Religion is not the stunted expression of a single faculty. It calls forth the expression of man's whole personality with all its powers and faculties. It brings into play not merely the intellect, but the will, the imagination, and the emotions. The

[6] *Bibliolatres*
[7] 1 *Cor.* 2:9

envisagement of the unseen world kindles the imagination. The consciousness of an offence against God elicits sorrow and stirs the will to amendment. The perception of the need of divine aid in times of perplexity and crisis intensify the fervor of our supplications and bring us in humility to His feet.

Our hearts go out in paeans of joy and gratitude in times of deliverance from suffering and danger. We exhaust the powers of the painter, the musician, and the poet in seeking to express the varied sentiments which fill our minds and the emotions which tug at our hearts as we turn to God in all the changing vicissitudes of human life. Hence we see how far off the mark are those writers who seek to limit religion to the exercise of a particular faculty, or to identify it exclusively with ritual or ethical conduct.

Hegel describes religion as "the knowledge acquired by the finite spirit of its essence as absolute spirit." Max Müller terms it "the perception of the infinite." Schleiermacher refers to it as "a determination of man's feeling of absolute dependence." Kant speaks of it as "the recognition of all our duties as divine commands." Matthew Arnold characterizes it as "morality touched with emotion." John Stuart Mill defines it as "the earnest direction of the emotions and desires toward an ideal object recognized as the highest excellence and as rightly paramount over selfish objects of desire."

These are, however, but fragmentary descriptions. They are but slender strands in the rich and varied tapestry of religion. Distortion and deformation can only result from the effort to limit religion to a single activity or faculty. Recognizing his dependence upon Almighty God for every sinew and fibre and faculty of his nature, man strives to render to God a full-orbed expression of his dependence, his gratitude, and his love, by pulling every element of his being into that acknowledgment. Hence religion involves the expression of the whole man, mind and heart and soul. If any element of his nature fails to participate in that manifestation, the homage is correspondingly incomplete.

Natural and Supernatural

Religion may be considered subjectively or objectively. Viewed subjectively, that is as resident in the person or subject who practices it, religion may be defined as the *disposition* prompting the individual to acknowledge through appropriate acts of homage, praise and love his dependence upon Almighty God.

Viewed objectively, that is as something external to the person or subject, religion may be defined as a system of truths, laws and practices which direct and regulate the rendering of homage and worship to God.

The most important division of religion is that which classifies it as *natural* and *supernatural*. Natural religion may be defined as the sum of man's duties to God in so far as they can be ascertained by the light of reason alone. In other words, it is the worship of God as prescribed by reason unaided by revelation. The duties of natural religion may be epitomized in the three great commandments which man's rational nature makes known to him, namely, to honor God, to subdue his passions, and to do unto others as he would have others do unto him.

The principal duties of man according to the law of nature find expression in the Ten Commandments with the exception that in the third, the day of designation would not necessarily be the Sabbath. Men would be obliged by the law of natural religion to set aside a day from time to time for the public worship of God, but the choice of a particular day would be at the option of each state or community.

Prompting man to observe these commandments would be the twofold motive, the love of God and the fear of His judgment in the life to come.

Supernatural religion is the sum of man's duties to God as known by divine revelation. Thus there are certain truths, such as the Incarnation and the Blessed Trinity, which transcend man's capacity to discover and which, if they are to be known at all, must be revealed to him. There are other truths which man could arrive at by his reason, such as, that God is one, necessary, eternal and infinite. Many such truths of natural religion are also divinely revealed. They are supernatural only in the manner in which they have been made known to us.

Divine Revelation

Divine revelation is a beautiful and striking expression of God's solicitude and love for mankind. For if left entirely to himself, man would fall into many errors and abominations, as the history of pagan antiquity abundantly discloses. The gods of the pagans were often patrons of theft, lying and lust. Licentious orgies were publicly performed in honor of Bacchus and Eros.

With such depraved notions of the deity, they lacked a fixed and unalterable standard of right and wrong. Even Plato (428–347 B.C.), one of the master minds of ancient Greece, favored a community of wives and the destruction of weakly and deformed children.[8] His great disciple, Aristotle (384–322 B.C.), who systematized so many branches of knowledge, entertained the same lax views in regard to infant life. Lacking a proper conception of human dignity, he regarded slaves as mere beasts who could be beaten, tor-

[8] *Rep.* Book V

tured or put to death by their masters without injustice.[9]

Seneca, one of the leading Stoic philosophers of ancient Rome, was emphatic in his approval of suicide. Even Marcus Aurelius, its last and noblest representative, was uncertain, now condemning, now approving the crime of self-destruction. In short, the best minds of pagan antiquity fell into grievous errors, while the masses were engulfed in sensual and licentious practices, destructive of the integrity of the home and of the dignity of the individual.

The light of divine revelation not only pointed the way out of these abominations but also gave mankind the necessary help to follow that path. For it spoke to mankind not in the faltering and uncertain tones of human reason but in the unfaltering and clear language of divine wisdom.

Revelation Affords Certainty

This is of great importance. For without that divine assurance of truth, mankind would be forever paralyzed by doubt. Thus, let us suppose that in some community there exists a master mind who devotes his whole life to the discovery of all the truths of natural religion and finally arrives at all of them. Then he undertakes to impart them to his fellow men. What chance of success would he have? Little or none.

The man, tempted to sin, might well say: "How do I know he is right? He is a man like myself. All his reasoning may be wrong. He is a hopeless minority, with no credentials of his authority to teach me the truth. I want and I need the assurance from God that this is wrong. Then only can I act with certainty."

Thomas Carlyle said of Robert Burns: "His religion at

[9] *Pol.* IV (VII) 16; 17, i, 5

best is an anxious wish—like that of Rabelais, a great Perhaps." Man cannot, however, resist a driving passion nor prepare himself to face the martyr's fire on the strength of a mere Perhaps. He needs a certainty—an unequivocal Yea, uttered in the clear tones of the divine Revealer. Then all doubt and uncertainty are washed away forever. Thus vividly and impressively do the mercy, the goodness, and the love of God shine forth through the revelation which He vouchsafed to man.

This deposit of supernatural truths, along with those discoverable by unaided human reason, forms a beautiful and harmonious mosaic of religious truth. There is a fundamental unity to all truth. For they all come from the same ultimate fountain. The supernatural truths buttress and reënforce those discovered by reason alone.

The human mind follows, as far as its finite tether will permit, the illimitable reaches of divine truth, and when reason falters and stumbles at the twilight of mystery, faith takes over and follows all the way. Faith rides on the donkey of human reason and, when the latter falters, it travels the remaining distance in the chariot of divine revelation. It is a lovely virtue which, like the beloved disciple, John, leans its head upon the bosom of the Lord and hearing the throbbing of His beating heart, knows that all is well. Faith is a genuflection of the will before the tabernacle of God's revealed truth, a gesture of love whereby the heart of man answers a cry from the heart of God.

CHAPTER XV

THE UNIVERSALITY OF RELIGION

There is no race so wild and untamed as to be ignorant
of the existence of God.—CICERO, *De Natura Deorum*

As THE belief in God has existed among all the races of mankind from the earliest times down to the present, so the practice of religion has been likewise universal. This is as true
today as it was at the dawn of history. Whether the race be
comparatively primitive or highly civilized, religion will
be found to play an important role. The practice of religion
would seem to follow as a direct and immediate consequence
of the recognition of the existence of a Supreme Being.
Man expresses that acknowledgment through prayer, sacrifice and ceremonial of varied kinds. "Nature herself," declares Cicero, "teaches us that God is to be venerated, and
of her law in this matter no man is free."

The findings of modern historic research corroborate the
truth expressed by Cicero. Reflecting the conclusions of investigators in this field, Professor C. H. Toy of Harvard
declares: "As far as our present knowledge goes, religion
appears to be universal among men. There is no community
of which we can say with certainty that it is without religion." [1]

Similar is the way Professor Tiele in his *History of Religion* sums up the findings of the researchers: "The state-

[1] *Introduction to the History of Religions*, pp. 5 f.

ment that there are nations or tribes which possess no religion rests either on inaccurate observations or on a confusion of ideas. No tribe or nation has yet been met with destitute of a belief in any higher being, and travellers who have asserted their existence have been afterwards refuted by facts. It is legitimate, therefore, to call religion, in its most general sense, the universal phenomenon of humanity."

Granting, then, that religious worship has been universal among all the tribes and races in the past, the question may be raised: Have we any assurance that it will persist in the future? Has not the advance of modern science been characterized by a progressive substitution of mechanical for personal agency in nature, with the inevitable result, as a sceptic has expressed it, that God will be escorted to the limits of His universe and then politely bowed out as no longer needed?

To this we may reply: The advance of modern science is fatal to all polytheistic forms of religion, in which the secondary causes are, through ignorance, mistaken for personal agents. The truth of the unity of nature's forces, so well established by modern science, is in perfect harmony with the monotheistic interpretation of nature. It is the polytheist, and not the Christian, who has a particular deity for thunder, another for lightning, and another for the earthquake. The monotheist recognizes all these phenomena as due to secondary or natural causes operating within the framework of universal law.

Far from being inconsistent with true science, Christian monotheism is necessary to supplement and complete the fragmentary interpretation of nature afforded by science. Being based on observation and experiment, science has for its legitimate field of study only secondary causes of nature. It can tell us nothing about origins, nothing about the great First Cause, from which nature with its network of myriad laws has come.

Science Deciphers God's Handwriting

In substituting physical laws for what was formerly thought to be the direct action of God, science has not accounted for the intelligent purposive action of nature. It has simply pushed the question farther back. But the demand for an Intelligent Cause, a Supreme Mind, remains as persistent and importunate as ever. Like the ghost of Banquo, it will not down. Dispense with Thor, explain thunder by physical laws, and you make not less necessary the need for the Legislator of such laws. "Let the chain of second causes be ever so long," observes George Lavington, "the first link is always in God's hand."

The discovery by science that the thunder, lightning, tornadoes, earthquakes are due to the operation of physical laws, prompts us to seek to know more about such laws. They show that we live in a *law-abiding universe*. On the basis of the regularity of the operations of the laws and forces of nature, we build the edifice of all our sciences, and chart the position of stars whose light has not yet reached our earth. In changing the picture of the universe from a fitful, capricious one, such as primitive man envisaged, to one characterized by the universal reign of law, science reveals the universe to be not less but more wonderful, more awe-inspiring than ever our forbears dreamed.

By the same logic, the Author of such a law-abiding universe is correspondingly enhanced. The adjectives, omnipotent, omniscient, infinite, which were becoming somewhat anaemic, are now seen to be filled with the red corpuscles of vital and startling reality. Far from dwarfing the expression of God's power, modern science aggrandizes it. Far from elbowing God out of the universe, science shows His omnipresence, through the power of His laws in the whirling electrons within a tiny atom and in the swing of Betelgeux through the vastness of immeasurable space.

Far from outmoding the worship of God, science confirms its reasonableness with ever more impressive evidence of His divine dominion over the whole vast universe. He has written His name, as Lord and Sovereign, in the nuclear structure of every throbbing atom, upon the heart of every flower, and upon the illuminated manuscript of the skies. The whole of creation mirrors His intelligence and His power. As long as man can see and reason, he will not fail to acknowledge the sovereign dominion of God over himself and all creation. In such an acknowledgment, religion finds its most basic and essential expression—an expression that is as universal and enduring as mankind itself.

CHAPTER XVI

ORIGIN OF RELIGION

There is in the nature of man a desire to know the cause
of the effects that he sees.—St. Thomas Aquinas

PRESCINDING for the moment from the testimony of Holy
Scripture, we ask: What was the natural origin of religion?
For religion, like morality, has a natural basis or origin. It
is the outcome of the use of reasoning whereby man con-
cludes from the observations of the forces of nature that
there must be some great Power, some supreme Intelligence
to account for them. Observing the unfailing sequence of
day and night, the regular order of the seasons, and other
such evidences of power, order and plan, it was possible for
primitive man to conclude by the light of human reason
alone that there must be a Being, possessing intelligence and
power, somewhere in the universe. In the absence of positive, historic data concerning the natural origin of religion,
we can only give a speculative answer.

The process by which primitive man arrived naturally
at a theistic interpretation of the world seems to have been
a *simple, spontaneous application of the principle of causality.*
So basic and far-reaching is this principle in enabling us
to arrive at the existence of causes, which often lie beyond
the range of our immediate vision, that it may be said to constitute the spinal column of the body of our scientific and
philosophic knowledge of man and of the universe. It is

the spinal column likewise of the philosophy of religion which seeks by reason alone to establish the basis of natural religion and to formulate its fundamental truths.

What was primitive man's view of nature? There is every reason to believe that it was to a large extent similar to that held by tribes and peoples who have not yet risen to a scientific knowledge of the laws of nature. The causes best known to him are living, personal ones, namely, himself and his fellow men. He has not penetrated to an understanding of secondary, mechanical causes of natural events. The result is that he attributes all the striking phenomena of earth, air and sky to personal agencies.

Personal Forces of Nature

His experience with lifeless objects, sticks and stones, utensils and weapons, shows him that they move and exercise force only when a person imparts energy to them. Consequently whenever he perceives a phenomenon showing movement and energy outside his limited experience of mechanical causation, he is prompted spontaneously to attribute it to some mysterious person. Thus, the thunder suggests the thunderer. He thinks of the sun and moon either as living things or as the instruments of an invisible living agency. It was easy for primitive man to perceive in and behind the phenomena of nature the operation of mind and will.

To perceive in the vast diversity of these phenomena the operation of but one supreme person was, however, far from easy. While such an inference was indeed possible, it was not a likely one. This becomes evident when we consider the enormous difficulty confronting primitive man in attempting in his inexperience to coördinate the widely different phenomena of nature and to trace them to one and the same source of intelligence and power. The more likely tendency would have been to attribute different phenomena to distinct personalities. This is what was done by the peoples of antiquity. In fact this is still done by savage and uncivilized tribes everywhere.

Dr. Charles F. Aiken thus sums up the situation: "Peoples, whose ignorance of the physical laws of nature has not been compensated by revealed teaching, have invariably personalized the forces of nature, and, feeling that their welfare depended on the beneficent exercise of these powers, have come to divinize them. From this danger of falling into a polytheistic interpretation of nature, primitive man was saved by Divine Revelation. Such, it would seem, was the simple philosophy forming the natural basis of religion in primitive times. It was theoretically capable of leading to a monotheism like that of the ancient Hebrews, who viewed clouds, rain, lightning, and tempest as the signs of God's immediate activity. But, apart from revelation, it was very liable to degenerate into polytheistic nature-worship. Its defect was primarily scientific—ignorance of the secondary causes of natural events; but it rested on a sound principle, namely, that the phenomena of nature are in some way the outcome of intelligent volition. This principle commends itself to the Christian philosopher and scientist." [1]

Conclusions Which Do Not Follow

Religion did not have its origin in fear, as a few modern writers assert. They picture early man as frightened by the thunder, lightning, tempests and earthquakes, and calling upon the deity for protection. The fallacy underlying this theory is that fear is a feeling, and no mere feeling can account for the *idea* of personality which may or may not be

[1] *Catholic Encyclopedia*, Art. "Religion," vol. 12, p. 744

associated with a dangerous or terrifying object. It is true that fear may stimulate man to call upon the deity for aid and protection. *But such supplication presupposes belief in such a deity.* When a man is attacked by a thug, his fear may prompt him to shout "Help! Police!" But he calls for the police only because he *already* knows of their existence and their willingness to come to his aid, when attacked by a robber.

Here we should advert to the attempts of other writers to discredit religion by calling attention to the large admixture of superstition and error found in the religious practices of savage and barbarous peoples. Volumes have been written, piling up instances of the use of magic, fetishes, totems and other superstitious practices. Let all that be frankly admitted. What conclusion follows therefrom?

"Religion," they reply, "is without any rational foundation. Present day religion is but the refinement of the worship, supplications, propitiation and thanksgiving of primitive man. Since those practices were infested with superstition and error, all religion is without a solid basis and is valueless."

The conclusion is, however, too wide for the premises. If that line of reasoning were to prevail there would not be left in the world today a single valid science. For in their early stages all branches of science were infested with error. Medicine is a capital example. How many false potions, treatments and remedies were mixed up with the early practice of the healing art. Up until a few centuries ago it was the custom to bleed people to relieve fever and to cure other ailments for which it was no remedy at all. Does it follow that the whole modern science of medicine is without any solid basis and is utterly valueless?

In its early days chemistry was entangled with many errors, not the least of which were the methods used in attempting to change the baser metals into gold and silver. Do those errors vitiate modern chemistry?

In past ages astronomers often engaged in astrological practices, seeking to foretell events by the position of the stars. Does it follow that the modern science of astronomy is without any solid foundation and that every textbook on the subject is as valueless as a fairy tale? To ask these questions is to answer them. Thousands of years ago Cicero punctured the fallacy of those who sought to discredit religion by pointing to the superstitions encumbering it, when he said: *"Religion is not removed by removing superstition."* [2]

The Principle of Causality

The simple fact is that the basis of primitive man's theistic interpretation of nature and therefore of his religious worship is the mighty principle of causality which constitutes likewise the enduring and rational basis of all the sciences. Far from scrapping that far-reaching principle by which man reduces the fragmentary and discrete phenomena of the universe to the marvelous unity of universal law, the findings of both science and philosophy reënforce its validity and extol it as a principle more potent than the lever for which Archimedes searched to move the earth. By the application of that principle, man has found truth and reality in all the domains of intellectual questing—in science, philosophy and religion.

"Without having recourse," observes Professor James Fox, "to psychological analysis of doubtful value, and contested assumptions as to the conditions which surrounded primeval man, we perceive an obvious inherent characteristic of the human mind common to all stages of development, which is amply sufficient to account for the appearance of religious

[2] *De Divinatione*, II

beliefs and practices. This characteristic is the impulse of ascribing every perceived effect to some cause." [3]

St. Thomas Aquinas likewise calls attention to this inherent characteristic of the human mind. "There is," he says, "in the nature of man a desire to know the cause of the effects that he sees. . . . If the understanding of a rational creature cannot reach at the first cause of things, the desire of its nature will remain unsatisfied." So man is forever climbing up the ladder of secondary causes to the First and Supreme Cause—God Himself. In the breast of every human being there is an echo of the words of the Psalmist: "He has made us, not we ourselves."

The conviction of early man that the universe cannot account for itself, that it demands an adequate cause, a Supreme Intelligence, is as true today as it was untold thousands of years ago. True, somewhat different and more enlightened expressions are given to that fundamental conviction, but its basic core is still essentially the same. That core is the principle of causality by which we arrive at the conclusion that the earth, its phenomena, its order, and the myriad forms of life thereon must have an adequate cause. That Cause mankind has called from time immemorial by the venerable name of God.

"Don't Cut Down the Tree"

The errors which were mixed up in primitive man's religious worship no more invalidate religion than the presence of a few bad apples destroys the value of the whole tree. Reason dictates that we pluck the infected apples, but it does not ask us to cut down the tree. Yet that is precisely what a few writers on the religious practices of early man would have us do—cut down the whole tree of religion.

[3] James Joseph Fox, *Religion and Morality*

The simple truth is that when the myriad customs, rituals and practices, followed by early man in religious worship, are carefully studied and properly interpreted, they emphasize in an impressive manner the basic fact that mankind always and everywhere has felt the duty of rendering homage to God and the need of asking His divine aid and guidance in all the vicissitudes of life.

Thus do the facts unearthed by painstaking research in the history of religion and by studies in comparative religion add their own distinctive undertones to man's age-old and unceasing cry for God—the creative womb from which he issued and the all-embracing arms to which he is destined ultimately to return. Far then from tending to undermine religious faith, the data supplied by these two branches of knowledge, when properly interpreted, afford a new and a striking reënforcement. They accent the universality of such faith, and show that for mankind as a whole it is a necessary and inescapable consequence of the capacity to think.

Theism is thus seen to be the inevitable conclusion from the application of the principle of causality to the phenomena of nature and to the order and harmony of the universe. The name of God is written on the silver lining of the cloud that veils our world and the radiance of that name is glimpsed ever and anon by all those who penetrate with seeing minds and understanding hearts beneath that mystic veil which we call the phenomena of nature. Look with reverent eyes, clear mind and pure heart and you will not fail to see the handwriting of God and catch something of the shining glory of His countenance.

ORIGIN OF RELIGION

151

CHAPTER XVII

RELIGIOUS WORSHIP—A DUTY

I am the Lord, thy God. . . . Thou shalt not have
strange gods before me.—*Exodus* 20:2

WE COME now to the consideration of the important question: Is there a duty upon all mankind to render homage and worship to God? "No," reply some, "that is a privilege which may be exercised or not according to the whim or option of the individual." True, man is physically free to worship God or not. Likewise the legislation of virtually every state grants its citizens the right to engage in religious worship, but refrains from any enactment compelling them to do so.

The fact is, however, that there exists a stern moral obligation upon every human being to render homage and adoration to God. Why? Since man owes his very existence to the Creator, and is dependent upon Him for both body and soul, it follows that man should acknowledge this dependence upon God, proclaim his gratitude to Him, and express by appropriate action God's sovereign and absolute dominion over him. This is a law of nature. This is a dictate of reason. This is a command of God. The failure to make such an acknowledgment constitutes a serious violation of the whole moral order.

Let us illustrate man's dependence upon God. A newborn babe is cradled in its mother's arms, drawing nourishment from her breasts. It is a picture of complete helplessness. Unable to ward off a hostile blow, unable to take a single step, unable to speak a word, unable to provide for a single one of its many needs, it is a perfect symbol of sheer and utter helplessness. Dependent upon its parents for its life, it is likewise dependent upon them for its maintenance. Deprive that tiny newcomer of the loving care of mother and father, and quickly the spark of life will flicker and die.

Our Dependence on God

Similarly we are dependent upon the Creator from whom all life proceeds. Our dependence is, however, even more absolute and universal. We are dependent upon God for body and soul, for every breath we take, for every movement we make, for every thought of our mind, for every decision of our will, and for every aspiration of our soul. All the faculties of the soul and all the powers of the body come to us as gifts from the Creator's bounty. We are indebted to the divine omnipotence not only for their existence but for their actions as well.

Withdraw the sustaining power of God for but a moment, and we should cease to be. Withhold the divine concursus by which we act, and we should not so much as utter the infant's cry of distress. Thus is God the ground of our being, the anchor of our preservation, and the sustaining power of our activity. So absolute and universal is our dependence upon Him that there is engraven upon every fibre of our being the indelible mark of God's unlimited and unconditioned ownership.

We may have the wisdom of Solomon, the strength of Samson, the beauty of Apollo, the riches of Croesus, the imagination of Shakespeare, and the genius of Pasteur. We may win the plaudits of our fellow men and bask in the sunshine of popularity. But we can never obliterate the birth-mark proclaiming the nothingness of our origin and the insufficiency of our being. Sounding as overtones of the world's applause is heard in the soul's inner ear the whisper of the Creator claiming the work of His hands: "You and your talents and achievements are all mine. For without me, you can do nothing."

The little babe may in time become independent of his parents, and provide for his own needs, but the creature can never become independent of the Creator. The umbilical cord binding the babe to its mother is severed at birth, but the cord of the creature's dependence upon his Creator remains forever intact.

The true picture of man is not that of lord of the universe. For with all his knowledge and scientific achievements, he still finds himself like an infant enveloped in a world of fathomless mystery. Everything he sees, hears, or touches, if pushed but a step or two, terminates in mystery. He has not yet learned the alphabet of nature's language, nor trained his ear to catch the music of the stars. Brief voyager on a planet lost in the skies, he is born today, to pass tomorrow into the Stygian darkness of uncomprehending night. The true picture of man is that of an infant crying in the night, with no language but a cry, a cry to the God who made him.

The title of the Creator's dominion over us is more absolute than any achieved by the creature. The picture painted by the artist, the poem penned by the poet, the statue carved by the sculptor, belong to their owners by virtue of their labor. They must be given, however, the material and the tools upon which they are dependent to achieve their products. Without the proper materials there would be no paintings, no books of poetry, no statues. God knows, however, no such dependence. Not only does He fashion our natures but He also creates the very substance of our being.

Hence God's title of ownership or dominion over us is as complete and absolute as the human mind can conceive.

Paying Our Debt

Now it is an ordinance of nature and a dictate of our moral nature that a debt should be acknowledged and paid. Since we are indebted to God for both our being and our continuance in existence, we should acknowledge that debt and seek to pay it by appropriate actions. That fundamental obligation we fulfill by acts of religion. For the essential element in all religious actions consists in the acknowledgment of our dependence upon God and His sovereignty over us.

What is the meaning of the bowed head, the folded hands, the bent knee? What is the significance of the act of adoration, the hymn of praise, the propitiatory striking of the breast, the song of thanksgiving? Are not all these so many efforts of the creature to acknowledge his indebtedness to the Creator for his life, his faculties, and for all that he may ever achieve? They are the language of adoration spoken with the accents of gratitude and love.

We can illustrate the duty of the creature to acknowledge his dependence upon the Creator by citing the universally recognized duty of a son to show honor and respect to his father. Why is he obliged to pay such homage? Because the father begot him and during the years of his dependence maintained him by his toil. The duty of respect flows therefore from the twofold gift he has received—procreation and maintenance. Acts of kindness, obedience, gratitude and love constitute the currency wherewith the son seeks to pay his debt. If he fail to pay his father the homage of his respect, gratitude and love, he is universally regarded as an ingrate of the blackest hue.

It is a debt from which the father cannot dispense his son. For it is rooted in the very nature of a son's relationship to his father—the relationship of dependence for his existence and maintenance. Hence it does not spring from any wish or whim of the father to be respected. It is grounded in the moral law which binds both father and son. It binds the father to require such respect and it binds the son to render it. That moral law is a reflection of the mind and will of God.

What would you think of a father who did not exact such filial respect? Suppose he were to say to his son: "True, I am your father. By my toil I provided for you during the days of your infancy and early youth. But you do not need to make any acknowledgment. You can ignore me altogether. You can treat me with utter indifference and neglect. You need not speak a kind, grateful or affectionate word to me. When walking with your friends, you need not speak or bow to me or indicate in any way that you so much as know me. You are free to disregard my wishes and to disobey my commands. I shall not complain if you forget all that I have done for you, not even if you return my love with hatred."

Would you not say that such a father was attempting to grant a dispensation which he had no moral right to grant? Would not every man and woman regard him as an unnatural father, a monstrosity, devoid of common sense as well as of the normal instincts of fatherhood? The fact is that procreation begets not only the right, but also the duty, of demanding honor, obedience and love from children. By failing to demand such respect the father would sin not less grievously than the son in failing to give it.

More greatly indebted is the creature to the Creator than the child to his father. Not only for his very being but for every act as well is he indebted to his Creator. The father gave of what he had received. God, however, gives of what is absolutely His own. The creature is under a moral obligation to acknowledge his complete and abiding dependence upon the Creator. So absolute is this obligation that not even God can dispense from it. For such a dispensation would constitute a subversion of the whole moral order and would be equivalent to an open denial of God's authority over the work of His hands.

Worship—Internal and External

Let us now set forth the different kinds of worship, conditioned by human nature. Man is a creature composed of body and soul. He is capable, therefore, of originating two different kinds of acts. Some of his acts, such as thought and volition, may remain entirely in the mental faculties from which they proceed. Others, such as speaking, singing, genuflecting, find outward expression in the body. The former are internal, the latter, external. Corresponding to these two kinds of activity are internal and external worship.

Internal homage consists in the inarticulate thoughts of praise and adoration and in the unspoken affections of the soul, leaning in reverence upon the bosom of divine love, and listening to the throbbing of the divine heart. External worship expresses the sentiments of reverence, obedience, praise, loyalty and love through vocal prayer, the singing of hymns, and through the moving ceremonies of the Church's ritual service.

Since God is the Author of soul and body, we must render to Him the worship of both. We must give Him the love of the former and the obeisance of the latter. Otherwise we would be defrauding God by paying Him only half of the debt.

Thus it becomes evident that the rendering of homage to God by acts both of internal and external worship is not a matter of option or caprice. It is a matter of strict obligation. It binds every creature born into this world, whether he be white or black, red, yellow or brown. It binds alike the rich and the poor, the king and the beggar, the scientist in his laboratory and the untutored redman in the forest. From this universal obligation no court can dispense.

As the debt man owes to the Creator is greater than any he could owe to his fellow man, the obligation for its discharge rests with correspondingly greater weight and pressure upon the conscience of every human. It is man's first obligation in justice, his most important and urgent debt. Hence, St. Thomas ranks religion as the first of all the moral virtues, since by it we pay the first and the most important of all our creditors, our Creator, what is due Him.

An Obligation of Justice and Truth

The duty of rendering homage to God flows not only from the obligation of justice but from that of truth as well. God is the most perfect of all beings. He is wisdom, truth, goodness, beauty and love unutterable. Out of His infinite goodness and generosity he has lifted us from the valley of nothingness to the mountain of being. Out of His infinite love, He vouchsafed to us His divine Son, to die for us upon Calvary's cross. To fail to recognize and acknowledge such goodness and such love is not only an offence against justice but against truth as well. It is man's monumental lie. In comparison with it all others are pygmies.

Take the case of a soldier who fought with distinguished bravery for his country in the South Pacific. As a pilot he risked life scores of times by attacking the enemy in the trackless skies, shooting dozens of them down, and thus saving the lives of thousands of men in the troopships below. At last he himself is shot down in flames. Badly wounded, he manages to drag himself from the burning plane. Through the jungle he gropes his way, suffering hunger, thirst, weariness and the stabbing pain of his wounds.

For months he barely manages to keep alive on a few berries and edible greens. By day the sun scorches his half-naked body. By night he shivers as the cold rain pelts him with icy pellets. Every nerve in his body is aching, while his mind is tortured with the fear of impending death in a wilderness where his body would never be found. At last when the cup of human misery is filled to overflowing, he drags himself, emaciated and wan, into a settlement of friendly natives. Invalided back to America, he has lost an arm and a leg, while an injured spine condemns him for the rest of his life to a wheelchair.

On being returned to his native land, let us suppose that he receives no word of recognition. No Purple Heart is pinned upon him. No Distinguished Service Medal adorns his uniform. His commander, his fellow officers, his countrymen utter no word of admiration, no word of gratitude, no single acknowledgment of all that he has done and suffered for his country.

What would be the feeling of the victim of such black ingratitude? Would not their failure to express a single word of appreciation cut him to the very quick? Would it not stab him with a pain sharper than any he had endured from wounds, or cold or hunger or thirst in his jungle prison? Sharper than a serpent's tooth is black ingratitude.

Let us now consider the feeling of the American people after being apprised of such a case. Would not every man, woman, and child in the land rise up as one to pay homage to such a hero? With a single voice they would say: Such heroism should receive the grateful acclaim of the nation.

Such bravery under fire should be fittingly recognized. Such suffering and sacrifice should receive the public recognition of the American people as long as they have any regard for justice, merit, and truth. Indeed, if we knew that there was one single such unrecognized hero in our midst, would we not be restless and unable to sleep peacefully until we had ferreted him out and given to him the public recognition which his heroism demanded? Why? Because both justice and truth require it. Not only would his merit entitle him to such recognition, but *truth* itself would likewise demand that we pay homage to such excellence. If we did not do so, we should experience not only the rankling sense of injustice but also the torturing guilt of participating in a public lie.

Public Worship—A Duty

God is the one infinitely perfect Being in the universe. All the perfections, such as goodness, kindness, honesty, truth, justice, mercy, generosity, love, which we find existing in a fragmentary manner in creatures, exist in God in an infinite degree. In giving us our very being and all the faculties of body and soul, God has given us more and has done more for us than any and all the benefactors and heroes who ever lived. Therefore truth itself demands that we give public recognition to such excellence and such beneficence. It is a dictate of simple honesty. It is the thunderous demand of strict justice.

This truth is well expressed by Dr. F. Hettinger: "As religion consists in the recognition of God as our Creator and the end of all creatures, so its immediate and formal expression is adoration. Man naturally pays homage to real greatness, wherever found; he is naturally attracted by goodness and love, of which he is the object; he naturally admires genius in works which bear its impress. But God is the plenitude of Life, of Love, and Power; when, therefore, man reads His greatness in the marvels of creation, His love and goodness in the order of nature and the pages of history, His providence in the ordering of his own life and in that of others, then he falls prostrate, and exclaims with child-like awe, '*Holy, holy, holy, Lord God of Sabbaoth!*' He confesses that both himself and all things are from God, by his prayer, 'Our Father, Who art in heaven'; that all things live and move in God, and are sustained by His might, by the 'Hallowed be Thy Name'; that he and all creatures are destined to serve God here, and to share His glory, by the prayer 'Thy Kingdom come.' And as long as man is man, so long will religion endure, and, with it, the obligation of worship." [1]

A Curious Myopia

There has been a curious myopia on the part of many people concerning this obligation. People recognize instantly the malice of theft, drunkenness, and murder. Each would be horrified to be called a thief. Each would slink away in shame if termed a drunkard. Everyone would be aghast if called a murderer. Yet they seem to perceive little or no malice in withholding from God the worship which is His due.

Thieves they are, nevertheless, and robbers too, not of men but of God. If it be a sin to rob a human being of his due, how much greater sin is it to rob God of His due? If we judge the malice of an offence by the dignity of the person offended, who is there who can measure the malice of a deliberate offence against the infinite majesty of God? Most crimes are the result of passion which blurs the reason and

[1] *Natural Religion*, pp. 277, 278

bends the will like a reed in a gale. They are usually the result of a passing disorder. But the crime of ignoring God and of withholding for a long time the worship due Him can plead no such extenuating circumstances.

Suffice it to say that the sin of irreligion is one of the most grievous which a creature can commit. To those who are less sensitive to the term, *sinful,* and more responsive to the term, *immoral,* we add that it is one of the most profoundly immoral acts which a creature can perform. For such a person places himself in direct and permanent opposition to the whole moral order because he is in opposition to the Author and Underwriter of that order.

The anarchist aims the assassin's bullet not at a private citizen but at the Ruler of a nation, because he wishes to destroy law and order and thus plunge the whole nation into disorder and strife. We look upon his dastardly deed with greater loathing because of the more far-reaching consequences of the act. Like the anarchist, the irreligious person points a revolver, loaded with ingratitude and treason, at the heart of the Creator, the one Being who has the greatest claim upon his gratitude and love. To worldlings and to irreligious this may sound like strong language. It is, however, well within the margin of the facts.

Considering the vast number of people who rarely or never darken the door of a church in our land, there is no truth that needs to be sounded so loudly or so persistently in the ears of the American people as that of the duty of rendering homage and worship to the God who made them. It is man's first and supreme duty. It is absolute, universal and indispensable. Anyone who violates it should feel upon his brow the mark of Cain, in his heart the treason of Benedict Arnold, and in his conscience the guilt of Judas.

Why Neglect God?

The overwhelming majority of the American people believe in God and in His Son, Jesus Christ. They possess many noble virtues and qualities which evoke the admiration of mankind. They are generous almost to a fault. With no thought of selfish gain, they entered World War I, and sent their sons across the sea to free the countries of the Old World from aggression. With lavish hand they poured out their blood and treasure for the freedom of lands they had never previously seen. For the first time in the history of the world, mankind saw a major power emerge from a bloody conflict, into which that people had poured their substance on a gigantic scale, *without taking so much as a grain of sand.*

In World War II they repeated the story, but on a larger scale. Fighting for the freedom of the Chinese, the Filipinos and the Australians in the Pacific, and for that of the occupied countries of Europe, they poured out their wealth on a scale never witnessed before. They sent millions of their young men to fight in the Seven Seas, on all the battlefields, and in the skies of all the world. This they did without a thought of gaining a penny of booty or a single inch of territory for themselves. It is no wonder that the oppressed peoples of the Orient and the downtrodden countries of the Old World, thrill at the thought of America and marvel at the feats of her people.

This is the flowering of the seed of religious faith and Christian idealism which the founding fathers planted deep in our land. Signs are not wanting, however, that the religious faith, which was once so sturdy in our national life, is waning through the failure of many millions to practice it. Religion, like all living things, grows through use and decays through disuse. The failure to teach religion in our public schools, because of the diversity of denominational creeds, is doubtless one of the important factors in the decay of religious life in our country. While it constitutes a serious administrative difficulty, it is one which, we believe, American resourcefulness and ingenuity can overcome.

Surely a way can be found, fair and equitable to all, whereby religion can be taught to the overwhelming majority of our children, sons and daughters of God-fearing men and women. Otherwise irreligion will grow by leaps and bounds, and the sturdy faith of our pioneer forefathers will be but a nostalgic memory. It will be a sad day for America and its future, when our children know more about Donald Duck and Mickey Mouse than they do about their Creator and His Son, Jesus Christ, our divine Redeemer. Yet that is the direction in which we are traveling at breakneck speed today.

It is time to call a halt. It is time to put first things first. It is time to put God on the throne of American life, to thank Him for the blessings which He has poured out so lavishly upon our land, to obey His divine commands, and to render to Him the homage of adoration, propitiation, and love which are His due. It is time for us to remember that we can kill a faith by failing to practice it.

The spiritual distemper of our day is indifferentism. This is the first stage in the sickness that leads to decadence and death. "*Nothing,*" warned Edmund Burke, "*is so fatal to religion as indifferentism, which is at least half infidelity.*" Similar, too, is the admonition of Samuel Johnson: "To be of no church is dangerous. Religion, of which the rewards are distant, and which is animated only by Faith and Hope, will glide by degrees out of the mind, unless it be invigorated and reimpressed by external ordinances, by stated calls to worship, and the salutary influence of example." [2] It is time for the American people to heed this warning. It is time for them to remember that since they have poured out their blood and treasure for nations all over the globe, they must not be miserly toward the one Being in the world who has the first claim upon their gratitude and love, the Creator, who gave them their very existence and who has showered upon them such a multitude of blessings.

[2] *Lives of the Poets: Milton*

CHAPTER XVIII

RELIGION AND SOCIETY

The task and triumph of religion is to make men and nations true and just and upright in all their dealings, and to bring all law as well as all conduct into subjection and conformity to the law of God.—HENRY VAN DYKE

MAN is both an individual with a certain independence of action and a member of society. He has been endowed by God with gifts of mind, heart and will, whereby he can think his own thoughts, direct his affections to whatsoever object he desires, and make his own decisions, independently of the thoughts and actions of others. But he has likewise been endowed with a social nature, with gifts which enable him to coöperate with his fellows and prompt him to associate with them in all the great enterprises of life. As a matter of fact, he lives and moves and has his being in the society of which he forms a part. He has a craving for the company of others and reaches a richer and fuller life by the use of his social endowments.

From this twofold nature of man arises the duty of private or individual worship and of social or public worship. As we have already presented at sufficient length the duty of internal and of external homage on the part of the individual, we shall develop with equal care the *duty of social worship*.

As man is obliged to acknowledge God's authorship of his body and his mind by using both these natures in conjoint acts of adoration, so man is in duty bound to use his social nature in rendering homage to God. This he does by uniting with his fellows in acts of public prayer, praise and worship. In endowing man with a social nature, God becomes the Author of society. That debt therefore can be paid, not by the individual, but only by the society which bows its corporate head in reverent acknowledgment of its dependence upon God and His dominion over it.

That is why the act of public homage in which the Ruler, the civil magistrates and the private citizens join is a well-rounded act of worship, especially pleasing to God and wholesome and salutary to the spiritual and moral life of society. Man is profoundly influenced by the example of his fellows. Social worship stimulates and reënforces individual worship and frequently adds order and regularity to expressions of devotion which, if left entirely to the individual, might become fitful, desultory and uncertain. Hence, the great advantage of having one day of the week set aside for the systematic, public worship of God by all members of society.

In such corporate action the devotion of the individual is greatly intensified by being blazoned forth in congregational singing, the joint recitation of prayer, and the performance of other acts of public worship. So closely knit are the physical and the psychical natures of man that the external expression of an inward sentiment serves to deepen and stabilize it and render it easier of recall.

"Why No Welcoming Committee?"

Social worship is not therefore to be viewed as a superfluous supplement to private worship, a supplement which springs merely from fashion or convention, and not from the deeper elements of man's nature. It is a profound moral obligation which arises from the social nature with which God has endowed man. We can make this matter somewhat clearer by an illustration.

Let us suppose that the President of the United States announces his intention to pay your city a public visit. He arrives at the depot, but alas and alack! there is no one to greet him and his party. He looks around for the mayor, the civil officials, the welcoming committee of prominent citizens and the usual concourse of private ones. But he looks in vain! People are hurrying to and fro, intent upon their own affairs. A few idlers, who recognize him, stare and pass on.

Finally he hails a couple of Yellow Cabs and he and his entourage go to the mayor's office. There the mayor's attention is divided between his cigar and the morning newspaper. Later on when his eye lights upon the President, he lays down his paper and says:

"Hello! Mr. President, welcome to our fair city."

When the President inquires why there was no welcoming committee, no manifestation of public respect for the Chief Executive of the nation, His Honor replies:

"Oh! We don't believe in those artificial and superfluous expressions. I, the other officials and the citizens here keep our esteem for you in our hearts. It would be silly and meaningless to have any public expression of such homage and esteem."

What do you think the President's reaction would be to such strange procedure? What do you think would be the sentiments expressed in every newspaper and upon the lips of every citizen of our land? Would they not be indignant against the magistrates and the citizens of that community for their gross lack of elementary respect for the President of our country? Regardless of any differences of political views which might exist, the members of that community, the nation would declare, should pay to the President the public respect which his exalted office justly demands. That is a debt which they owe him, and if they failed to pay it, they would be the objects of the indignation and the scorn of all the other citizens of the land.

From that conclusion, no citizen will dissent. Yet, if it be universally admitted that the President is entitled to that public expression of the respect and esteem of society, how can society withhold the expression of the honor and reverence due to the Creator? Is He not the God of presidents, the King of kings, the Lord of lords? At His name should not every knee bend, of those that are in heaven, on earth, and under the earth? Is not God the source of all authority, the fountainhead of all rights? Is it not in His name that kings rule and lawmakers issue just decrees? Does not the whole moral order derive its sanctions from God? What authority is there in human society that does not stream from God? For society to fail then in giving to the King of kings the public expression of its reverence and homage is to fail in its first and most important duty. This is the capital sin.

An Impersonal Force?

So reasonable and obvious is this conclusion that it admits of no equivocation or escape. Why is it then that there are so many of our fellow countrymen who fail to give God the public homage and worship due Him? The causes in our opinion are fourfold. First is the tendency of many people to think of the Deity in terms of a vague power or impersonal force far off in the universe. Secondly, many wonder or doubt if God wants such homage. Thirdly, many fail to realize that they have a strict duty to render public worship to God. Fourthly, many are so engrossed in their own mundane concerns as to forget about God almost completely. Let us look briefly at these considerations.

The conception of God as a force operating throughout the universe, without intelligence and will, and hence devoid of personality, is easily disproven. Wherever we look at nature, whether it be at a blade of grass, a leaf on the tree, a flower, a bird, or man, we see the evidence of plan and purpose, the blueprint of means carefully arranged to secure a previsioned end. But such a careful dovetailing of a multitude of means to achieve a predetermined end is the unmistakable evidence of intelligence and will. Therefore the Author of nature must be a Personal Being, and not a blind force.

The same conclusion is reached by the following simple line of reasoning. One of the basic principles of logic declares that every effect must have an adequate cause, that the effect cannot transcend the cause any more than water can rise higher than its source. In other words there cannot be anything in the effect which does not exist in some way in the cause. Before a sculptor carves a statue he must have the idea or image of that statue in his mind. Before an artist paints a picture, he must have the picture in his mind. Since man possesses intellect and will and personality, it follows with inescapable logic that the Creator must possess personality. Otherwise we would have an effect without a cause, and all possibility of logical thinking would collapse.

Thousands of years ago the Psalmist proclaimed this mighty truth, which all the findings of science and philosophy have but underlined. "He has made us," declared the Psalmist, "not we ourselves." God is the supreme personality of the universe. We are but tiny echoes of Him. "Trailing clouds of glory do we come," said Wordsworth, "from God who is our home."

Does God Want Our Homage?

Now in regard to the second point. Does God really want our homage? What does He gain from it? We are so small. God is so great. Isn't it somewhat presumptuous to think that the God of a million worlds and of the immeasurable spaces would be interested and pleased by our expressions of reverence and love? The answer is simple and direct. God does want our worship and our love. He has proclaimed that time after time in Holy Scripture. This is the burden of the prophets and the focal point in the Savior's message to mankind. This is the duty proclaimed in the first of the ten commandments, given by God to Moses amidst the thunders on Mt. Sinai. "I am the Lord, thy God. . . . Thou shalt not have strange gods before me."

A doctor of the law asked Christ:

"Master, which is the great commandment in the law?"

"Thou shalt love the Lord thy God with thy whole heart," replied Jesus, "and with thy whole soul, and with thy whole mind. *This is the greatest and the first commandment.*" [1]

The structure of one's moral character rests upon the shifting sands of expediency if it is not built upon the rock of compliance with this, the greatest and the first commandment. One's whole life is topsy-turvy, if it is not ordered on obedience to God's primal and supreme demand. This mandate is written not only upon the tablets of stone but also upon the fleshy tablets of the human heart. Our whole nature reaches out to Him in aspiration and love. He is our Father and our God.

Does a father want the love of his child? Is he indifferent as to whether his son ever gives him any expression of respect, any tribute of love? Let us picture a father returning after the day's toil to his home. His three little children, aged

[1] *Mat.* 22:36-39

five, seven and nine are at the door. Instead of running to greet him, to take his hand and welcome him with gleeful shouts of joy, they stand motionless and silent. Entering, he holds out his arms to them. But instead of running to him to enfold themselves in his loving embrace, instead of struggling to be the first to climb upon his knee and give him the tender expressions of children's love, they turn and walk silently away.

What would the father think of such behavior? Would it not cut him to the quick? Would it not break his heart? What could hurt him more? Why, the very thought of such unnatural conduct fills you with indignation. What monstrous children must they be, you would exclaim, who could show such ingratitude to the father who begot them and who maintains them in existence by his toil.

A Contrast

Contrast with that the opposite scene. As soon as the children catch sight of their father, they make a mad dash for him. They seize his hands, tackle him about the knees, and seek almost to devour him with their greedy expression of love. His youngest, a daughter, climbs upon his knee and tells him with the eloquence of little arms twined tightly round his neck how much she loves him. Go to that man as he sits there, basking in the sunshine of his children's love, and say to him:

"That's all meaningless . . . silly . . . nonsense."

"Why," he would reply, "you amaze me. Don't you have any mind or any heart? Don't you know that nothing is dearer to a father than the expressions of his children's love? This means more to me than all the yellow gold in the mines of Solomon. This is something which money cannot buy—the sincere and tender expressions of children's love."

Yes, those expressions mean much to the father because they are rooted in the very nature of children's relationship to a father—a relationship which demands the expressions of respect, gratitude and love. Not less, but more, does the expression of His children's homage and love mean to God, our Heavenly Father. What a monstrous conception it would be to think that, after creating us and endowing us with hearts to love and mouths to speak, God would cut us adrift and have no interest in hearing the cry of our love. Why, that would be to degrade Him to a status below our own human fathers!

Deep Calls Unto Deep

The seashell echoes of its ocean home. Deep calls unto deep. The creature cries out to his Creator. To that cry, which is like the mystic radio wave heard round the earth, God turns a listening and a loving ear. Of no fact in life can we be more certain than that God wants the expression of our gratitude and love. This we know from reason and from divine revelation.

Indeed, it is the very essence of religion. For without prayer and worship, religion vanishes into thin air. These expressions of trust, obedience, reverence, thanksgiving, atonement, adoration, supplication and love constitute the golden bond that ties the heart of the creature to the heart of God. This is the truth which Tennyson expresses so beautifully:

> More things are wrought by prayer
> Than this world dreams of.
> For what are men better than sheep or goats
> That nourish a blind life within the brain,
> If, knowing God, they lift not hands of prayer
> Both for themselves and those who call them friends?

For so the whole round earth is every way
Bound by gold chains about the feet of God.

A mind greater than that of Tennyson, namely, that of St. John, who rested his head upon the bosom of Christ and felt the throbbing of the divine heart, gives us the basic reason why the creature should pay homage to his God. "Thou art worthy, O Lord our God," declares the beloved disciple, "to receive glory and honor and power: because thou hast created all things, and for thy will they were, and have been created." To that divine Being there is due, he tells us, "benediction and glory, and wisdom and thanksgiving, honor and power and strength, forever and ever."

They Don't Realize Their Duty

Now for the third reason why so many people fail to render public homage to God. That reason is because they fail to realize the duty of rendering such worship. This, we are convinced, is the chief reason why so many of our fellow countrymen rarely if ever darken a church door. Receiving scarcely any religious education at home, they attend public schools wherein the teaching of religion is forbidden by law. The result is that they know little or nothing about religion. They do not understand the claims that God has upon them, and not understanding, they do not satisfy them.

Like everything else that is to be understood, religion must be taught—and taught in a thorough and systematic manner. How much of the history of our country would its citizens know, if it were not taught in school? They would have but a hazy and sketchy knowledge of the great and moving events which brought our nation into being. So it is with religion. It is apparently regarded by great numbers of our citizens as exercising no weighty claims upon them. It is an optional affair with them.

They feel free to go once in a while, or to remain away altogether. The latter alternative is unfortunately too often followed. Only in times of crisis, of great emotional upheaval, when the bottom of their world seems to be dropping out, do many of them turn to God.

The fact that man is *physically* free to worship God or not, should never be construed to mean that he is *morally* free to ignore his Creator. We are physically free to commit theft or murder. But we are under a *moral* restraint. So it is with the worshiping of God. While physically free to turn our backs upon Him, we are under the most serious and compelling moral obligation to render to Him the homage of gratitude, worship and love due Him in strict justice.

This truth perhaps above all others, needs to be driven home to the people of America. This means that a way must be found, and found quickly, if our nation is not to continue to fall deeper and deeper into a form of veneered paganism, of bringing in a systematic manner to the vast masses of our people the saving truths of religion. This is the crying need in America today as it will be in the days ahead. This is the appeal that should be sounded from every pulpit, echoed in the press, flashed upon the screens of our cinemas, and burnt into the conscience of the people of our land.

We need to write upon the skies of America the truth, which the experience of humanity the world over has proven to the hilt: An education which sharpens the intellect but does nothing to strengthen the character, to purify the heart, and to sensitize the conscience to the undertones of the moral law, may render a person a more clever but not necessarily a better citizen. The conscience which does not sink its roots into the subsoil of religious faith, nor shoot its antennae beyond the roof of the skies, misses alike the music of divine inspiration and the thunder of divine commands. To strengthen the character and to quicken the conscience to the duties of citizenship, religion is of vital value and of supreme importance. "Educate men without religion," observed the Duke of Wellington, "and you make them the creatures of circumstance."

Lest We Forget

A word about the fourth reason why many of our citizens fail to give God the public homage due Him. That is because they are so engrossed in their mundane affairs as to forget about God and their duties to Him. Man has never been short of alibis for busying himself with his material pursuits to the neglect of the divine invitation to spend one hour with Him. Down through the ages come the echoes of those who, in Christ's parable of the supper, spurned the king's invitation to the banquet table: "I have bought a farm, and I must needs go out and see it." "I have bought five yoke of oxen, and I go to try them." "I have married a wife, and therefore I cannot come." [2] Old as Ur of the Chaldees, they are as up-to-date as this morning's newspaper.

Especially subject to absorption in material pursuits are the American people. Busy for a century in pushing forward the frontiers of an expanding civilization, our people move to a tempo which astonishes visitors from other lands. They have compared the bustling energy of our people to bottled lightning. Only when an American lives abroad for a year or two does he begin to realize the abnormal speed at which our nation moves and lives. Pep, speed, and action have become our national watchwords.

We are a nation of "go-getters," engrossed night and day in the frenzied pursuit of the almighty dollar. Unending streams of autos shoot along our streets at a speed that spells danger to the occupants and to the pedestrians. Thus have

[2] *Luke* 14:18-21

we been killing more than 30,000 and maiming more than a million a year. Crowds rush hither and yon in our cities. We are eternally on the go. But where? No one seems clearly to know. Many pile up wealth which exceeds all the needs of body, mind and soul. In a little more than a century we have become the richest and the mightiest nation on the face of the earth. Virtually all others now look to America for favors, help and largesse.

It is time for the American people to remember that man does not live by bread alone, but by every word that proceedeth from the mouth of God. It is time to remember that they have souls as well as bodies. It is time to remember the God who has showered such riches, wealth and prosperity upon our land as no other nation in all history has ever known. When Great Britain was at the zenith of her imperial power, exercising a tributary sway over one-fourth of the earth's surface and population, Rudyard Kipling, the poet laureate, sounded a note of warning in the famous *Recessional*, lest the nation forget the Source from whom all power and blessings flow. He wrote:

> God of our Fathers! Known of old,
> Lord of the far-flung battle line
> Beneath whose awful hand we hold
> Dominion over palm and pine.
> Lord God of hosts! Be with us yet,
> Lest we forget. Lest we forget!

A Warning to America

That is the note that needs to be sounded in America to-day. We must not forget the divine Being who has poured out His blessings and favors upon us with so lavish a hand. Common decency requires us to acknowledge our indebtedness to our Creator and to return to Him the homage of our worship, gratitude and love. That is the note that we fain would sound today through all the sections of American life, that every man, woman and child would fall upon their knees to thank God both for the blessings they have received as individuals and as members of the most favored nation on earth.

Such is the dictate of our minds. Such too is the clamorous demand of our hearts. As America has achieved the first place among the nations of the world for its wealth, let it now achieve eminence for its gratitude to God. For upon the brow of a nation distinguished for its power and influence there rests no crown so regal as that which is composed of the gold of gratitude and the pearl of humility.

The failure to render such homage constitutes a double sin—the sin of ingratitude and of injustice. Against such a sin there is warning America today a voice mightier and more impressive than that of Kipling. It is the voice of the great Apostle of the Gentiles who is addressing to America today the warning he uttered to the Romans of old: "The wrath of God is revealed from heaven against all ungodliness and injustice of those men that detain the truth of God in injustice: because that which is known of God is manifest in them. For God hath manifested it unto them. For the visible things of him, from the creation of the world, are clearly seen, being understood by the things that are made; his eternal power also, and divinity; so that they are inexcusable. Because that when they knew God, they have not glorified him as God or given thanks; but became vain in their thoughts, and their foolish heart was darkened. For professing themselves to be wise, they became fools. . . . Who changed the truth of God into a lie; and worshipped and served the creature rather than the Creator, who is blessed forever. Amen." [3]

[3] *Rom.* 1:18–25

CHAPTER XIX

RELIGION AND MORALITY

Christianity is the good man's text; his life is the illustration.—CHARLES MONTESQUIEU

WHAT is the relation between religion and morality? Are they separate and independent? While there has been some confused thinking which has pictured them as unrelated, the fact is that they are so intimately related as to constitute but different aspects of the same basic reality. As it is of enormous practical importance both for religion and for morality to understand their true relation, we shall discuss this point at some length and offer a few illustrations.

First, a definition. Morality may be defined as human conduct in so far as it is freely subordinated to the ideal of what is right. It is antecedent to ethics, and denotes those concrete actions of which ethics is the science. The evolutionary, positivist and idealist schools have brought much confusion into popular thought by seeking to substitute an independent morality for that based on belief in God.

Ethical Culture Societies have carried on a propaganda whose general thesis is that people can be made good citizens by inculcating in them ethical ideals and standards with no reference to God or the supernatural. In the education of the young they would substitute discussions of codes and criteria of ethics, for religious training. They would take the eyes of youth away from God and place them entirely on man.

We can perhaps best show the close relationship between religion and morality by pointing out that the *obligation for both types of conduct stems ultimately from God.* Thus, after Christ had enunciated the duty of loving God with one's whole heart and soul as the first and the greatest commandment, He added: "And the second is like to this: Thou shall love thy neighbor as thyself. On these two commandments dependeth the whole law and the prophets." [1] To love one's neighbor implies the duty of being just, fair, kind and generous to him in all the relations of life. To do this is not merely a dictate of right reason, but it is also a divine command.

A Divine Command

In His Sermon on the Mount, Christ proclaimed the law which may be said to be the basic rule in all human relations and the fundamental principle of all *morality*. It is the famous golden rule: "All things therefore whatsoever you would that men should do to you, do you also to them. For this is the law and the prophets." [2] From these two utterances of the divine Founder of the Christian religion it is clear that one's relations with his fellow man are not merely matters of expediency or of social propriety. They are regulated by a divine command which binds every rational creature, regardless of race, color or creed.

Now in obeying that divine ordinance we are acknowledging, with the eloquence of deeds and not merely of words, God's sovereign dominion over us. We are rendering to Him a most pleasing homage. It is a homage comparable to that which we give to God when we praise, adore and love Him. The worship of God is direct homage. A good moral act,

[1] *Mat.* 22:39-41
[2] *Mat.* 7:12

such as a kindness to one's neighbor, is *indirect* homage. God exacts of His creatures not only the direct homage of worship but also the indirect homage of virtue and morality.

Thus the love which we bestow upon our fellow man may be said to be the completion of the homage which we render to God when we love Him directly and immediately. The common Fatherhood of God makes us all His children and therefore imposes upon all of us the duty of loving one another as brothers.

We are to see in the countenance of the poorest and the most afflicted of men the lineaments of the face of Christ. We are to minister to the outcast, to the hungry, the thirsty, the naked and to those in prison as we would minister to Christ Himself. For Christ has assured us: "As long as you did it to one of these, my least brethren, you did it to me." [3] It was the realization of this truth which held St. Peter Claver at his post of duty ministering to the Negro slaves at Cartagena with the tenderness and kindliness with which he would have ministered to the wounded Christ. It was this realization which has prompted all the saints of God to love His children and to spend themselves in sacrificial service for them.

"Bring Him In"

During the American assault on Attu Island, our soldiers came across a Jap, named Ito, badly wounded in his foxhole. He and a companion had exhausted their ammunition. Each had held his last grenade against his stomach and pulled the pin. Ito's proved to be a dud. But his comrade's grenade exploded, disemboweling Ito and shattering his leg. When our soldiers found him several days later, he was still clutching his dud grenade.

[3] *Mat.* 25:40

His leg had now become a greenish, muddy, bloody mass of gas gangrene. The stench was terrific.

"Throw that stinking mess overboard," barked out a wounded gunner on the hospital ship, "before he suffocates us all."

"Gimme my trench knife," yelled an infantryman with a bayonet slash in his hip, "and I'll operate on the ———."

A few nights before, the Japs had broken through our lines and slaughtered some of our unarmed medical corpsmen. The situation was tense—loaded with the dynamite of hatred, needing only a spark to ignite the fuse.

Lights had burned all night over the operating table. Finally the last American had been lifted from it. Dr. Cass Stimson, the chief surgeon, stepped forward.

Did he have the right to use the blood plasma, donated by an American to save an American's life, for the hated Jap? Did he have the right to endanger his life and those of his assistants by coming in contact with the highly infectious gas gangrene? Wasn't it their business to *kill* Japs, not to *save* them?

Here too were the passions of hatred and vengeance pounding at the central dogma of the Christian faith, the teaching that all men are brothers. Would religion gird him with the power to resist the flaming passions of nationalism and the clamor of hatred and vengeance?

"Bring him in," ordered Dr. Stimson.

When the operation was over, tears of joy streamed down Ito's cheeks as he grasped the surgeon's arm, and sobbed, "A-mer-REEK-A! A-mer-REEK-A!"

Here was the flowering of the central teaching of the Christian religion into a deed of service, kindliness and love for one's enemy. So knit together are we all as members of the mystical body of Christ, that we cannot unjustly harm any of our fellow men, even the most loathsome of our enemies, without injuring ourselves. Any cruelty inflicted upon that helpless Jap—even the refusal to relieve his pain —would have degraded those who inflicted it. There is no cave deep enough for us to hide in, when the cry of suffering is heard, even though it be the cry of our enemy. Thus does religion stretch out her hands, full of healing, of beneficent service, of loving kindness to all mankind.

The Homage of Virtue

Well does St. John declare: "If any man say, I love God, and hateth his brother; he is a liar. For he that loveth not his brother, whom he seeth, how can he love God, whom he seeth not?" Then the Beloved Disciple sums up the case thus briefly and simply: "And this commandment we have from God, that he, who loveth God, love also his brother." [4]

No man therefore can be said to render to God the perfect homage of love, if that love does not extend to his fellow men and embrace even his enemies. From all this it is clear that our moral duties to our fellow men are based ultimately not upon the theoretical conclusions of ethicians, the dictates of self-interest, or even the ordinances of human reason, but upon the express will of God. Remove God from the scheme of human life and you remove the basis not only of religion but of morality as well.

The concept that religion is largely a matter of lip service to almighty God, of oral prayer and hymn singing, with little or no connection with moral conduct is a grotesque caricature of Christ's teaching. "By their fruits," the Master declared, "you shall know them." Then he reminded His hearers and all His followers in future ages: "Not every one that saith to me, Lord, Lord, shall enter into the kingdom of heaven: but he that doth the will of my Father who is

[4] 1 *John* 4:20–21

in heaven, he shall enter into the kingdom of heaven." [5]

This truth is central in the teachings of Christ. It is stressed by every writer on the spiritual life. It is echoed by Thomas à Kempis in his great masterpiece, *The Following of Christ:* "Sublime words make not a man holy and just, but a virtuous life maketh him dear to God."

Hence God wants not only the worship of prayer, but also the homage of virtue. To render Him the former without the latter is to hand Him a branch from which the fruit has been plucked. It is like the action of the man who places on the collection plate on Sunday an envelop, orthodox and imposing enough on the outside, but empty within. Religion is not an empty sham. It is a living tree, producing the fruit of morality, and both the tree and the fruit derive their vitality from God.

God and the Moral Law

As this point is of great practical importance, let us supplement the above considerations, drawn from the revelation of Christ, with the evidence of a philosophical character. We have already indicated that man is indebted to God both for his existence and his faculties. Furthermore, he is dependent upon God for the operation of his faculties.

The nature of this dependence we may illustrate with the following example. A watch owes its existence to a watchmaker. But if that watch is to operate, the watchmaker must do more than simply put together the various parts of its mechanism. He must convey to the spring a portion of his own energy which is there stored up in the form of tension. It is only in virtue of this stored-up power that the watch can function.

In a somewhat similar manner, the Creator must place

[5] *Mat.* 7:20–22

His own energy at the disposal of His creatures, if they are to be able to use the faculties with which they are endowed. Without the divine concursus the creature could not perform a single act. Hence God's coöperation is essential in all our thoughts and actions. As God is infinite holiness and perfection, the action in which He coöperates cannot be a matter of indifference to Him. He must necessarily will that it be in accordance with His own divine nature. Hence the Creator's will must be the ultimate norm of all the conduct of His creatures.

This is true, irrespective of the specific natures of the creatures. Whether they be living or inanimate, rational or irrational, they are all under the Creator's jurisdiction and must conform to His will. The expression of the divine will is accommodated to the specific nature of each creature. In beings devoid of reason, God's direction finds expression in the physical determination of the precise manner in which they are to act, so that they cannot swerve therefrom by so much as a hair's breadth. In creatures endowed with intellect and free will, the divine direction is reflected in the moral law, enunciated by the practical reason.

"It is a law," observes Bernard J. Otten, S.J., "written in the intellect after the manner of knowledge, and communicated to the will as a moral obligation." [6] While leaving man physically free, it binds him to a type of conduct from which he may not swerve. What is the binding force of that law? It is identical with the binding force of the Creator's sovereign will, since it is but the manifestation of that will in rational nature.

Morality, like religion, is thus seen to consist essentially in the free acknowledgment of man's dependence on God. Both are thus linked together in a union strong and inseparable.

[6] *The Reason Why*, B. Herder Book Co., St. Louis, Mo., p. 84

Two seashells, though of different size and color, tell by their echo of the common ocean home from which they come. So religion and morality, differ though they may in outward form and expression, tell by the echo of the binding force within them both, of the *common* source from which they come—God, the Ruler of the far-flung heavens and the Moral Governor of the questing hearts of men. The slanting rays of light that splash the skies at sunset with the colors of the rainbow point like fingers to their fountain. So religion and morality, that paint on the multicolored canvas of human life the shining deeds of man's love of God and of his fellow man, point like stabbing arrows of light to the common Source of all Light, the Author of all holiness, the Fountain of all perfection—the Light that enlighteneth every man that cometh into this world.

The Need of Sanctions

This vital truth may be established with equal clarity by the consideration of the *need of adequate sanction to make the moral law effective.* By sanction we mean a proper reward for the observance of the law, and a condign punishment for its violation. Since the moral law extends to all rational activity, whether internal or external, it follows that its sanction must do likewise. But most of man's actions, whether good or bad, escape the eyes of men. This is true of all of man's unexpressed thoughts wherein so much of his life consists. It is true likewise of most of his private actions. If the only sanction is that which comes from human justice, then most of man's rational life would be devoid of proper reward or punishment.

The seeds of action lie in thought. Whoever seeks to control his action must therefore begin by shepherding his thoughts. "As a man thinketh in his heart," says the author of the *Book of Proverbs*, "so is he." Thoughts constitute the core of one's mental life, issuing forth later in words and deeds. The policeman cannot arrest a man for murderous thoughts or larcenous desires. For he knows nothing of them and can therefore take no cognizance of them.

God, however, labors under no such disadvantage. He holds a man to strict accountability for his thoughts and secret desires. "You have heard," said Christ, "that it was said to them of old: Thou shalt not commit adultery. But I say to you, that whosoever shall look on a woman to lust after her, hath already committed adultery with her in his heart." [7] *It is only God who can surround that segment of man's rational life with adequate sanctions.*

Proponents of a system of morality independent of religion are fond of quoting the adage: Virtue is its own reward; vice, its own punishment. This cannot, however, stand close scrutiny. For in this life, this is only partly true. Instances all too numerous can be found, by anyone who takes the trouble to investigate, of persons who violate the moral laws and grow fat upon their ill-gotten gains. Indulging their appetites and passions, they scarcely know the meaning of self-denial or self-sacrifice. The just man not infrequently lives in penury, and the martyr dies at the stake.

Moreover such an abstract and doubtful speculation is not likely to deter a person from the satisfaction of an inveterate passion. Will the average person struggling with the raging passion of anger, jealousy, hatred, revenge, or lust be aided in quelling the tumult within him by such a consideration? All around him he sees persons taking what they want and, in the language of the day, "getting by" with it. Why should he be an exception? How warm and enticing is the voice of human passion. How cold and unappealing, if not positively unreal, is the voice of the abstract speculation.

[7] *Mat.* 5:27–29

"Carve the Granite with a Razor . . ."

What such a man needs, and needs desperately, is the clear, stern voice of God, reminding him that he cannot throw dust in the eyes of the Almighty, and that he will be punished with unfailing certainty for any violation of the moral law by an omniscient and eternal God. To Him our most secret thoughts are as the pages of an open book. Considerations of conventional propriety are no more capable of restraining the individual in whose bosom a tumultuous passion is raging than are chains of straw. No brass-buttoned policeman is near. No prying eye of a neighbor will detect his deed. No empty, verbal rhetoric will restrain him. Only the thunder of God's stern command, heard in the inner ear, is competent to encompass the whole cycle of man's rational life, both internal and external, with sanctions that grip the muscles of his will like bands of steel.

One may echo the words of Kipling's poem about wishing to be "east of Suez, where there ain't no ten commandments." But he would speedily find, if he went there, that God's commands and His mighty sanctions embrace the globe, and know no barrier of border, breed or race. When the storms of human passion are beating tempestuously against our frail bark, threatening at any moment to capsize it, it is only the divine voice commanding "Peace! Be still," that is able to save the day.

Knowledge, without religion, will no more sanctify than painted fire will burn, or the sight of water cleanse. Mere human knowledge or intellectual subtlety will not avail. No one has brought this out more strikingly than the great scholar of Oxford, Cardinal Newman, when he said: "Carve the granite with a razor, moor the vessel with a thread of silk, then you may hope with such keen and delicate instruments as human knowledge and human reason to contend against those giants, the passions and the pride of men." In that immortal utterance there is epitomized a whole volume.

Those words came back to the writer when walking one July day in the famous cemetery of Père La Chaise in Paris. Here are buried many of the notables of France. Suddenly we came upon the grave of one we least expected to find in the soil of France. It was that of Oscar Wilde. Poet, playwright, orator, he wrote and spoke our language with a brilliance and an eloquence which has rarely been surpassed. He was a symbol of refinement, learning, and culture. Yet he fell to the lowest depths of degradation and fled in shame and disgrace to seek refuge in the alien soil of France. The weeds, growing high and luxuriously upon his neglected grave, seemed to proclaim with myriad tongues:

"Education, refinement, culture cannot save. Intellectual subtlety, cleverness, sophistication offer little protection against the tumultuous waves of human passion. They are but broken reeds in a storm. A man may walk intellectually among the stars and grovel morally among the swine. The mighty power of religion which purifies the mind, chastens the heart, tames the passions, and energizes the weak muscles of the will with a divine strength, is an indispensable requisite for a life of sustained moral rectitude. Let the nations of the world know that they are but heading the way of Nineveh and Tyre if they seek to educate their youth without the saving leaven of religious truth."

True, a religious person may stumble and fall. For he is a man and not an angel. But he will not remain complacent in the mire. His conscience will give him no peace until he rises and with his tears and penitence washes away his defilement. Religion bears down upon him with its stern requirements for contrition, purpose of amendment and penance. Not content with general resolutions for betterment, it demands the avoidance of the proximate occasions of sin. Stay away, it thunders, from whatever has led to your downfall in the past.

For frail mortals, perfection is achieved not by never falling, but by rising every time we fall. It is the man who refuses to stay down who eventually wins the fight. Religion will not let a sincere believer remain prostrate. It lifts him up and puts his unsteady feet upon the right path. It instills courage into his soul and strengthens the will for more determined effort. Peter thrice denied his Lord. But tears of repentance wore furrows in his cheeks, and he climaxed a life of heroic service in the Master's cause by shedding his blood for the faith of Christ.

Religion—Basis of Morality

Religion is the basis of morality. If morality is to be functional, it must have the sanctions which only religion can provide. This truth has been borne out by the experience of the centuries. It is writ large in the history of the rise and decline of civilizations. It has been recognized by all the profound students of society, regardless of philosophical or religious belief. "He who destroys religion," observes Plato, "overthrows the foundations of human society." Recurring to this theme, he declares: "It is an incontrovertible truth that if God presides not over the establishment of a city, and if it has only a human foundation, it cannot escape the greatest calamities. . . . If a State is founded on impiety and governed by men who trample on justice, it has no means of security." [8]

Long before Plato the Royal Prophet had expressed this same truth: "Unless the Lord build the house, they labor in vain that build it. Unless the Lord keep the city, he watcheth in vain that keepeth it." [9]

[8] *Ibid., tom.* VIII
[9] *Psal.* 126, 1

The social philosopher, J. J. Rousseau, voices this truth in a brilliant passage in *Emile:* "Attempts have been made to constitute reason the basis of virtue, but I find that religion is the only solid basis for morality. Virtue, it is said, is the love of order. But am I bound to sacrifice my happiness to this order? Granted that wherever intelligence exists, there is a certain moral order; but the difference is that the just man subjects himself to the whole moral order, whilst the unjust man subordinates the whole moral order to himself, and constitutes himself the center of all things. If God does not exist, then the unjust man reasons rightly in thus regarding himself."

It will come as a surprise to most admirers of our public school system to learn that Horace Mann, who is generally regarded as its founder, laid down the stern warning: "If the intellect, however gifted, be not governed by a sense of justice, a love of mankind, and a devotion to duty, its possessor is only a more splendid, as he is a more dangerous barbarian. *For we are fully persuaded that the salt of religious truth can alone preserve education from abuse.*" The rejection of that saving salt, unwittingly brought about by the diversity of creeds and the resulting administrative difficulty, has caused such a decline in the morality of the youth of our land that educators, social planners and legislators are now struggling desperately to find a way to restore the lost leaven.

That penetrating student of political science, Edmund Burke, proclaimed this truth to the people of Britain, when he declared: "True religion is the foundation of society, the basis on which all true civil government rests and from which power derives its authority, laws their efficacy, and both their sanction. If it is once shaken by contempt, the whole fabric cannot be stable or lasting."

"Reason and Experience Both Forbid . . ."

The voice, however, which will strike the most responsive chord in the hearts of the American people is that of the beloved Father of our country, George Washington. In his *Farewell Address*, Washington took particular pains to warn his countrymen of the importance of religion for political welfare and as a basis for public morality. Above the portals of every school, library, and public building, and framed on the walls of every home in our land, should be these memorable words of our first President:

"Of all the dispositions and habits which lead to political prosperity, religion and morality are indispensable supports. In vain would that man claim the tribute of patriotism, who should labor to subvert these great pillars of human happiness, these firmest props of the duties of men and citizens. And let us with caution indulge the supposition that morality can be maintained without religion. Whatever may be conceded to the influence of refined education on minds of peculiar structure, *reason and experience both forbid us to expect that national morality can prevail in exclusion of religious principles.*"

Those are words of mellow wisdom, which America can afford to neglect only at a cost of national morality and welfare. The unfortunate circumstances, which have unintentionally issued in the complete divorce of religion from public education, are bringing youthful morality to the lowest ebb in our nation's history. Appearing recently before a Congressional Committee in Washington, Mr. Edgar Hoover, F.B.I. chief, testified to the alarming increase of juvenile delinquency and pleaded for remedial action. "Return to the old-fashioned home and Church life," declared Mr. Hoover, "is essential if we are to provide an effective remedy for the situation."

In a recent symposium, *Democracy—Will It Survive?*, Walter Lippmann sounds the same urgent note of warning. "I venture to submit," he declares, "that the prevailing education is destined, if it continues, to destroy western civilization, and is in fact destroying it. . . . By *separating education from the classical religious tradition*, the school cannot train the pupil to look upon himself as an inviolable person because he is made in the image of God. . . . The teacher has no subject matter that even pretends to deal with the elementary and universal issues of human destiny. The graduate of the modern school knows only by accident and hearsay whatever wisdom mankind has come to in regard to the nature of men and their destiny."

The testimony of careful students of society, men of every shade of political and philosophical faith, could be piled sky high to the effect that religion is the basis of public morality and the foundation of good citizenship. The witnesses we have cited, however, will suffice to carry conviction to all open minds. There is in their testimony a note of warning, and a call for action, which cannot longer be delayed if we are to protect our nation from the growing tide of delinquency, lawlessness and crime.

A Reasoned Conclusion

To sum up. We have shown from the words of Christ that man is under a divine command to love his fellow man as well as God. In other words the obligation to be moral and the duty to be religious stem from the same source— God Himself. We then presented the philosophical evidence showing that since God's coöperation is essential for our every act, He cannot be indifferent as to the character of our conduct, but must will it to be in accordance with His nature. *Therefore the divine will constitutes the norm for the conduct of all creatures.* In irrational living creatures as well as in inanimate ones that divine norm finds expression in the physical determination of the precise method of acting, from which no deviation is possible. In rational creatures the divine will finds expression in the moral law, known by the intellect and communicated to the will, resulting in moral, but not in physical obligation.

The second philosophical consideration was drawn from the necessity for adequate sanctions for all rational activity, which only God and religion can provide. We then presented the testimony from the history of civilization, as expressed by philosophers, social scientists, educators and statesmen, showing that religion is a necessary basis for public morality and good citizenship. From all this we have seen that morality is the fruit which grows upon the tree of religion, and that the best way of cultivating that fruit is by nourishing the tree upon which it grows.

CHAPTER XX

THE VALUE OF RELIGION

> Religion is the final centre of repose; the good to which
> all things tend; apart from which man is a shadow, his
> very existence a riddle, and the stupendous scenes of
> nature which surround him as unmeaning as the leaves
> which the sibyl scattered in the wind.—ROBERT HALL

WHAT is the value of religion? We can best answer this question by indicating its values first to the individual and then to society. *Its supreme worth to the individual lies in the fact that it answers his deepest questionings:* Whence have I come? Whither am I going? What is the meaning and the purpose of human existence? Unless these questions are correctly answered, man walks about in a daze and life becomes a jig-saw puzzle from which essential parts are missing. Uncertainty paralyzes the springs of action, and no man can chart his course intelligently if he is ignorant of his destination.

Religion floods our darkness with a divine light. It reveals to us the God who is the Alpha and the Omega, the Beginning and the End of our existence. Not only does it disclose to us our ultimate destiny, but it also provides us with the means of attaining it. Religion brings into the focus of attention the two supreme values—God and the human soul. It makes clear to us that only in the possession of God, who is infinite Beauty, Truth and Love, will the human soul find the answer to its ceaseless questing.

195

Thus does it enable us to form a true hierarchy of values by appraising all things in accordance with the degree in which they aid us in the achievement of eternal life. It enables us to put first things first. It guides us in offering our supreme loyalty to God and in putting ourselves in the right relationship to God. "If you are not right toward God," wrote Lord Chatham to his nephew, "you can never be so toward man; and this is forever true, whether wits and rakes allow it or not."

Without religion we cannot be right toward God, toward man or toward ourselves. With religion and with the faithful fulfillment of all of its commands we look out upon life and the universe with a serene eye and a peaceful heart. Clasping His almighty hand, we know that no evil can befall us. We can see His face in earth and sky, His laughter in the running brook, and His voice in every song bird's call. To the believer, as Hood points out:

> Each cloud-capped mountain is a holy altar,
> An organ breathes in every grove;
> And the full heart's a Psalter,
> Rich in deep hymns of gratitude and love.[1]

Strengthens Character

Secondly, *religion helps the individual in the proper formation of his character by supplying him with adequate incentives for the observance of the moral law.* Character means that a man acts according to principle, not on motives of expediency. But this demands that the principles of morality be clothed with proper sanctions to secure their observance even in the teeth of passion, at the risk of unpopularity with the crowd, yes, in the face of death itself. Religion alone, as we have pointed out previously, can supply the

[1] Thomas Hood, *Ode to Rae Wilson*, l. 385

sanctions which are coextensive with all man's actions, whether they be private or external, whether they be seen by the eyes of our neighbor or known only to God and conscience.

There is but one rule of conduct for a man. That is always to do the right thing. The cost may be high in money, in friends, in sacrifice. The cost not to do right, however, is infinitely higher. For a temporal gain we barter the infinities. But how are we going to develop the character and acquire the strength to pay so dearly in pleasure, in popularity, in life itself, if we do not sink the roots of our being in the infinite might and wisdom of God Himself?

Seed that is placed on rocks and stones cannot develop a harvest. Neither can the character that rests upon motives of opportunism develop the power necessary to fight through to victory when money, power and good weather friends have fled. In contrast with the worldling's dependence upon external factors, the religious person knows that God and one constitute a majority, and that with God on his side, he cannot fail. Who is there who can hurt you, if you be zealous of good?

The importance of religion for character is thus ably set forth by Daniel Webster: "Political and professional fame cannot last forever, but a conscience void of offence before God and man is an inheritance for eternity. Religion, therefore, is a necessary, an indispensable element in any great human character. There is no living without it. Religion is the tie that connects man with his Creator, and holds him to his throne. If that tie is sundered or broken, he floats away a worthless atom in the universe, its proper attractions all gone, its destiny thwarted, and its whole future nothing but darkness, desolation and death. A man with no sense of religious duty is he whom the Scriptures describe in so terse but terrific a manner, as 'living without hope and without

God in the world.' Such a man is out of his proper being, out of the circle of all his duties, out of the circle of all his happiness, and away, far, far away from the purposes of his creation."

Without the zest which only religion can give, the individual puts up but a faint-hearted struggle. He feels bewildered, helpless and alone. "No one," observes Jean Paul Richter, "is so much alone in the universe as a denier of God. With an orphaned heart, which has lost the greatest of fathers, he stands mourning by the immeasurable corpse of the universe." [2]

During World War II, as during the previous one, the press has recorded thousands of instances wherein soldiers, sailors and aviators have testified to the strength and help received from God in circumstances of dire plight. Fighting with their backs to the wall, at the end of their own tether, men have turned instinctively to God for strength to endure, and courage to carry on. When his soldiers were being hemmed in on all sides, their ammunition running out, their food almost gone, their strength exhausted, and they still fought on, General MacArthur made the significant announcement: "There are no atheists in the foxholes of Bataan." No, for it takes character to fight on when all seems lost. And character, consciously or not, is rooted in faith in God and in His ultimate vindication of right.

Writing to his former teacher, Father R. C. McCarthy, S.J., at Marquette University, a young bombardier who had gone out on repeated missions of the utmost danger over Germany, said: "Believe me, Father, when you're miles up in the air with flak bursting all around and fighters spraying you with hot lead, rockets, and 20 mm. cannon shells, it is mighty comforting to know that there is Someone in Whom you can put your trust and realize that He is watching you!

[2] *Flower, Fruit and Thorn Pieces*

It's at times like that a fellow fully realizes what his religion means to him." In the words of that young gladiator of the skies there is reflected the sentiment of the myriads of warriors who in all ages have battled at the very brink of the abyss and knew not at what moment they might disappear into its all-embracing darkness.

Sharpens Individual Responsibility

Thirdly, *religion sharpens the sense of individual responsibility*. By its central teaching that God will reward or punish the individual according to his deserts, and that no one can hide behind the skirts of his neighbor, religion quickens the sense of accountability for one's own deeds. This is of enormous importance in a society in which the tendency to shift the blame and to forge alibis is so common. Since society is but an aggregate of individuals, the place at which to begin the improvement of society is with the individual. All social reforms, to be effective, must grip the conscience of the individual and start him on the upward plane. Otherwise there is noise, agitation and excitement, but no real improvement.

The answer to the Totalitarian heresy that man was made for the state lies in the truth which Christian philosophy has taught for twenty centuries that man, and not the state, has been endowed with an immortal soul. "There will never be," observes Thoreau, "a really free and enlightened State until the State comes to recognize the individual as a higher and independent power, from which all its own power and authority are derived." Another New England thinker, Henry Ward Beecher, expressed this truth when he wrote:

Christ did not die for laws and governments.
He did not die to build a nation up.
He died for men, the separate souls of men.

When this basic truth of Christianity is lost sight of, man becomes the mere chattel of the all-powerful state which uses him as mere cannon fodder in a war about which he has never even been consulted. "There is something appallingly wrong," declares Alfred Noyes, "something tragically wrong with a world in which hundreds of millions of those individuals whom Christ died to save, are hurled helplessly into bloodshed by half a dozen men whose plans and motives have been completely hidden from all but perhaps another half dozen; so that entire nations, which in their general level of individual character and intelligence—not to speak of their outstanding individuals, a Beethoven, a Pasteur, a Shakespeare, a Galileo—have far surpassed the general level of the half dozen manipulators of the political machinery, suddenly find themselves helplessly slaughtering one another." [3]

Social Value of Religion

Now let us look at the values of religion to society. First, *religion ennobles the relations between man and man by teaching that we are all the children of God and therefore are all brothers.* The implications of this central dogma of religion are tremendous. It was the perception of these implications which was chiefly responsible for the abolition of slavery and of a thousand other forms of blatant human injustice. How could a man enslave a person and treat him as a beast of burden when his religion proclaimed in the inner citadel of his conscience that that person was his brother and was as dear in the eyes of God as he?

It is this central teaching of Christianity that constitutes the basis of human dignity and therefore the basis of true

[3] *The Edge of Darkness*, E. P. Dutton & Co., N.Y., 1942, p. 35

democracy. When the essential dignity of the human personality is lost sight of, men are regarded as chattels, serfs, and slaves, and the evils of dictatorships and totalitarian regimes follow apace. In vain shall we crush military dictatorships if we do not root out the ideological heresy which constitutes their spawning ground. We must keep forever before the eyes of men the true basis of the dignity of every man, be he peasant or king.

That basis lies in the fact that personality is the high creation of Almighty God, who has vested therein the dignity of a human soul, endowed with understanding and free will. That soul is created in the image of God, and transcends all earthly commodities as heaven transcends earth. Since an infinite God saw fit to vest in that temple of clay the tremendous gift of free will, by which the creature becomes the sculptor of his own destiny and can choose either Heaven or Hell, can obey God or defy Him, how can a mortal man undertake to impose upon him a compulsion which God Himself refused? If the infinite Creator thus respects the freedom of the human personality, how can a mere creature undertake to shackle it with the chains of slavery?

Be it noted, however, that man's essential dignity stems ultimately from God, whose image and superscription he bears. Remove God from the scheme of human life and you remove the basis of man's unique dignity. Man becomes a chattel, a beast of burden. Dictatorships and totalitarian regimes, which ride roughshod over the individual and enslave him, are the ruthless tracing out in society of the logical implications of the banishing of God from human life. Remove the sun and you extinguish the reflected glory of the moon. Remove God and you strip from man every vestige of that reflected glory wherein his unique dignity lies.

Elevates Family Life

Secondly, *religion elevates and ennobles the family life.*
It emphasizes the sacredness of the marriage contract and
stands steadfastly for the permanence of the Christian home.
It proclaims to both husband and wife their solemn obligation to shoulder the responsibilities of marriage and bids
them pass on in a generous manner the precious heritage of
life. It stresses the duty of parents to set a good example to
their children and to train them in virtue and holiness of life.
Offering uncompromising opposition to marital infidelity,
religion constitutes the strongest bulwark for the life-long
union of husband and wife.

It reminds a married couple that the observance of that
solemn vow which they make when they take one another
"for better or for worse, for richer or for poorer, in sickness
and in health, until death," is an obligation which transcends
all considerations of pleasure or expediency. It is the test of
character and the hallmark of honor. Only in homes where
children have the care and guidance of both father and
mother do they get that well-balanced upbringing which
is so important a factor in the development of good citizens.

If children see their own parents breaking their solemn
vow of life-long love and loyalty and entering into new
unions, how can the offspring of such broken vows and
broken homes escape the demoralizing influence of such
examples? All too often they are thrown out to shift for
themselves, soon to appear in courts as delinquents, incor-
rigibles and criminals. Religion raises its voice against such
marital delinquents and warns them in stern tones that
almighty God will demand a strict accounting for the
precious souls entrusted to their charge.

She points out that there would rarely, if ever, be juvenile
delinquents if parents did their full duty and were careful

to rear their children in the fear and love of God. Religion is the strongest cement holding together the members of a family. It safeguards the sanctity of the family fireside and converts it into a house of God and a gateway to Heaven. The home is the solid bedrock upon which civilization rests. In safeguarding the home, therefore, religion constitutes the strongest bulwark for the protection of society against inward decay and the mightiest rampart for the preservation of human civilization itself.

Renders Morality Functional

Thirdly, *religion provides society with the most effective sanctions for the observance of law and the fulfillment of duty*. The performance of one's duty is in the last analysis a matter of conscience. If conscience does not prompt one to fulfill his duty to his fellow man, what force can compel him? Policemen, you say, and constables. But if the voice of conscience be stilled, who will police the policemen, and who will watch the constables? The simple fact is that no external guardian of the law can take the place of that internal monitor which touches off the springs of action and holds the reins of conduct.

Quickly would society fall into the abyss of anarchy and strife if conscience did not curb the rapacity, restrain the animosities, and hold in leash the tumultuous passions of men. But what is the agency which quickens the conscience and keeps it responsive to the gentle tug of the moral law? That agency is religion. To seek to quicken conscience without an appeal to God and the sanctions which religion provides is like a person seeking to lift himself by pulling at his bootstraps.

Convince a citizen of the existence of a Divine Legislator, the Supreme Source of all law, by whom "Kings reign, and

lawmakers decree just things." [4] Convince him of the truth
of the inspired utterance of St. Paul that "there is no power
but from God, and that those that are, are ordained of God,
and that, therefore, he who resisteth the power resisteth the
ordinance of God." [5] Convince him that an incorruptible
Judge, who knows all his thoughts, words, and deeds, will
mete out to him, with unfailing accuracy, the rewards or the
punishments which are his due. Convince him of these
truths and you place within him a guardian of law and a
sentinel duty which never sleeps but which walks with him
in the sanctuary of the home, in the crowded marketplace,
in the arena of public life and in the loneliest mountain pass.

In convincing us of these great truths, religion provides us
with the strongest incentives for the observance of law and
the fulfillment of all the duties of good citizenship. Thus does
religion constitute the firm foundation of society and its best
insurance against the corrosive influence of vice and crime.
Thousands of years ago the author of the *Book of Proverbs*
proclaimed this truth when he said: "Righteousness exalteth
a nation." [6] Only that nation is great which is great in justice, in generosity, in truth—in short, in righteousness, the
offspring of religion.

Champions Social Justice

Fourthly, *religion is the champion of social justice*. The
special objects of its predilection, as of Christ's as well, are
the poor, the downtrodden, the underprivileged, and the
afflicted. It is not the sycophant of kings or of the rich and
powerful. It is the one voice which proclaims fearlessly to
the king his duty to his subjects and threatens him with di-

[4] *Prov.* 8:15
[5] *Rom.* 13
[6] *Prov.* 14:34

vine punishment if he treats unjustly the lowliest in his realm.

It warns the employer, who defrauds his laborers, of the divine wrath which shall come upon him. "Behold the hire of the laborers," says St. James, "who have reaped down your fields, which by fraud has been kept back by you, crieth: and the cry of them has entered into the ears of the Lord of sabaoth." [7] It admonishes the servant to discharge his duties faithfully and well, "not serving to the eyes as it were pleasing men, but as the servants of Christ, doing the will of God from the heart." [8]

By championing the rights of all classes and emphasizing that the welfare of society is best attained by giving every man his due, religion renders a powerful service in removing the grounds of class warfare and in promoting the unity and the brotherhood of all. No agency is so effective in sterilizing the grounds of antagonism and strife between employer and employees as social justice. This is the medicine which religion uses to heal the wounds in the social organism and to promote the harmonious growth of all its members.

Promotes Stability of Government

Fifthly, *religion promotes the stability of government*. This is no small benefaction. For the welfare of society is safeguarded by a stable and responsible government, hedged round with constitutional limitations, and responsive to the will of the people. Anarchy is the enemy of law, order and civilization. By teaching that all just authority comes from God, and by stressing the duties of civic obedience, religion rears a mighty bulwark against lawlessness and strife.

[7] *James* 5:4
[8] *Eph.* 6:6

"Render therefore to Caesar," it ordains, "the things that are Caesar's; and to God, the things that are God's." [9] The terrors of the French Revolution, when the junta in power rushed their enemies to the guillotine only to be rushed there themselves when they fell from power, remain as a blood-stained page in history to warn posterity of the bloodshed, ruin and destruction which the apostles of anarchy never fail to inflict upon a country. The scaffold becomes their altar. The shrieks of victims become their incense. Ribald songs are made their hymns. Lust, rapine, and bloodshed become the idols at whose shrines they worship with a cruel and bloody fanaticism. During the few months of the reign of terror in France, the apostles of anarchy accumulated, as De Lamennais observes, "more ruin than an army of Tartars could have left after a six years invasion." [10]

Neither they, however, nor the Bolsheviks in Russia were able to stamp out religion. They could kill religious people. But they could no more kill religion than they could extinguish the sun. "Religion," says Thomas Carlyle, "cannot pass away. The burning of a little straw may hide the stars of the sky, but the stars are there, and will reappear."

Anterior to society and more enduring than political parties, religion is the focus of the social virtues of patriotism, obedience and respect which underlie all governments and give them stability and endurance. "Every philosopher and statesman," points out Cardinal Gibbons, "who has discussed the subject of human governments, has acknowledged that there can be no stable society without justice, no justice without morality, no morality without religion, no religion without God." [11] The recognition of God as the Fountainhead of rights and the ultimate Source of the

[9] Mat. 22:21
[10] Our Christian Heritages, p. 467
[11] Essai sur l'Indifference, p. 431

authority of governments runs like a thread of gold through the warp and woof of our own Constitution and Bill of Rights and is responsible in no small degree for the marvelous stability of our American system of government.

Founds Institution of Charity

Sixthly, *religion brings into existence the institutions of charity, mercy, and philanthropy which pour such a mighty stream of healing and benediction upon society.* Up until comparatively recent times the Christian Church bore almost alone the entire burden of establishing and maintaining such institutions as hospitals, asylums, orphanages, homes for the aged, homes for the incurably afflicted, and many other institutions to minister to the poor and the afflicted. "The highest flights of charity, devotion, trust, patience, bravery," observes William James, "to which the wings of human nature have spread themselves have been flown for religious ideals." [12]

Similar is the note sounded by Theodore Parker: "Silence the voice of Christianity, and the world is well-nigh dumb, for gone is that sweet music which kept in order the rulers of the people, which cheers the poor widow in her lonely toil, and comes like light through the windows of morning to men who sit stooping and feeble, with failing eyes and a hungering heart." [13] The Church is a tender and a loving mother who has reached her arms out through society in every age and has gathered to her nourishing breasts the poorest and the most afflicted of all God's children.

With her, charity is not cold, stinted or statistical. It is the warm milk of human kindliness which runs through her whole being, and which she dispenses, with all the love with

[12] *Varieties of Religious Experience*, p. 259
[13] *Discourse of the Transient and Permanent in Christianity*

which a mother feeds her helpless babe. She brought into being different types of institutions to minister to every human need. Communities of men and women sprang up to staff these institutions and to dedicate themselves by sacred vows to a life-long ministry to the sick, the lepers, the poor, the aged, the afflicted of every kind. Not the least remarkable of these institutions and brotherhoods were those who dedicated themselves to the ransom of captured Crusaders. Brave and noble men they were, who offered themselves to the Saracens to secure the release of imprisoned and enslaved Crusaders.

Here was the bright flowering of the social teachings of religion. Here was a noble and inspiring love of man with one's whole heart and soul, and the willingness to lay down one's life for one's fellow man. "By this," said Christ, "shall all men know that you are my disciples, if you have love one for another." [14] These mighty institutions of charity, mercy and benediction which Christianity has bequeathed to civilization constitute the monumental evidence of the earnestness with which the Church has sought in all ages not only to hearken to those words of Christ but to implement her obedience to them.

Mother of Education

Seventhly and lastly, *religion is the mother of education, enlightenment, scientific progress, and the most zealous worker for the outlawry of war and the organization of international institutions for the stabilizing of the peace of the world*. For many centuries the Church bore alone the burden of education. She founded many of the great universities of the world. She has taught in all ages the holiness of wisdom and the wisdom of holiness. She has been the generous

[14] *John* 13:35

and munificent Patroness of art. She has inspired many of the world's masterpieces in painting, sculpture, music and poetry. "Religion," observes A. E. Haydon, "is the mother of dreams. Over the gray world, ruined by deluge and death, it has sought ever, and found the arching rainbow of hope." [15]

She honors those who push back the frontiers of our darkness and give us new glimpses of nature and of her marvelous network of law, wherein we see the handwriting of nature's God. For God reveals Himself to us not only through the inspired books of the Bible but also through His handwriting in the vast book of nature from tiny atom to the farthest star. All truth streams from Him and all truths lead us back to Him.

Religion and science walk hand in hand in giving us a deeper appreciation and a greater reverence for the Supreme Architect of the universe and the Ordainer of its every law. This truth finds expression in the words of Asa Gray, inscribed beneath his bust in the Hall of Fame: "I confidently expect that in the future even more than in the past, faith in an order, which is the basis of science, will not be dissevered from faith in an Ordainer, which is the basis of religion."

The greatest evil that plagues humanity with ever increasing devastation and death, is war. By teaching that all men are brothers and that the human race constitutes one family, religion has provided mankind with a principle which ultimately will secure the eradication of the vicious institution of war. She fights against the narrow nationalism which would blind men to the virtues of peoples of other lands.

She proclaims in clarion tones to all mankind that the time has come when nations must build the framework of those juridical institutions which will settle by reason and conscience the disputes which arise between nations. Likewise

[15] *The Quest of the Ages*, p. 205

does she insist upon the necessity of sanctions which will secure the enforcement of those decisions. When her voice is hearkened to by the nations of the world, war will become but an ugly nightmare of the race's past. Thus "religion is," in the words of Homer, "the golden chain which suspends the earth from the throne of the eternal." Not less striking are the words of Eugene Savage, Professor of Art at Yale University: "All that separates the white man from barbarism is the Christian Church." In short, religion offers to both the individual and to society the highest values of life. On the rungs of her divine commandments, the individual climbs up the golden ladder of service to humanity and of love toward the Creator, till he reaches the very throne of God. For religion is the golden bond that binds the heart of man to the heart of God.

PART III

THE SOUL: GOD'S IMAGE IN MAN

Its Spirituality, Freedom and Immortality

What doth it profit a man if he gain the whole world,
and suffer the loss of his own soul?—*Matthew* 16:26

Man differs from all the living creatures on this earth because he possesses a rational soul. Herein lies his kinship with God. For the soul is God's image in man. By virtue of this spiritual principle, man towers above all the beasts of the field in knowledge, in power, and in value. He possesses intelligence and free will. Thus he is unique among all the creatures which science has discovered in all the visible universe.

Let us turn the searchlight upon the soul, the element which makes man distinctively human. It is not a mirage, a process, a wave of thought. It is the substantial principle by virtue of which man thinks. It is simple, immaterial, spiritual. While it operates in union with man's physical nature, it is essentially independent. Moreover, it enables man to choose freely.

This freedom of the will is the basis of man's moral responsibility. Because it is in itself spiritual and immaterial, transcending in some of its operations the powers of matter, it is not subject to disintegration or death. After the dissolution of the body, man's personality lives on because of his indestructible and immortal soul.

CHAPTER XXI

GOD'S IMAGE IN MAN

"Two things," the wise man said, "fill me with awe;
The starry heavens and the moral law."
Nay, add another wonder to thy roll——
The living marvel of the human soul!

HENRY VAN DYKE, *Stars and the Soul*

SUPREME among all the values on this earth stands the human soul. It ranks next to God. Indeed it is God's image in man and His pledge of human immortality. "Of all things which a man has," observes Plato, "next to the gods, his soul is the most divine and most truly his own." [1] Because he possesses a soul, man may be said to be an amphibian, capable of living in two worlds—in the world of time and in that of eternity. Destroy his body and his spirit remains unquenched, destined for an eternal life with God in heaven. It is this spiritual nature which elevates man above all the beasts of the field and renders him a being of unique dignity and of transcendent worth.

"Whether or not," observes John Erskine, "the philosophers care to admit that we have a soul, it seems obvious that we are equipped with something or other which generates dreams and ideals, and which sets up values." [2] S. T. Coleridge goes to the very nub of the question when he says: "Either we have an immortal soul or we have not. If we have

---

[1] *Laws*, Bk. IV, sec. 252
[2] Durant, *On the Meaning of Life*, p. 39

not, we are beasts, the first and wisest of beasts, it may be; but still true beasts. We shall only differ in degree, and not in kind; just as the elephant differs from the slug. But by the concession of all the schools, or almost all, we are not of the same kind as beasts—and this also we say from our own consciousness. Therefore, it must be the possession of a soul within us that makes all the difference." [3]

Long before Coleridge, the Roman philosopher, Seneca, pointed to the soul as the source of man's true nobility. "The soul alone," he says, "renders us noble. . . . Do you ask where the Supreme Good dwells? In the soul. And unless the soul be pure and holy, there is no room in it for God." [4] A Teacher greater, however, than Plato, Erskine, Coleridge or Seneca, reveals to us the surpassing value of the human soul. Making this the focal point of His gospel to mankind, Jesus Christ, the divine Founder of the Christian religion, declares: "What doth it profit a man, if he gain the whole world, and suffer the loss of his own soul? Or what exchange shall a man give for his soul?" [5]

Pile up all the riches and treasures of this earth, and place them on one side of the scales. Add to them all the honor, glory and fame of this world. On the other side of the scales, put the soul of the most ragged and neglected waif that roams our city streets. That soul will outweigh all the earthly treasures on the other side. Why? Because it is spiritual and will live when all the things of earth are but dust and ashes.

Recognized by Primitive Man

Belief in the existence of a principle distinct from the body stretches back into the remote past till it is lost in the

[3] *Table Talk*, Jan. 3, 1823
[4] *Epistulae ad Lucilium, Epis.* 44:5 and 87:21
[5] Mat. 16:26

twilight of antiquity. It appears as an almost inevitable inference from the observed facts of life. In the lapse of consciousness during sleep and in swooning, in the mysterious dreams which haunt his sleep, even in the common operations of imagination and memory, which abstract a man from his bodily presence, the lowly savage perceives the existence of something besides his visible body. That something is within the body, he realizes, but to a large extent is independent of it, and leads a life of its own.

In the rude psychology of the savage, the soul is often depicted as traveling to and fro during dreams and trances, and after death haunting the vicinity of its body. Almost invariably it is thought of as something volatile, a perfume or a breath. The Samoans have a name for the soul which means "that which comes and goes." Other savage peoples, such as the Dyaks and Sumatrans, are accustomed to bind various parts of the body with cords during illness to prevent the escape of the soul. In short, the scientific study of primitive peoples shows that the belief in a soul, distinct from the body, like the belief in a Supreme Being, was well-nigh universal among them.

In Ancient Philosophy

In the philosophy of the ancients, the soul has had likewise a long and eventful history. In the *Rig-Veda* and other liturgical books of India are found numerous references to the coming and going of *manas*—mind or soul. In Indian philosophy, whether Brahminic or Buddhistic, with its various systems of metempsychosis, the distinction between soul and body is so accentuated as to make the bodily life a mere transitory episode in the existence of the soul.

In Greek philosophy, Plato focussed attention upon the soul. In his *Phaedo,* he bases his argument for the immortality

of the soul on the nature of intellectual knowledge interpreted on the theory of reminiscence. Soul and body are
conceived as distinct orders of reality, with bodily existence
involving a kind of violence to the life of the soul. Thus the
body is viewed as the "prison" or "tomb" of the soul. Aristotle's definition of the soul as "the first entelechy (activat-
ing principle) of a physical organized body potentially possessing life" stresses the closeness of the union of soul and
body. He recognizes the spiritual element in thought and
describes the active intellect, νοῦς ποιητικός, as separate and
impassible.

The Stoics conceived the soul as a breath pervading the
body, calling it a particle of God, αποσπασμα τοῦ θεοῦ. In Epi-
cureanism the atomist theory of Leucippus and Democritus
was widely held. This represented the soul as consisting of
the finest grained atoms in the universe, finer even than those
of wind and heat. Thus they explained the exquisite fluency
of the soul's movements in thought and sensation.

In the Old Testament the distinct reality of the soul is
clearly taught. Later Jewish thought was greatly influenced
by Philo of Alexandria who infused into it many Platonic
concepts. He taught the immediately divine origin of the
soul, its pre-existence and transmigration, contrasting the
pneuma, or spiritual essence, with the soul proper, the source
of vital phenomena. He revived in Hebrew philosophy the
old Platonic Dualism, attributing the origin of sin and evil
to the union of spirit and matter.

In Christian Philosophy

It remained for Christianity to purge these ancient phi-
losophies of their vagaries and errors and to bring their scattered elements of truth into full focus. The teaching of
Christ tended to center all interest in the spiritual side of

man's nature, making the salvation of the soul the supreme issue of human existence. The dualism of body and soul is explicitly recognized and their values are frequently contrasted, as in the passage: "Fear ye not them that kill the body, and are not able to kill the soul: but rather fear him that can destroy both soul and body in hell." [6]

St. Thomas Aquinas developed the philosophy of the soul into the form substantially held by the Schoolmen today. We summarize the four principal points in his doctrine thus:

1. The rational soul, which is one with the sensitive and vegetative principle, is the form of the body.

2. The soul is a substance, but an incomplete substance. By this is meant that it has a natural aptitude and exigency for existence in the body, in conjunction with which it makes up the substantial unity of human nature.

3. While connaturally related to the body, it is itself absolutely simple. This means it is of an unextended and spiritual nature. It is not completely immersed in matter, as its higher operations are intrinsically independent of the organism.

4. The rational soul is produced by special creation, at the moment when the organism is sufficiently developed to receive it. The vital principle has merely vegetative powers in the first stage of embryonic development. Then a sensitive soul educed from the evolving potencies of the organism, comes into being. Later on this is replaced by the rational soul, which is essentially immaterial and so demands a special creative act. This last point is now generally abandoned by modern Scholastic philosophers who hold that a completely rational soul is infused into the embryo at the first moment of its existence. [7]

[6] Mat. 10:28
[7] Cf. Soul, by Michael Maher and Joseph Boland, in Catholic Encyclopedia

Universal Belief

This brief historical review brings into clear relief the universality of the belief of mankind in a soul distinct from the body. Like the belief in a Supreme Being, this universal conviction of mankind is the result of the simple spontaneous application of the principle of causality to the observed facts of life. While the concept of the soul has differed widely in details among peoples in various stages of development and civilization, the core of all of them is that something, distinct from the body, exists within it, and is independent, at least in some of its actions, of the body.

The fact of the matter is, that it is impossible for anyone, ancient or modern alike, to look inward upon himself without being led to think of a thinking, aspiring agent who is not completely identified with flesh and blood and bones or any form of matter under the sun. Call that principle by which one thinks, ψυχή, πνεῦμα, *anima, ego, I, soul,* or any other name, the reality underlying all of them remains. Man can no more divest himself of the conviction of a unitary principle underlying his manifold thoughts than he can divest himself of the consciousness of his own identity amidst all the ebb and flow of his mental life.

CHAPTER XXII

THE SOUL: SUBSTANTIAL AND SIMPLE

The human soul is a silent harp in God's quire, whose
strings need only to be swept by the divine breath to
chime in with the harmonies of creation.
—H. D. THOREAU, *Journal*, August 10, 1838

WE COME now to a consideration of the nature of the human soul. We shall treat briefly of its substantiality, simplicity, spirituality, freedom, and immortality.

The soul may be defined as the subject of our mental life,
the ultimate principle by which we feel, think, and will, and
by which our bodies are animated. The term *mind* generally
denotes this principle as the subject of our conscious states,
while *soul* denotes the source of our bodily activities as well.
For all practical purposes they are used as interchangeable
terms.

The Substantiality of the Soul

The human mind or soul is a substantial principle. By this
we mean that the ultimate basis of our conscious life cannot
be a *mode* or an *accident*. A principle is that from which
something proceeds. Substance, as its etymology indicates, is
that which *stands under*, or supports something else, namely,
accidental modifications. We may define it as being which
exists *per se*, which subsists in itself, in contrast to accident,
which cannot so subsist but must inhere in another being as
in a subject of inhesion.

219

In short, substance "stands by itself." An accident, however, leans, clings, inheres in the subject which it modifies, and has no ground in itself for its own being. Imagine before you a piece of *rounded* wax. That shape illustrates what is meant by accident, as the roundness could not exist by itself but needs a substance in which to inhere.

Now the ultimate foundation of our psychical existence, the last ground of our mental life, must be a substantial principle. Thought and volition do not exist by themselves. They do not spring out of a void and go floating about like cobwebs in the autumn air. They cannot declare, like Topsy in *Uncle Tom's Cabin*, that they "never had no father, nor mother, nor nothing." They proceed from something and inhere in it. Where there is motion there is *something* that is moved. So likewise where there is thought, there is *somebody* that thinks. Where there is a feeling, there is a *being* which feels. In other words thinking, willing, feeling are accidental modifications of a thinking, willing, feeling subject.

This conclusion holds with equal rigor, even if states of consciousness be regarded merely as aspects of cerebral processes and not as involving the operation of a spiritual principle. For in the former case, not less than in the latter, they would still have their root in a substantial principle. Hence even a materialist, who admits the existence of sensations, cannot deny the general principle that a modification necessarily implies a subject. This ultimate substantial principle, the subject of our thinking, feeling, willing, and of all our conscious states, is what is meant by the soul.

The Simplicity of the Soul

The human soul is a simple or indivisible, substantial principle. By this we mean that the soul, unlike the body, is neither extended nor composed of quantitative parts nor separate principles of any kind. This excludes all forms of composition, that of extended parts as well as of separate, unextended principles, whether homogeneous or heterogeneous. For the *unity of consciousness* is incompatible with a multiplicity of component elements of any kind whatsoever. Thus the soul is something *distinct from the body*. This does not mean that the soul is "a *detached* existent, *sufficient unto itself*." In thus interpreting the Scholastics, William James [1] and many other modern writers failed to understand the position of the Schoolmen. By representing the latter as believing in the existence of a detached entity, sitting inside the brain and pulling the reins of action this way or that in complete independence of the bodily organism, many modern writers have made a grotesque caricature of Scholastic teaching. In refuting the existence of such an entity, they mistakenly thought they were refuting the Scholastics, whereas they were simply destroying a man of straw, which they themselves had erected. Scholastic philosophy teaches that the soul, though *distinct* from the body, is actually *united* to the body to form one complete substance with it. Soul and body are *complementary parts of man*. As long as this union lasts, the soul is far from being "sufficient unto itself," it neither exists apart from the bodily organism nor acts independently of it.

The line of reasoning by which we establish the simplicity of the soul may be put into the following syllogistic form: Every composite or extended substance consists of an aggregate of distinct atoms or parts. But the subject of our conscious acts cannot consist of such an aggregate. Therefore it is not an extended or composite substance. The major premise is evident. The minor is demonstrated by a multitude of facts in our mental life, of which we shall cite a few.

[1] *Principles of Psych.*, vol. I, p. 6

The Simplicity of Intellectual Ideas

One of the certain facts of our mental life is that we form various abstract ideas or concepts, such as truth, goodness, beauty, unity, honesty. One of the abstract ideas mentioned in virtually every issue of the press these days is patriotism. That idea as well as the others mentioned are by their nature simple indivisible acts. But acts of this character cannot flow from a composite or extended substance, such as the brain. This becomes evident from a brief analysis. If such an indivisible idea as, say, patriotism, were to be produced by the brain, it would have to be produced in one of three ways. Either different parts of the idea must inhere in different parts of the brain, or each part of the brain must be the subject of an entire idea, or the whole idea must pertain to a single part of the brain.

The first alternative is untenable. Why? Because the act whereby the mind apprehends *patriotism, truth* and the like, is an indivisible thought. It is directly contrary to its nature to be distributed or scattered over an aggregate of separate atoms. The second alternative is equally impossible. If different cells or atoms of the brain were each the basis of a complete idea, we would have in our mind at the same time not one, but a multitude of ideas of the object. This is, however, directly contrary to the testimony of our consciousness. The third alternative likewise collapses under inspection. For if the complete idea were contained in one part or element of the brain, then this part is itself either composite or simple. If the former, then the old series of impossible alternatives again stare us in the face. If the latter, then our thesis, that the ultimate subject of thought is simple or indivisible, is established.

The Simplicity of the Intellectual Acts of Judgment and Inference

We can establish the simplicity of the soul likewise from an analysis of an act of judging. Any judgment, no matter how simple, involves the comparison of at least two distinct ideas which must be simultaneously apprehended by one indivisible agent. Let us take the simple statement: "Man is mortal." If the agent which entertains the two concepts, *man* and *mortal*, is not indivisible, then we must assume that one of these concepts is held by one part and the other concept by a second part; or else that separate parts of the divisible agent are each the seat of both ideas.

In the former case, however, we cannot formulate any judgment at all. The part A entertains the idea of *man*, the different part B entertains the idea of *mortal*. But does this yield any comparison or judgment? Not any more than if my right-door neighbor, John Smith, thinks of *man* and my left-door neighbor, Thomas Murphy, thinks of *mortal*. What is absolutely necessary for the act of judgment is that a *single* agent should apprehend the two ideas of *man* and *mortality*, and after comparing them should formulate the judgment: *Man is mortal*.

In the second alternative, if part A and part B each simultaneously entertained the idea of *man* and *mortal*, we should have not one but a multiplicity of judgments, which is contrary to the testimony of our consciousness.

Neither can one escape the above conclusion by conceiving our conscious states, as William James does, as "a stream of thought" without an abiding subject. How could even the simple judgment, which we have already formulated, take place? Let us say that one section of that stream, A, apprehends the idea of *man*. Another section, B, apprehends *mortal*. Now how can a judgment be formed, when the idea, *man*, is apprehended by one wave of thought, and the idea, *mortal*, is held by a different wave? There can be no escape from the conclusion that a judgment can be passed only by a *single* agent which apprehends both subject and predicate and affirms their likeness or lack of it.[2] The same line of reasoning establishes the simplicity of the soul from the unity of consciousness presented in acts of volition as in acts of judgment.

Proof from Memory

The operation of memory furnishes another striking proof of the simplicity and indivisibility of the human soul. Through memory we are aware of our own abiding personal identity in the midst of all our varied experiences. We know with the most absolute certainty that we are the same persons who yesterday, a month ago, many years ago, went through experiences that are still vivid to us. Thus the writer can recall as vividly as though it were but yesterday an event that took place nearly half a century ago. As a youngster of five, he had started off for his first day at school. After going a block, he was seized with fright at the thought of that strange institution looming up before him. Turning on his heels, he fled homeward in something close to tears. Every reader can duplicate the incident with experiences of his own.

Such recollections would be impossible, however, were the mind composed of successive states, or were the material organism the substantial principle in which these states inhere. It is an established fact of physiology that the constituent elements of the body are completely changed, not merely every seven years, as was formerly thought, but every few months. "None of the flesh of our body," points out Flam-

---

[2] Cf. Michael Maher, S.J., *Psychology*, Stonyhurst Series. The work is distinguished for its lucidity and penetration, and we commend it highly.

marion, "existed three months ago; the shoulders, face, eyes, mouth, the arms, the hair—all our organism is but a current of molecules, a ceaselessly renewed flame, a river which we may look upon all our lives, but never see the same water again." [3] Fleeting mental operations which did not inhere in a permanent subject could no more be remembered than could Peter recall the experiences of Paul whom he has never known or seen. It is only an indivisible principle, abiding unchanged amid the transitory experiences, that is able to afford an adequate basis for the operation of memory.

The helplessness of materialism to explain the operation of memory is well brought out by Dr. Alger: "A photographic image impressed on suitable paper and then obliterated is restored by exposure to the fumes of mercury. But if an indefinite number of impressions were superimposed on the same paper, could the fumes of mercury restore any one called for at random? Yet man's memory is a plate with a hundred millions of impressions all clearly preserved, and he can at will select and evoke the one he wants. No conceivable relationship of materialistic forces can account for the facts of this miraculous daguerreotype-plate of experience, and the power of the mind to call out into solitary conspicuousness a desired picture which has forty-nine million nine hundred and ninety-nine pictures latent lying above it, and fifty millions below it." [4]

How could one possibly remember experiences that took place years ago, and in the interim undergo the loss of every atom of his bodily organism and its replacement by new matter, if there is not some indivisible principle which retains its identity in the midst of such repeated renewals? The abiding

---

[3] Camille Flammarion in *The Proofs of Life After Death*, edited by R. J. Thompson, p. 97
[4] *A Critical History of the Doctrine of a Future Life*, 10th ed., p. 628

identity of the *ego*, that knits together by the thread of memory the scattered and varied experiences which stretch from the cradle to the grave, is one of the most certain facts of the conscious life of every person. Thus the proof from memory, while simple and within the comprehension of a child, is complete and absolute in its convincing power.

The Unity of Consciousness

The three proofs, which we have developed, may be said to be illustrations of the fundamental fact of our mental life, namely, the *unity of consciousness*. This fact is fatal to every form of materialism. By the unity of consciousness is meant that our manifold conscious states are either explicitly referred to a single indivisible unity, or are apprehended in reflection to be possible only as acts of such a simple subject. Lotze presents this fact and its implications with penetration and insight in the following brilliant passage:

"We come to understand the connection of our inner life only by referring all its events to the one *Ego* lying unchanged alike beneath its simultaneous variety and in its temporal succession. Every retrospect of the past brings with it this image of the *Ego* as the combining centre; our ideas, our feelings, our efforts are comprehensible to us only as its states or energies, not as events floating unattached in a void. And yet we are not incessantly making this reference of the internal manifold to the unity of the *Ego*. It becomes distinct only in the backward look which we cast over our life with a certain concentration of collective attention. . . . It is not necessary and imperative that at every moment and in respect to all its states a Being should exercise the unifying efficiency put within its power by the unity of its nature. . . . If the soul, even if but rarely, but to a limited extent, nay, *but once* be capable of bringing together variety into the unity of consciousness, this slender fact is sufficient to render imperative an inference to the indivisibility of the Being by which it can be performed." [5]

The evidence which we have presented, demonstrates the simplicity and the indivisibility of the substantial principle lying at the root of our mental life, and shows that it cannot be an extended or composite substance. Indeed, the evidence proves not merely the *simplicity* of the soul but also its *spirituality*. We shall, however, develop this latter truth with further considerations dealing with it explicitly. It is sufficient to point out here that the evidence already presented refutes the cardinal dogma of Materialism—that thought and volition are functions of the brain.

True, most modern materialists shrink from the vulgar frankness of Cabanis and Vogt, and no longer speak of thought as a "secretion of the brain." Sloughing off many of the crudities of the older school, its modern exponents deck it out with many refinements and present in euphonious phrases a more subtle form of Materialism. We hope to make its overthrow still more complete by demonstrating explicitly that the substantial, simple, indivisible soul of man is spiritual and immaterial. For in the demonstration of the spirituality of the soul is sounded most clearly the death knell of Materialism both as a philosophy of life and as a method of interpreting the phenomena of the mind.

[5] *Microcosmus*, Bk. II, c. i, 4

CHAPTER XXIII

THE SPIRITUALITY OF THE SOUL

Mount, mount, my soul! thy seat is up on high,
Whilst my gross flesh sinks downward, here to die.
SHAKESPEARE, *Richard* II, V

THE essential dignity of man lies in his possession of a spiritual and immortal soul which reflects the nature of God. It is that spiritual nature which elevates him above all the animal kingdom and renders him a creature made in the image and likeness of the Creator. Strip a man of that spiritual soul and he would differ not in kind, but only in degree from the beasts of the field. With that likeness of the divine within him, however, man can never be permanently reduced to the status of a chattel or mere beast of burden. For that spark of the divine within him burns with a lustre which no tyrant can extinguish—a lustre that points to his divine origin and proclaims his divine destiny. Indeed, it heralds the essential equality of the serf or slave with the tyrant or the king who wears a crown and sits upon a gilded throne. The mark of man's true dignity and essential worth lies not in these external trappings, but in the divinely bestowed endowment of a spiritual and immortal soul.

We now undertake to demonstrate that the human soul is spiritual or immaterial. We distinguish carefully between *simplicity* and *spirituality* which are not infrequently confused. When we say that a substance is simple, we mean that it is not composed of parts. By affirming that it is spiritual, we mean that in its existence, and to some extent in regard to its operations, it is independent of matter. Thus the principle of life in lower animals is generally held by Scholastic philosophers to be a simple principle but not spiritual, because it is absolutely dependent upon the organism, and unable to exist without it.

The general line of reasoning by which we establish the spirituality of the human soul runs as follows: The human soul is the subject of various activities which are essentially immaterial or spiritual. But the subject of such spiritual operations must itself be a spiritual being. Therefore the human soul must be a spiritual being.

The minor premise is evident. Water cannot rise higher than its source. An effect cannot transcend its cause. An action cannot contain a greater perfection or a higher order of reality than is possessed by the being which is the cause of the action. If we can show that some of the operations of the human mind transcend the properties of matter then it is evident that the principle from which those operations flow must likewise transcend matter and in some respects be independent of it. Let us now look at some of the operations of the human intellect which unmistakably reach the heights of an immaterial, spiritual order of reality.

Comparison and Judgment

Man may be compared to a city with five gates through each of which messengers come with reports of happenings in the outer world. The gates are the five senses. Each allows a special kind of imagery or sense impression to enter, to be carried to the intellect. Man is dependent upon the testimony of the senses of sight, hearing, taste, smell, and touch for the raw material of his knowledge of the external world.

Man shares these senses with many creatures of the animal kingdom.

His knowledge does not end, however, with the mere piling up of the reports of the senses. He works over these reports, classifies, analyzes, and compares them. The distinctive work of the intellect begins where the work of the senses end. Mere sense impressions would never result in judgments, comparisons, and abstract ideas, if a higher power did not enter to transmute them into purely intellectual concepts devoid of all sense attributes. A caveman could draw a picture of a monkey, as G. K. Chesterton has observed, but no monkey ever drew a picture of a man.

The supra-sensuous character of the intellectual operations is clearly manifested in the acts of comparison and judgment. In comparing the roundness of an orange and an apple, we ignore their color, taste, size and weight and, concentrating upon the single attribute of circularity, declare that attribute to exist in greater measure in the orange. While this judgment presupposes the sensations or images of both objects, it is obviously distinct from either one.

In fact, it involves an intellectual act distinct from the related impressions by which the relation subsisting between them is apprehended. In addition to the pair of compared ideas, it demands a superior force which holds them together in consciousness and examines the relationship of comparative roundness existing between them. The mere successive impingement of the sense images of an apple and of an orange could never result in the analysis of their comparative circularity, unless there be a third distinct activity of a higher order in which both are present, and which is capable of discerning, measuring, and judging the common attribute under comparison.

It is to be noted, as T. H. Green has pointed out, that "a feeling qualified by a relation of resemblance to other feelings is a different thing from an *idea* of that relation, different with all the difference between feeling and thought, between consciousness and self-consciousness." [1] The assumption of the materialist which obliges him to dissolve the mind into a series of conscious states devoid of all real unity renders impossible of explanation not only the persistence of personal identity in all the far-flung operations of the mind but also the formulation of the simplest act of comparison between two successive ideas. For this obviously requires the operation of a higher power, an immaterial or spiritual element, which scrutinizes, measures, and compares the specific relationship involved and passes judgment on the same. The element which in its operations thus clearly transcends the properties of matter must itself be spiritual, else the effect would transcend the cause. That spiritual immaterial element which is so plainly manifested in acts of comparison and judgment is what is meant by the rational soul of man.

Universal and Abstract Concepts

The operations of the mind in the formation of universal and abstract concepts likewise demonstrate the spirituality of the human soul. By abstract ideas we mean those from which all individuating notes or attributes have been withdrawn, so that they reach the high plane of universal concepts which completely transcend the scope of the senses. We have, for example, ideas of honor, truth, righteousness, beauty, possibility, futurity. Did any man ever see, hear, feel, smell, taste or touch honor? Did anyone ever take a walk with truth? If it be material, then it must have the properties common to matter, such as size, shape, color, weight and the like. What size is truth? What is its shape? What color is it? How much does it weigh?

[1] *Introduction to Hume's Treatise on Human Nature*, p. 213

The simple fact is that truth, like all other abstract and universal concepts, has none of these properties. It cannot be perceived by the senses. It is arrived at by the speculative intellect which has stripped it of all individual notes or marks so that it will embrace in its universal grasp any and every truth, whether it be in science, mathematics, aesthetics, philosophy or in any other conceivable domain. Our senses convey to us the image of a particular man. Images are always particular. It is the intellect which seizes upon the essential features which constitute the common nature of the class. Our consciousness of this community constitutes the universal idea.

Long ago Plato called attention to the importance of universal concepts for both philosophy and science and pointed out that they transcend the scope of the senses. It is in the capacity to form abstract universal concepts that the dignity of man, as a thinker, lies. The concept of relationship, causal or merely concomitant, lies at the basis of all science. The capacity to form such universal concepts completely transcends the power of animals which are dependent upon the senses and instinct for their operations. Abstract concepts such as truth, goodness, righteousness, justice are spiritual realities since they are devoid of all material attributes. But the intellect which forms such purely spiritual concepts must likewise be spiritual, else the effect would transcend the cause. "If the understanding were a corporeal substance," points out St. Thomas, "intelligible ideas of things would be received in it only as representing individual things. At that rate the understanding would have no conception of the universal, but only of the particular, which is manifestly false." [2]

A purely physical organ can react only in response to physical impressions, and can only yield representations of a

[2] *Contra Gentiles*, Bk. II, C. XLIX, p. 3

concrete character, portraying contingent, individual facts. Truth, honor, causality, futurity, however, do not constitute such a physical stimulus, and therefore could not be apprehended by a purely organic faculty. Accordingly the formation of abstract and universal ideas transcends the sphere of all actions depending essentially or intrinsically by their nature on a material instrument and must be acknowledged to be of a spiritual character. The acknowledgment of the spiritual character of the intellectual activity resulting in abstract concepts is, however, but another way of saying that the human soul is itself a spiritual and immaterial being.

Reflection and Self-consciousness

Even more striking is the evidence drawn from the facts of reflection and self-consciousness. It is only man who can turn his mind inward upon himself and study his own sensations, emotions and thoughts. We can analyze them, compare them with previous states, and recognize them as our own. Even while reflecting on these states we can apprehend the identity of the subject of these states. It is only because we possess a supra-sensuous faculty that we can recognize ourselves as something more than our transient states of consciousness.

While that spiritual element is evidenced in the perception of relationships, comparison, judgment, the formation of abstract and universal concepts, and in the intuition of the necessary character of certain judgments, it shines forth most conspicuously in the reflective observation of our own conscious states. Profound and thoughtful scholars have characterized this phenomenon as the most marvelous fact in the universe. In scrutinizing our own consciousness there occurs an instance of the complete or perfect turning of an indivisible agent back on itself. I apprehend an absolute identity between myself thinking about a situation, and my-self reflecting on that thinking self. The *Ego* thinking and the *Ego* thought about is one and the same. It is at once *subject* and *object*.

This is without parallel in all the world of matter. Such an action is not merely unlike the known properties of bodies, but it is in direct and violent conflict with all the fundamental characteristics of matter. Here we have an act in absolute and flagrant contradiction with the essential na-ture of matter. We can understand how a piece of rubber can be bent back so one part of it will act upon another part. We can understand how one atom may repel or attract an-other, or in various ways influence it. But that one atom can act *upon itself*, that the same identical piece of matter can be simultaneously both agent and patient in its own case, is in plain contradiction to common experience and to all the teachings of physical science. In other words, the action of a material atom must always have for its object something other than itself.

If then this unity of subject and object, of agent and patient, is so directly opposed to the very nature of matter, certainly an organ whose every act is intrinsically depend-ent upon matter cannot be capable of self-consciousness or self-reflection. Self-knowledge and the unity of conscious-ness would be clearly impossible for such a bodily organ. Therefore there is a spiritual power within us, and the source from which it issues must be intrinsically independent of the body. This is but another way of saying that the hu-man soul is spiritual and immaterial.

St. Thomas states this argument in the following clear and cogent manner: "Of no bodily substance is the action turned back upon the agent. But the understanding in its action does reflect and turn round upon itself; for as it understands an object, so also it understands that it does understand, and so endlessly. Hence Holy Scripture calls intelligent, subsistent beings by the name of *spirits*, using of them the style which it is wont to use for the incorporeal Deity." [3]

The evidence establishing the power of self-determination, the capacity to choose freely between various alternative courses of conduct, demonstrates not only the freedom of the will but also the spirituality of the soul. For if some of man's volitions are free, if they are not the mere resultants of forces operating upon him, there must be within him an inner center of causality, an internal agent enjoying at least a limited independence of the bodily organism. That inner principle of free volition which is able to go directly against the current of sensuous appetite and the urgings of the carnal passions is but another name for the spiritual soul of man. The evidence of that liberty we shall present in detail in the treatment of the freedom of the will. It is sufficient to indicate here the bearing of the freedom of volition in reenforcing the previous lines of evidence demonstrating the spirituality of the soul.

Let us now turn our attention to the chief difficulties urged against the spirituality and the simplicity of the soul. As the objections to both merge into one another, we shall not undertake to separate them.

Thought: A Secretion of Brain?

The coarser forms of materialism identify thought with a secretion of the brain. "There subsists," says Vogt, "the same relation between thought and the brain, as between bile and the liver." Cabanis flatly asserts: "Thought is a secretion of the brain." [4] Moleschott describes thought as "a

[3] *Contra Gentiles*, XLIX, 7 and 8
[4] *La pensée est une secretion du cerveau*

motion in matter" and also as a "phosphorescence" of the brain.[5]

The answer to objections of this sort really lies in a better understanding of the essential character of thought. To describe thought as a mere "secretion" of cerebral tissue or as a "movement" of the atoms in the brain is to betray a failure to grasp the nature of consciousness. Thought is essentially unextended. The concept of relationship, causal or concomitant, the judgment that man is mortal, the metaphysical concept of being, the idea of a categorical imperative, the appraisal of moral values, are by their nature devoid of all spatial relations. The organs of secretion produce products which possess weight, size, shape, color and all the attributes of matter. The operations of the organs as well as their products occupy space and can be apprehended by the external senses. Even when unperceived, they continue to exist and to run their course.

Consciousness not only has nothing in common with these, but it is the exact opposite of all these material properties. What does it look like? How much does it weigh? What is its size, its shape, its color? The microscope cannot find it. It has no weight, color, shape, or any of the properties of matter. When not perceived, it is non-existent. Its only *being* is to *be perceived*. Its *esse* is *percipi*. To talk of consciousness as a secretion of matter, or as the movement of one atom against another or in any direction whatsoever, is to miss its essential nature completely. Such descriptions of thought are crude caricatures which have about as much resemblance to the mental reality as they have to the man in the moon. Thought and matter, as John Stuart Mill has pointed out,

[5] Cf. Janet, *Materialism of the Present Day*, c. i; also Margerie, *Philosophie Contemporaine*, pp. 191–226 for an account of German and French Materialism.

are "not merely different, but are at the opposite poles of existence." [6]

Movements of atoms, secretions of organs, are in a different category of reality altogether. They have not bridged even the first gap between matter and *sensation*, to say nothing of the gap that yawns between matter and man's higher *thought* processes. Long ago Herbert Spencer pointed out the futility of attempting to reduce mental states to physical processes. "No effort," he declares, "enables us to assimilate them. That a feeling has nothing in common with a unit of motion becomes more than ever manifest when we bring them into juxtaposition." [7]

Dr. Tyndall thus proclaims this same truth: "The passage from the physics of the brain to the corresponding facts of consciousness is *unthinkable*. Granted that a definite thought and a definite molecular action in the brain occur simultaneously, we do not possess the intellectual organ, nor apparently any rudiments of the organ, which would enable us to pass by a process of reasoning from one to the other. They appear together, but we do not know why. Were our minds and senses so expanded as to enable us to see and feel the very molecules of the brain, were we capable of following all their motions, all their groupings and electric discharges, if such there be, and were we intimately acquainted with the corresponding states of thought and feeling, we should be as far as ever from the solution of the problem— How are these physical processes connected with the facts of consciousness? The chasm between the two classes remains still intellectually impassable." [8]

[6] *Essays on Religion*, p. 202
[7] *Principles of Psychology*, vol. I, p. 62
[8] *Address to the British Association at Norwich*

Thought: A Function of Matter?

Shying away from such crude descriptions of thought as "a secretion of the brain," Huxley, Broussais [9] and others seek to smuggle in an interpretation, equally materialistic, but somewhat more subtle and refined. "Thought," declares Huxley,[10] "is as much a function of matter as motion is." Amplifying this a year later, he asserts: "There is every reason to believe that consciousness is a *function of nervous matter*, when that matter has attained a certain degree of organization, just as we know the other actions to which the nervous system ministers, such as reflex action, and the like, to be." [11]

The use of the term "function" conceals some of the crudity of the "secretion" theory only because it is less explicit. It does not, however, render the materialistic interpretation one whit more plausible with those not contented with payment in obscure words. Function is a delightfully generic "cover-all" term, while secretion is painfully specific. But what is a "function of matter"? The only "functions" of matter which physical science recognizes consist of *movements* or *changes in matter*. Consciousness, as we have already pointed out, cannot be reduced to such movements of atoms of matter. It is something utterly different and belongs in a different category of reality from physical matter, whether in rest or in movement. If we are going to make words reflect realities and not caricatures, we can speak of thought or consciousness only as a function of a reality utterly opposed in nature to all known subjects of material force.

True, when intellectual processes occur, there are movements within the neurones of the cerebrum. The movements of each of these neurones involve the movements of millions

[9] *Macmillan's Mag.*, May 1870
[10] *Ibid.*
[11] *Contemp. Rev.*, Nov. 1871

of atoms and of billions of protons and electrons. In this material sense, the brain may be said to "function" and to expend energy. But do the movements of billions and billions of particles of matter within the cerebrum and the expenditure of physical energy bring us any nearer to the reality of consciousness? Would anyone be so rash as to say that the expenditure of physical energy and the whirling together of millions of particles of matter within the cerebrum constitute *consciousness?* The chasm, as Dr. Tyndall points out, between the two classes of fact, the two categories of reality, still remains "intellectually impassable."

No matter how complex may be the molecular action within the brain cells, we cannot bridge the gap yawning between such manifold physical activity and the unity of consciousness. "Fifty million molecules," as Ladd observes, "even when they are highly complex and unstable phosphorized compounds, gyrating in the most wonderful fashion with inconceivable rapidity certainly do not constitute *one thing.* They do not, then, by molecular constitution and activities, even constitute a physical basis which is conceivable as a representative or correlate of one thing." [12] The simple truth is that any attempt to explain thought as a function of the brain or the whirling together of millions of complex molecules of matter breaks down utterly when it comes face to face with the *unity of consciousness.* This prodigious fact, as undeniable as it is portentous, may be said to be the mighty Gibraltar against which all the waves of materialistic explanations of consciousness dash themselves to pieces.

A Sculptor and His Tools

An objection to the spirituality of the soul is advanced from the findings of physiology and pathology. These find-

[12] *Physiological Psychology,* p. 595

ings, it is alleged, show the absolute dependence of the mind upon the brain. Thus if a portion of the brain is injured, the mind will be impaired in its activities.

The concluson is too wide for the premises. The soul is extrinsically dependent in some of its activities upon the brain. This does not mean, however, that it is identical with the brain. A sculptor is dependent upon his tools, his hammer and chisel, to carve a statue. If those tools are seriously damaged, the character of his work will be correspondingly impaired. But does this mean that a sculptor *is* his tools, or that he cannot *exist*, if they are completely destroyed? Similarly the mind uses the brain as an instrumental tool and generally speaking will be affected by the character of that instrument.

Fritz Kreisler, using a poor violin with some of its strings broken, will produce one kind of music. Playing the same composition on a Stradivarius in perfect condition, he will produce a vastly better melody. Yet is not Fritz Kreisler the same identical person in both cases? Yes, it is the difference in the instruments used which is responsible for the difference in the quality of the two performances. That is the analogy which holds in a general way for the soul. There are, however, some of its intellectual operations, as in the formation of abstract ideas, which even though preceded, accompanied, or followed by movements in the brain, nevertheless transcend all the properties of matter. Who, listening to a rendition of Lalo's *Symphonie Espagnole* by Fritz Kreisler, would attempt to explain the rapid bursts of melodic fluency and the deep pathos of the adagio, by saying they are the mere result of the moving of a few strands of horsehair across a piece of cat gut, with no conscious intelligence behind the elaborate process?

Localization of Brain Functions

The localization of the functions of the brain and the discovery that an injury to one of those parts impairs the mental correlate does not militate, as some materialistic writers have imagined, in the slightest way against the Scholastic position. Long ago St. Thomas stressed the intimate union of soul and bodily organism and pointed out the close interdependence of their operations. There is no finding of physiology or pathology which sheds any particularly new light upon this long recognized relationship.

Writers who imagine that the scientific data, emphasizing the marked influence of changes in the brain upon mental processes, are hostile to the scholastic teaching, are really confusing it with the theory which Descartes brought into the world in rebellion against Scholasticism. It was Descartes who inaugurated the theory of the soul existing within the brain but in complete independence of it. In contrast to Descartes who placed the soul in the pineal gland of the brain, the Scholastics made no attempt to localize it but conceived it as existing everywhere in the body. "It is enough to say," declares St. Thomas, "that the whole soul is in each part of the body by the totality of perfection and of essence." [13]

It is worthy of note, moreover, that the foremost authorities in cerebral physiology are the first to admit that the nature of consciousness is as much a mystery as it ever was. All the vivid descriptions of currents and discharges of nervous energy, of neural tremors, and of molecular waves along the afferent and efferent neural paths, so frequent in popular magazines, stop where the process of consciousness begins. Taking to task writers who glibly assert "that *all* mental phenomena whatever their varied characteristic shading,

[13] Q. LXXVI, A. 8

have exact equivalents, as it were, in specific forms of the nerve-commotion of the living brain," Professor Ladd remarks:

"Our first impression on considering the foregoing way of accounting for mental phenomena is that of a certain surprising audacity. The theory, standing on a slender basis of real fact, makes a leap into the dark which carries it centuries in advance of where the light of modern research is now clearly shining." He then shows that even such inferior and comparatively simple problems as the determination of the physiological conditions of variations in the quality, quantity, time-rate of sensation, and "almost everything needed for an exact science of the relations of the molecular changes in the substance of the brain and the changes in the states of consciousness, is lamentably deficient." When we come to the neural conditions of spiritual acts, such as the conception of the principle of causality, or the idea of substance, Ladd observes that science is, and will remain, in absolute ignorance.[14]

The Need of a Guiding Principle

Let us assume for the moment, however, that science will one day discover the intimate relations between neural conditions and intellectual life, and will even photograph the molecular changes taking place in the brain cells. Would that prove more than the extrinsic dependence of the soul upon the body? No, it would merely be a filling in of the details of the process, which we all now admit, that every psychosis involves a neurosis, that all thought involves activity of the cerebral organism.

If we were to take a moving picture of every action of a

[14] *Op. cit.*, pp. 592–597; cf. also Janet's *Materialism of the Present Day*, pp. 132 f.

great artist in painting a masterpiece, so that we knew every detailed movement of his hands, arms, shoulders, eyes and head, every stroke of the brush, be it ever so light, and perceive the blending of all the colors and the play of light and shade, would that demonstrate anything more than the artist's extrinsic dependence upon his instrumental tools? Would it lessen by so much as an iota the need for a directive intelligence behind the thousand and one detailed movements of hands, arms, eyes and brush? Would it show that it was the work of an automaton, a robot? Not at all. All such detailed knowledge of the movements of the physical tools would serve but to emphasize the indispensable necessity of a guiding intelligence behind the whole process.

So likewise whatever advances we have made thus far, or ever shall make, in the study of the detailed neural and molecular processes concomitant with the operations of the intellect, will serve but to emphasize the indispensable need for a principle, spiritual and immaterial, to account for the spiritual and immaterial concepts achieved in the processes of abstract thought. In other words, the fullest knowledge of molecular motion in the brain throws no single ray of light upon the essential nature of consciousness. It is as much a mystery as before the cerebral physiologist began his work. The gap between the movement of atoms of matter and consciousness still remains as wide and deep and impassable as ever.

The ultimate factors in the higher thought processes, particularly those affecting the quality of the reasoning, are still a mystery to the physiologist. It is obvious that the *absolute weight* of the brain cannot be a measure of intelligence. For on that basis the elephant and the whale would exceed Shakespeare, Pasteur and Einstein. Neither can it be greater *relative* weight. For in this respect man is surpassed by many of the smaller birds, such as the titmouse, and the adult by the child. Neither do the multiplicity, complexity, and thickness of the convolutions on the surface of the brain afford the answer. For on this basis the ox would be of distinguished mental capacity. Equally ineffective are the appeals to the chemical constitution of the cerebral substance and the richness of the brain in phosphorus. For here again the superiority of the human cerebrum is challenged by two proverbially stupid animals, the sheep and the goose.

Body Without Soul Is . . . ?

The objection is sometimes urged that we never find mind apart from body. The implication is that it is nothing distinct from the body. Mere concomitance does not, however, prove identity. A child may never have seen his mother without her wedding ring. Would that prove the identity of the ring with the finger? Furthermore we do find bodies without minds. A corpse may weigh exactly the same as the body when vivified by a soul. Yet it is now a radically different entity. Why? Because the soul which was the source of its vital and intellectual activities is gone. In the difference between a cadaver and a living personality one secures a good picture of the role played by that immaterial principle of mental life which we call the human soul.

The difficulty has been proposed that the different functions which man performs would seem to imply three distinct souls: a vegetative soul for growth, an animal soul for sentiency, and a spiritual soul for thinking. But principles or beings are not to be multiplied without necessity. Moreover, the different parts or powers coöperate closely with one another for the welfare of the whole, thus indicating that they are under the direction of a single vital principle. Then, too, man's consciousness of feeling and of thinking testifies that he is the same identity who both feels and thinks, thus pointing to a common principle behind both operations. But if it be thus admitted that his soul can combine spiritual with animal powers, no difficulty arises from ascribing vegetative powers to it also.

Furthermore, if man had three separate souls, would he not need a fourth to coördinate the workings of the other three for his common welfare? But how would such a fourth soul act on the others, and guide each one in its operations, unless it possessed the three powers which we ascribe to the one human soul? These three considerations all converge upon the conclusion that man possesses a single soul capable of directing all the manifold activities of a human being.

One last difficulty. The soul, it has been argued, cannot be simple and indivisible, because it is present throughout an extended body. The answer lies in a distinction. A simple, indivisible force or substance cannot be *quantitatively* present throughout an extended subject. This means it cannot have parts alongside of parts throughout a spatial object. But it can be *essentially* present by the exercise of its power or influence ubiquitously in such a subject. Thus God is essentially present throughout the universe, exercising His power everywhere, from the whirling electrons in a grain of sand beneath our feet to the movements of the farthest star in the trackless sky.

We have presented at considerable length the evidence of the spirituality of the human soul and have considered with care all the important objections and difficulties. We have done this with such thoroughness because of the importance of the subject and of its far-reaching consequences. For once we have established the great truth that man possesses an immaterial and spiritual principle, called a soul, the freedom of the will and the immortality of the soul follow with irresistible logic. It is this precious possession, a spiritual soul, which marks man off from all the material universe as a being of unique dignity and of transcendent worth. It is by virtue of that incalculable spiritual treasure that man establishes his freedom from all the compulsions of matter and authenticates his claim to everlasting life. The freedom of the will and the immortality of the soul are the towering pillars of man's spiritual edifice, which rests upon the enduring foundation of an immaterial human soul.

CHAPTER XXIV

THE FREEDOM OF THE WILL

Where we are free to act, we are also free to refrain from acting, and where we are able to say No, we are also able to say Yes.
—ARISTOTLE, *Nicomachean Ethics*, Bk. 3, ch. 5, sec. 2

THE foundation of man's moral responsibility lies in the freedom of the will. Upon this mighty truth have been based our conceptions of reward and punishment, our codes of ethics, and our system of laws with all their varied sanctions, social, economic and penal. This basic truth of philosophy and of psychology branches out into ethics, natural theology, ontology, cosmology and into all the departments of metaphysics. Its importance can scarcely be overestimated.

Its demonstration should logically determine one's theory of morality and one's philosophy of life. It offers striking evidence of the existence within man of a spiritual principle whose operations cannot be explained by the pull and tug of material forces. Along with the capacity of rational thought, it constitutes the basis of man's unique dignity among all the creatures of God.

Thousands of years ago Confucius recognized this truth, when he thus proclaimed the inalienable endowment of a free will: "The commander of the forces of a large State may be carried off, but the will of even a common man cannot be taken from him." [1] Over in ancient Greece, the

[1] *Analects*, Bk. ix, ch. 25

mighty genius of Aristotle, after peering deeply into the springs of human conduct, etched deeply into his *Nicomachean Ethics* his conviction of man's untrammeled freedom. "Where we are free to act," he wrote, "we are also free to refrain from acting, and where we are able to say No, we are also able to say Yes." Epictetus expressed the conviction of both Confucius and Aristotle in the memorable utterance: "No one can rob us of our free will." [2]

Among the philosophers of ancient Rome, we find the wise Seneca proclaiming: "No action will be considered blameless, unless the will was so, for by the will the act was dictated." Crystallizing the thought of the Romans, comes to us the Latin proverb, whose origin is lost in the mists of antiquity: *Voluntas non potest cogi*. The will cannot be forced. The conception of the Anglo-Saxon world finds expression in the classical lines of Milton's *Paradise Lost:* [3]

> Good he made thee, but to persevere.
> He left it in thy power, ordained thy will
> By nature free, not over-ruled by Fate
> Inextricable, or strict necessity.

Lodged deeply in the mind of the race is the conviction that man possesses liberty of the will and is responsible for his actions.

Meaning of Free Will

Freedom of the will has sometimes been misunderstood and misrepresented. This has been true particularly in recent years. Much of the ostensible opposition to it is really not against it, but against its caricatures. Let us first remove these misconceptions by making clear what free will does

[2] *Discourses*, Bk. III, ch. 22, awx. 105
[3] Bk. V, l. 525.

not mean. It does not mean a *causeless* volition, a willing to do something for no motive at all. This would be the characteristic not of a free man but of an insane man. For only the latter acts for no motive or reason. It is the mark of a rational person to weigh reasons and motives and to choose the weightier one.

Neither does free will mean that *all* of a person's acts are free. Many are not. Some are automatic, such as breathing and winking. Some are conditioned reflexes, such as the knee jerk. Control over our thoughts seems to cease in large measure during sleep. A long series of thoughts may pass through our mind before we, by an act of self-consciousness, avert to their indeliberate and spontaneous character, and only then render them deliberate and voluntary.

By *will*, or rational appetite in general, we mean the faculty of inclining toward or striving after some object intellectually apprehended as good. Free will may be defined simply as the *capacity of self-determination*. It means the power to choose between alternative courses of conduct, the power to do an act or to refrain from doing it. It affirms that the individual is not compelled by external circumstances or by the internal forces of heredity to make all his choices and issue all his volitions. While these may profoundly influence him, and even in some cases tip the scales in one direction or another, our thesis contends that man is the master of his own decrees, that he has the essential freedom to choose between various alternatives, to do a thing or to refuse to do it. Free will thus implies that volitions are freely exerted by the *Ego*, by that spiritual principle which is back of man's cognitive and volitional acts, and which owes allegiance to no sovereign under the sun.

It is to be noted that freedom implies the capacity to conceive of an end of action and to choose the means by which it may be attained. No being can be free, unless he is capable

of the perception of an end and of the relation of the means
to that end. Intelligence which manifests itself in the perception of relations is thus seen to be the *foundation* and the
guarantee of freedom. Freedom does not imply indifference
to one end rather than to another. Man is driven by his
very nature to seek happiness. Thus we are not free to will
happiness or not to will it. It is a necessary volition.

The means of achieving happiness, however, are by no
means perfectly clear. A great variety of means looms up
before the imagination. These the intellect can explore, and
scrutinize the closeness of their relationship with the end
sought. Among these various means the will can freely
choose. Freedom manifests itself not in choosing to be
happy, but in choosing the *means* that make one happy. This
does not reduce freedom to a mere question of intellectual
discernment. For the search for happiness involves the in-
hibition of desires and the restraint of impulses driving to
contrary ends. "Happiness has so many forms," observes
Prof. T. V. Moore, "and human beings have so many desires, that to know happiness and to seek it involves not only
the power to understand ends and the relation of means to
ends but the ability to drive the steeds in the chariot of human nature." [4]

The Evidence from Consciousness

The first line of evidence which we shall present is the
direct testimony of our own consciousness. The reasoning
runs as follows:

That which consciousness universally testifies, within the
sphere of its legitimate jurisdiction, must be true. Otherwise
man would be deceived by his very nature, and to distin-

[4] *Dynamic Psychology,* p. 392

guish between truth and error would be forever impossible. But consciousness universally testifies to the freedom of some of our actions. Therefore, they must be free.

Our major premise affirms that in the domain of mental phenomena consciousness is the ultimate court of appeal. Beyond this neither the philosopher nor the psychologist can go. Who can tell me as authoritatively and as accurately concerning the character of my own choice as my own consciousness? Who else is present to perceive it and to testify to its precise character? Obviously no one. Just as we are obliged in all philosophical investigations to grant the validity of the human mind to know, so too are we obliged to concede the truth of that which consciousness universally testifies. The failure to recognize either of these primary truths would lead inevitably to the denial of knowing anything whatsoever, and would plunge mankind into universal scepticism.

If any conclusions of philosophy or any generalizations of science appear to conflict with the immediate truths of consciousness, they must be re-examined and modified until they harmonize with the latter. If they cannot be so harmonized, then they stand disproved. Such generalizations are, at best, inferences reached by a process of reasoning whose liability to error is generally in proportion to the number of links in the chain. A scrutiny of all such links, involving initial assumptions, alleged facts, judgments, and inferences from such combinations of principles and facts, and the final generalization, discloses that none of them can claim an authority higher than the direct and immediate testimony of consciousness. No final result of such a lengthy and involved procedure, with error besetting it at every step, can usurp the unique authority of the immediate affirmation of consciousness.

The Testimony of All

Now for the minor premise. Here we can only affirm the fact that our own consciousness clearly testifies to the freedom of our volitions and that the testimony of mankind is to the same effect. "Universal usage," observes Professor Thomas Dwight, "throughout civilization, and indeed in uncivilization, tells us that in every detail of intercourse among men we recognize the existence of free will. The state of mind that denies it is not one of enlightenment, but of muddleheadedness." [5] Neither riches nor the dungeon, neither the gallows nor the martyr's fire, can coerce the naked soul of man. Wordsworth [6] epitomizes all history when he says:

> But who would force the Soul tilts with a straw
> Against a Champion cased in adamant.

Why do the peoples of every land, regardless of race, environment and civilization, affirm unhesitatingly that certain actions are deserving of reward and others of punishment? Why, in fact, do they actually administer those rewards and punishments? Is it not because they perceive that men are free to do such acts or not to do them? If they perceived that they were compelled to do them, and thus had no choice in the matter, they would have no such sense of merit or blame.

Why does our country, in common with every other country, confer awards for valor and gallantry in action upon soldiers, sailors and aviators? Because she knows that they were free to expose themselves to added dangers to life and limb or not to do so. Otherwise they would be no more worthy of reward than the leader who deserts his soldiers

[5] *Thoughts of a Catholic Anatomist*, p. 155
[6] *Ecclesiastical Sonnets*, Pt. III, 7

in the heat of battle, or the traitor who betrays his country for yellow gold. George Washington and Benedict Arnold would differ not a whit in moral character, in merit or in blame, if they were both mere automata responding to the compulsions of forces within or without them, and thus enjoyed no measure of freedom. The conviction that men are free in deciding their course of conduct is thus seen to be embodied in the laws of all nations, in their remunerative and in their penal codes, and to be mirrored in the ethical judgments of all mankind.

To the individual who should persist, however, in affirming that he is different from the rest of mankind in experiencing no such consciousness of freedom in his choices, we would make two observations.

First, we would point out that such an individual, differing so radically from the rest of mankind, might well seek the attention of a psychiatrist. This would be particularly true if his statement, that he experienced no testimony of consciousness as to the freedom of his actions, was borne out by the repeated commission of actions, such as stealing, setting buildings on fire, which he morally disapproved, but which he felt powerless to resist doing. Pathology may affect the mind as well as the body, and such a case would obviously call for psychiatric treatment. Society recognizes the existence of mental abnormalities and, when they are socially dangerous, provides asylums for such cases.

Secondly, if the denial of the consciousness of freedom were not corroborated by the commission of deeds contrary to the choice or volition of the individual, then we would seek to elicit more clearly the consciousness of his evident freedom. This we would do by a simple illustration, in which we address ourselves directly to the individual.

"Take this book in your hand and hold it a foot above the table. Now are you free either to continue to hold the book or to drop it? Before answering, listen for a moment to the testimony of your own consciousness. Does it not tell you with unmistakable clearness that you are free to do either of these actions? Throw aside all pride of opinion. Listen attentively to the testimony of your own consciousness. Then speak aloud its verdict. If you will perform that simple experiment, and be honest in proclaiming the verdict of your own consciousness, you will find that you do not differ in the matter of freedom from the rest of mankind."

The affirmation of consciousness comes out most clearly in the moment before the deliberate choice is made. This affirmation is thus described with accuracy and penetration by Henry Sidgwick: "It is impossible for me to think at such a moment that my volition is completely determined by my formed character and the motives acting upon it. The opposite conviction is so strong as to be absolutely unshaken by the evidence brought against it; I cannot believe it to be illusory. So far it is unlike the erroneous intuitions which occur in the exercise of the senses; as e.g., the imperfections of sight and hearing. For experience soon teaches me to regard these as appearances whose suggestions are misleading; but no amount of experience of the sway of motives even tends to make me distrust my intuitive consciousness that in resolving after deliberation I exercise free choice as to which of the motives acting on me shall prevail." [7]

How To Make a Motive Prevail

The observation is sometimes made that what really determines every decision is the strongest motive. This would reduce the matter to one of mere intellectual discernment and not of will. The matter, however, is not that simple.

[7] *Methods of Ethics*, Bk. I, ch. v, p. 2, 1st Edition

For the will can *make* a motive strong or weak as it chooses. How? By focusing attention upon one motive, and considering exclusively the advantages to be derived from following it, that motive actually grows in psychological power and strength. Contrariwise, by keeping the attention away from the motive and by refusing to consider the advantages it offers, that motive though it might be, intrinsically and objectively considered, the weightier of the two, actually grows weak and becomes psychologically feeble and ineffective.

Here then is disclosed the enormous and decisive role played by the will in determining the outcome of the struggle of initially conflicting motives. It holds the reins of power. It can tip the scales one way or the other as it chooses. It can do this, as we have pointed out, by choosing to focus attention exclusively upon the one motive which it wishes to prevail. Hence the freedom of the will in our judgment is manifested even more vividly in the moment or moments *antecedent to the decision, while the will is focusing the searchlight of attention upon the motive of its choice,* than in the actual act of decision issuing often in some overt act. Freedom of the will, of course, is apparent in both acts. We merely wish by this piece of careful psychological analysis to point out how conspicuously it is present in the moments immediately antecedent to the final decision—moments wherein its freedom has not commonly been noted or stressed.

The fact that a motive can be strengthened or weakened, by the deliberate direction of the attention upon it or away from it, has far-reaching implications for both psychology and ethics. It reveals the close relation between attention and the act we decide to perform. Even in matters of a non-moral nature, it is important to know the psychological technique of strengthening the motive which you wish to have prevail. In matters of a moral character, the importance of this insight can scarcely be overstressed.

"Let's Join the Boys"

Let us illustrate. John Smith is strongly tempted to accept the invitation of some boon companions to go with them to a certain tavern where he knows from past experience he is likely to drink excessively.

"Come, John," they say, "let's join the boys at the tavern. You've been working hard all week. This is Saturday night. You need to blow off some steam. Besides," they add, "you only live once."

The image of the tavern, the sound of the music from the juke box, the smell of the liquor in his nostrils, its taste in his mouth, the thought of the carefree camaraderie of his customary companions, all swoop upon him with powerful appeal. If he allows himself to dwell exclusively upon these considerations, the appeal of the tavern and the already kindled appetite for liquor will become so strong that his chance of resisting will speedily go a-glimmering. What is it supremely important for him to do? To turn the spotlight of attention from these alluring features to the advantages of remaining at home.

Let him consider the promises which he has already made to himself, to his wife, to his confessor to remain away from that tavern in which he has been squandering his pay-check, his health and the happiness of his family. Let him recall the warning of the doctor that a continuance of his drinking habit will incapacitate him for his work, impair his nervous system and bring him prematurely to a drunkard's grave. Let him remember the misery and shame which he has brought upon his wife and children by his drunkenness.

Let him consider the after-effects of his over-indulgence,

the torture of his abused nerves, the head that seems as if it would burst with pain. Let him hold the spotlight firmly upon these considerations, coupled with the thought of the joy which he will bring to his family, and the growing sense of redemption from his own shame and misery, and he will win the victory.

"No, boys," he will be saying, "I've had enough of that; yes, too much of it. It has brought me too much grief already. Include me *out*. I'm staying home with my family."

"He Who Hesitates . . ."

While the influence of attention in strengthening all motives is great, its influence upon those involving sexual gratification is especially marked. The ideo-motor theory finds its best and speediest exemplification in sensual images and imaginations. They tend to kindle motor responses with the speed and violence of dynamite explosions. Hence spiritual writers are unanimous in pointing out the danger of dilly-dallying with any such thoughts or imaginations, and the supreme importance of turning the attention instantly from them to thoughts of an opposite character. Here, above all other fields, is exemplified the truth of the motto: "He who hesitates, is lost."

The experience of temptation, the siren voice urging us to tone down our ideals for some passing pleasure or consideration, is universal among mankind. Who is there who has not felt the pull and tug of conflicting motives, of opposing forces in our inner life? The struggle is not always easy, nor is it invariably successful. But what conviction emerges more clearly from those experiences than the conviction that the decision, at which we finally arrive, represents our own *free* choice? Whether the decision be favorable to my ideals or not, I feel no inclination to attribute the outcome to anyone but to my own self. "I willed the act," I say, "and I will take the consequences, good or bad."

Let us now address ourselves in a friendly manner to a Determinist: "Let us suppose for the moment, that we are really free. *How could consciousness give any clearer or stronger testimony than it now gives that we are free?* It thunders unequivocally at every moment of my struggle against a predominant passion that I can yield or I can painfully persevere. Throughout the conflict I realize clearly enough that it is *wrong* to yield, and I admit that the ideal of virtue has a genuine attraction for me. But it is by no means true to say that my perception of the ideal renders its reduction to practice such a pleasure that it outweighs the agreeableness of the gratification and inexorably tips the scales in its favor."

It would be just as credible to say that the temptation does not exist at all, as to say that I am not freely resisting, freely struggling against the easier and the more pleasant course. The fact is then that the human mind cannot *conceive* how consciousness could tell me more clearly or more unequivocally that I am free than it now so testifies. *Hence if consciousness gives us any assurance at all, it is the assurance that we are free.* From that conclusion there can be no escape.

The Ethical Argument

Moral liberty is the basis of ethics and the indispensable condition of morality. Without it, there can be neither duty, obligation, responsibility, nor merit. While Kant differs from us in some of his concepts of ethics, he is one with us in acknowledging that without free will there can be no ethics. He appeals to the undisputed fact of moral obligation as irrefutable evidence of liberty. "Thou canst because thou oughtest" is a familiar note sounded in his writings and in those of the greatest ethicians. "To deny the freedom of the will," points out James A. Froude, "is to make morality impossible." [8] The inference is well grounded. "It is a moral postulate," declares Professor William James, "that what ought to be can be, and that bad acts cannot be fated, but that good ones must be possible in their place." [9]

The ethical argument may be thus epitomized: The sense of moral obligation, of "oughtness," is present in all mankind. But the sense of oughtness implies the power to do a thing or not to do it. It would be absolutely meaningless, if the individual had no alternative open to him. Therefore man has the power of choosing between alternative courses of conduct, or, in other words, he enjoys moral freedom.

Belief in moral freedom alone harmonizes with the universal practice of mankind, to which we have already referred, in rewarding good deeds and in punishing evil ones. On the Determinist theory, man has no more control over his movements than has a cork, tossed hither and thither by the waves, over its own movements. Like the brute or the maniac, man feels, though the cork does not. But there is no essential difference as to the voluntariness and consequently as to the morality of his acts. His actions are the inevitable resultants of his heredity, his environment, and of the forces playing on him at the moment.

He is like a bird without wings, a king without a throne. He is like a ship without a rudder, unable to steer his course, but must go wherever the waves of heredity and the winds of environment drive him. Such a view not only is contrary to the testimony of our own consciousness but also does violence to the universal sense of moral obligation present in mankind. The waves may beat fiercely against his bark,

[8] *Short Studies: Calvinism*
[9] *Principles of Psychology*, vol. II, p. 573

and the winds may blow in a directly opposite direction, but man is conscious from his own experience that he can hurl defiance at these elements and steer the vessel of his soul toward whatsoever port he chooses. It is not the winds but the set of the sails that determines the way he goes.

The Sense of Remorse

The reality of the sense of moral obligation is further verified by the sense of remorse present at some time or other in every human. Remorse is essentially different from mere regret. Remorse is the gnawing pain of guilt which follows from the twofold conviction: 1. That we were free in committing an act. 2. That we ought not to have done it. A person stubs his toe and regrets it, because of the pain which ensues. An individual loses his pocketbook, and regrets the loss immensely. But in neither case does he experience the gnawing of remorse. Why? Because he did neither of these acts deliberately or freely, but only accidentally. Between the sense of mere regret and of remorse there is a world of difference, as every person who has experienced both, can testify.

The feeling of repentance stems from that of remorse and mirrors both the sorrow of the penitent and his purpose of amendment. Who has not felt remorse, sorrow, and purpose of amendment? Why, they are among the most profound and universal experiences of mankind. As the slanting rays of light, falling across the western sky at sunset, point to the source whence they come, so do these deep human emotions point to their common source in the universal sense of moral obligation. This sense would be without rhyme or reason, however, if man were not free to do other than that which he ought to do. Hence we are again driven by a different line of evidence to the conclusion that man possesses moral freedom.

The Metaphysical Argument

The freedom of the will is also established by a line of reasoning known as the Metaphysical Argument. While somewhat more subtle than the preceding considerations, it has the advantage of showing the cause of our freedom and the natural continuity of that freedom as long as reason remains with us in this life.

The will, we have already pointed out, is a *rational* appetite. It embraces nothing of necessity, save what is apprehended as *desirable in every respect*. Now the rational will can be irresistibly drawn only by that which the intellect proposes as so completely and absolutely attractive that it contains no disagreeable element. As long as the intellect is able to detect any such element, the will does not have that for which it is naturally yearning, namely, perfect happiness, and is consequently able to reject the proposed object. By concentrating the attention upon the undesirable feature, the object can always be made to lose its enticing force.

In this life, however, there is no object which presents itself as attractive under *all* aspects. Any finite good has its disagreeable features, either in the difficulty of its acquisition, or in the uncertainty of its retention, or in its possible incompatibility with our highest good. Even the infinite Good, God Himself, is so imperfectly and obscurely apprehended in this life that the will is not drawn irresistibly. The intellect perceives all too readily the difficulty of duty, the disagreeableness of restraining the carnal appetites, and the thorns which beset the path of virtue. Easy indeed is it for the intellect to concentrate on the hardship of carrying the cross, so that the will turns away from the *via dolorosa* to tread the primrose path of pleasure. Hence the will is not drawn irresistibly to any object, but is free to choose between the manifold kinds of goods conceivable by the intellect.

Free will is thus seen to be a result of man's possession of a spiritual faculty of cognition which is capable of conceiving unlimited and unalloyed good. Where such a spiritual faculty is absent, as in brute animals, moral liberty does not exist. The power of choosing freely, uncoerced by forces within or without us, shows that independently of the intellect, we are endowed with a spiritual faculty whose operations transcend matter and its forces as heaven transcends the earth. *For such spiritual activity must proceed from a spiritual and immaterial substance,* which is what we mean by the human soul. The establishment of the freedom of the will thus offers additional and striking corroboration of the mighty truth that man possesses a spiritual soul which elevates him above all the visible creation and renders him like unto God.

Conservation of Energy

We have completed the presentation of the evidence for moral freedom from consciousness, ethics and metaphysics. Let us now consider the difficulties. Most of these arise from a failure to understand what is meant by freedom of the will and to recognize the limitations we place upon it. Many of the objections stem from the false notion that the freedom of the will implies motiveless or causeless volitions. Others think that the libertarian view holds that man is always free and that heredity and environment exercise no influence upon volitions. These, as we have pointed out, are caricatures of our true position.

One objection, however, remains. It asserts that freedom of the will would be a violation of the law of the Conservation of Energy, as it would introduce new fountains of energy of an utterly incalculable character, which would thus change indefinitely the existing quantum. This difficulty is based on a misconception. The will does not *create* but simply *directs* the application of energy already in existence. By directing the application of existing forces, the will can change their alignment and hence the resultant.

The law states that "the sum of the kinetic and potential energies in the universe remains constant." This simply means that when one form of physical energy is transformed into another, the quantity of the second form is equivalent to that of the first. The generalization is confined to physical energy and consequently does not apply to the activity of a spiritual, immaterial principle. Physics as such knows nothing about psychical activity as forces and hence makes no attempt whatsoever to enclose them in a framework of physical laws.

This is clearly pointed out by the eminent authority on physiological psychology, Professor Ladd of Yale: "The law of the conservation and correlation of energy—as far as it has been observed, or can reasonably be assumed to hold good—offers no valid objection to the existence of a real causal connection between the mind and the brain. The present position of this law is that of *an empirical generalization,* found to hold approximately true for a large number of classes of phenomena, and presumably true for yet other cases. *To exalt it to the place of a universal and necessary relation among all phenomena of every class—mental as well as physical—would be unwarrantably to extend its application.*" [10] In other words the law of the Conservation of Energy does not touch the question of the activities of a spiritual principle, the human soul, the source of volitional operations.

Striking corroboration of this truth comes from the lead-

[10] *El. of Phy. Psychology*, p. 657

ers of modern physics. Mirroring the conclusions of Millikan, Compton and others, A. E. Eddington declares: "In the old conflict between will and predestination, it has seemed hitherto that physics comes down heavily on the side of predestination. . . . Here I have set forth the position of physical science on this matter so far as it comes into her territory. It does come into her territory, because that which we call human will cannot be entirely dissociated from the consequent motions of the muscles and disturbance of the material world. On the scientific side a new situation has arisen. It is a consequence of the advent of the quantum theory that physics is no longer pledged to a scheme of deterministic law. Determinism has dropped out altogether in the latest formulations of theoretical physics." [11]

Theory vs. Practice

Let us now advert to a few general considerations which bring out vividly the untenable and inconsistent character of the determinist view.

In theory Herbert Spencer was a determinist; in actual life and practice, however, he was the direct opposite. Thus he wrote two huge biographical volumes in which he portrays in microscopic detail his difficulties and discouragements and his strength of will in overcoming them. The claims which he makes for himself, as W. H. Mallock rightly observes, "are intelligible only on the supposition that he possessed a free will of his own, which, while dismissing it in theory as a village gossip's illusion, *he, like everybody else, accepted it in practice as a reality.* Thus one of the few deterministic thinkers who have deliberately attempted to interpret concrete life by determinism is in his own person one of the most interesting witnesses to the impossibility of interpreting

[11] *The Nature of the Physical World*, pp. 293, 294

it intelligibly without a covert reintroduction of the plain man's belief in freedom." [12] In this respect Spencer is a typical example of all the other determinists who, after proclaiming in the lecture room that they have no free will, proceed to use it conspicuously, not once, but a dozen times every hour of the day.

"You Didn't Do It on Purpose . . . ?"

The unreasonableness of the determinist viewpoint becomes apparent when one undertakes to interpret human life and action in accordance with its basic assumption. Prof. James cites the case of a particularly atrocious murder which occurred in his day at Brockton. Deciding to get rid of his wife, a man inveigled her to a deserted spot in the country. Disentangling his hand from hers, he pulled out a revolver and shot her four times. Lying on the ground, she said:

"You didn't do it on purpose, did you, dear?"

"No," he replied, "I didn't do it on purpose," as he raised a rock and smashed her skull.

Who is to blame for this dastardly deed? The murderer? "Not at all," replied the determinists. "The universe is to blame. The laws of matter and energy, working out their fixed and inexorable course, are responsible for this act, as they are for all actions on this planet." The determinists spare the villain by indicting the universe. They jump from the frying pan into the fire.

Hitler—Not to Blame?

We think that the irrational character of the determinist view may be even more vividly shown by applying it to the case of a man, who not merely has killed one person, but

[12] *Reconstruction of Religious Belief*, p. 87

who has given orders for the killing of vast multitudes. We refer to the late archvillain—Adolf Hitler. Putting thousands of Jews to death by starvation and torture in concentration camps, dropping bombs on the people of Poland without a word of warning, invading one neutral country after the other, sending his military machine to run like a Juggernaut over the men, women and children of Russia, with whom he had a "friendship" pact, he brought suffering, agony and death to incalculable millions of people. In the far-reaching consequences of his villainy, the Brockton murderer, Jesse James, John Dillinger, Al Capone are but babes in the woods. Upon him is heaped the execration of the world as upon no other man in all history.

Yet according to the teaching of determinists, he is utterly blameless. He is no more responsible for his murderous deeds than is the mother who keeps her night vigil by the bedside of her sick child. Who then is responsible? The universe. For its forces, acting upon him from without and from within, compel him so to act. Can any sensible person believe that? It is difficult to see how he can. Instead of placing the blame, where it belongs, upon the perverse will of this murderous villain, the determinist places it upon the whole universe.

Even here, however, he runs into a flagrant contradiction. For the universe that compels Hitler to perpetrate his wholesale murders is the same universe that inspires the rest of humanity with horror and repulsion at his crimes. Thus does the determinist run headlong into a contradiction, direct, violent and irreconcilable. What could bring out more vividly the utter absurdity and the sheer bankruptcy of the whole determinist theory?

The Death Knell of All Thought

Its inconsistency, however, does not stop here. Determinism spells a denial of the freedom not only of our actions but of our thoughts as well. This means then that one person is compelled to accept determinism, while another is compelled to reject it. Intellectual judgments become as mechanistic as volitions. Thinking loses all meaning. Thus the determinist rejects the freedom of the will not because his arguments are superior, but simply because heredity and environment determine that he shall think so.

"Accordingly, if the determinist is right," observes Professor B. H. Streeter of Oxford, "reasoning can prove nothing: it is merely an ingenious method for providing us with apparently rational excuses for believing what in any case we cannot help believing. But if all reasoning is a 'pathetic fallacy,' then the reasons for believing in determinism itself are fallacious. Not only that; unless reason is that which can *discriminate*, there is no criterion of truth and falsehood, all knowledge collapses; one hypothesis is as good as another, and Science itself is a fairy tale." [13]

The determinist view would thus sound the death knell of all thought as well as of all volition. Stemming from a thoroughly materialistic view of life and the universe, it conceives of all life, even the mental life of man, as but the play of matter and energy in accordance with physical laws. Human life and all the thoughts and aspirations of humanity are predetermined with an iron-clad necessity by conditions obtaining in the cosmos a billion years ago. The dreary view of such a materialistic fatalism is vividly portrayed in the lines quoted by Professor William James: [14]

[13] *Reality*, p. 76
[14] *The Dilemma of the Determinist*, p. 150

With earth's first clay they did the last man knead,
And there of the last harvest sowed the seed
And the first morning of creation wrote
What the last dawn of reckoning shall read.

To Sum Up

To sum up: We have demonstrated the freedom of the will by the testimony of consciousness, by the universal sense of reward and punishment, of responsibility, duty, merit and blame, of remorse and repentance. We have presented the metaphysical argument showing that the will can choose from among the unlimited number and forms of good, conceivable by the intellect, the one closest to its heart's desire. We have shown that the law of the conservation of energy offers no difficulty to the freedom of volition, when both are properly understood. We have pointed out the untenableness of the necessitarian view by disclosing how it escapes placing the blame upon the perverse will of an individual only by placing it instead upon the whole universe. The inconsistency and bankruptcy of that viewpoint were further revealed by showing how it leads to the denial of the validity and significance of all thought and of all volitions.

Doubtless by this time the reader is asking: Why go to such pains to prove a truth which virtually every man and woman of good sense will readily admit? Why pile the evidence sky high, when our own consciousness testifies, with an intimacy and a clarity which cannot be surpassed, that we are free? We have done so, not because the average reader needs to be convinced, but because we want him to be forewarned and forearmed against the determinist sophistries, no matter how specious and enticing, which he may encounter at any time.

We think it desirable to have him perceive the truth of moral freedom, from its center to its circumference, because it constitutes the spinal column of moral responsibility and the foundation of man's ethical life. A clear and profound insight into the rational bases of this great truth will constitute for the individual an invaluable stimulus to initiative, courage and determination in struggling to convert his velleities into volitions, his aspirations into realities, and will be his best insurance against the crippling spirit of defeatism, fatalism and pessimism.

While the will is free, it may lose its freedom and become enslaved through habits of indolence, passion and vice. Like all living faculties, the will is subject to the laws of habit formation. It is of supreme importance to form as early in life as possible habits of labor, of persistent effort in the realization of high ideals, of resistance to the passions, and of self-control. Not only do such habits safeguard the freedom of the will, but they also strengthen and develop it. They make it, what the will should be in every well-rounded and integrated personality, the ready and obedient servant of a sensitive conscience. In the attainment of will power, human character sounds its climactic note and finds its crowning glory. It is the indispensable key to achievement and success in all the fields of human life.

CHAPTER XXV

THE IMMORTALITY OF THE SOUL

It must be so—Plato, thou reason'st well!
Else whence this pleasing hope, this fond desire,
This longing after immortality?
Or whence this secret dread and inward horror
Of falling into nought? Why shrinks the soul
Back on herself and startles at destruction?
'Tis the Divinity that stirs within us;
'Tis heaven itself that points out an hereafter,
And intimates eternity to man.

ADDISON, *Cato*, Act V, Sc. 1

OLD as the race is the question of life after death. "If a man die," asked Job of old, "shall he live again?" This is the question which confronts every man born into this world. It is not merely of speculative interest. It is of deep practical concern for all mankind. Charged with vital human interest, and laden with consequences which jut into eternity, it looms up like the Sphinx of Thebes, posing to every wayfarer a question fraught with life or death. Its importance can scarcely be exaggerated. Along with the existence of God and the freedom of the will, it constitutes the third in the trinity of problems which lie at the heart of philosophy.

While a few may affect indifference as to whether or not they survive, the overwhelming majority of mankind finds no inclination to strike that pose. They are unable to see in such an attitude any surcease from the restless yearning for continued existence, which throbs like a fever in their veins. Neither can they work out a reasoned scheme of things, nor a moral order with adequate motivation, until they have answered the question of a life beyond the grave.

And they are right. With this question remaining unanswered, man goes through life as in a daze, uncertain alike as to his origin and his destiny. Life becomes a jig-saw puzzle with the essential parts missing, "a tale, told by an idiot, full of sound and fury, signifying nothing."

It is well at the outset to clear up some misconceptions which have clustered around this subject and which have tended to create disaffection. Persons are sometimes heard to remark that they are not interested in the prospect of thrumming a harp all day before a throne, or of flitting on celestial wings from one hymn meeting to another. Such conceptions are of a piece with those which picture heaven as having pearly gates and streets of gold, and God as an elderly gentleman forever seated on a throne far off in the cobwebbed attic of the sky.

Such conceptions, it should be needless to point out, while forming the imagery for children's stories, are entertained by no serious theistic thinkers. They are puerile and should have no place in an adult's thinking. Yet not infrequently have we found persons who thought they were arguing against immortality when in reality they were only arguing against caricatures of it. We shall present toward the end of the discussion conceptions of supernal felicity not incommensurate with the intellect and the will of man.

The Nature of the Evidence

Some have contended that the question cannot be answered with definiteness and certainty because of the lack of sufficient evidence, that the most that can be achieved is a degree of probability of survival. When such a conclusion is formed, it is traceable in our judgment to two chief causes.

First, such writers fail to recognize that every branch of learning has a method of demonstration that reflects the character of its own subject matter and achieves validity within its own field. Thus truths of physics are established by a process of physical demonstration, those of mathematics by mathematical reasoning. Truths of philosophy are established by philosophical induction; those of aesthetics by aesthetic evidence and reasoning. How would you prove that *The Last Judgment* by Michelangelo is a greater painting than the amateurish water-color daubs of Adolf Hitler? Certainly you cannot provide a physical or mathematical proof. You can prove it, however, by applying the canons of art, the principles of aesthetics. And you can prove it to the hilt.

Similarly the immortality of the soul, being a question of philosophy, is established by philosophical evidence and reasoning. Not being susceptible of demonstration by the methods of physics or of mathematics, which play so large a role in establishing the facts of modern science, some have concluded that the immortality of the soul does not admit of proof. This is erroneous. It admits of proof, and of conclusive proof, but not of the kind which they have in mind. The evidence is of a philosophic character, such as is used to establish the existence of God and the freedom of the will.

The second reason for the unsatisfactory and inconclusive results achieved by not a few writers is that they undertake to treat immortality as a detached and isolated theme, torn out of its proper setting. They fail to perceive that human survival is a corollary of two antecedent facts, namely, the spirituality of the soul and the rational organization of the universe, with God as its author and guarantor. From these two great primary truths, the persistence of the human personality, at least for some time after the disintegration of the body, necessarily follows. Whereas if it be treated independently of these two antecedent facts, the treatment is likely to be sentimental, to abound in wishful thinking, and to be inconclusive. For it is a treatment in which the two chief fountainheads of evidence have been either ignored or tapped only incidentally.

The Immaterial Cannot Disintegrate

We have already demonstrated that the human soul is a substantial being, that it is simple or indivisible, that it is immaterial, spiritual and not *intrinsically* dependent upon the body for its activity or existence. By death is meant the disintegration of part from part. But the human soul, being simple and immaterial, has no parts and is therefore incapable *per se* of such dissolution. Moreover, since it is spiritual, and does not intrinsically depend upon the body for its existence, it is therefore exempt from corruption *per accidens*. Consequently the human soul is incapable of corruption in either of these ways. Its incorruptibility is thus seen to be a corollary of its immateriality.

The mind, as we have shown, is as distinct from the brain as a sculptor is from his hammer and chisel. If the mind were merely an aspect of the nervous system, a function of the brain, it would not enjoy this immunity from the corruption to which the physical organism is subject. In establishing with great care the immateriality of the soul and its intrinsic independence of the bodily organism, we not only extracted the fangs from cerebralistic materialism but we also established the intrinsic incorruptibility of the soul and hence its immunity to disintegration or death. Far from being of a sentimental or a wishful nature, the evidence and the reasoning by which we demonstrated these facts were of a rigorously philosophical character, which will carry conviction to any open mind.

The only way in which the human soul could cease then would be through annihilation, by itself, or by any created thing, or by God. By annihilation we mean the reduction of something to nothing. But neither the human soul, nor any other created thing, is capable of causing any being to disappear completely. The most that human power can do is to modify. Annihilation is possible only to God, through the withdrawal of His conserving power. Annihilation and creation are correlative terms, and both necessitate the action of divine omnipotence.

Now, not only is there no reason to believe that God would destroy the work of His hands, but there is every reason to believe that He will sustain in existence that part of creation which most resembles Himself, the soul of man. We know that even our corruptible body does not perish completely. Are we to believe that God, having created the soul of an incorruptible nature, would cause it to perish more completely and utterly than the corruptible body which it animates? Well does Edward Young ask:

> Can it be?
> Matter immortal? and shall spirit die?
> Above the nobler, shall less noble rise?
> Shall man alone, for whom all else revives,
> No resurrection know? Shall man alone,
> Imperial man! be sown in barren ground,
> Less privileged than grain on which he feeds? [1]

This dictate of our rational nature is confirmed by the revelation of Christ, as we shall see in detail later, that the soul of man is destined for everlasting life, and that God

[1] *Night Thoughts*, p. 114

does not contradict the work of His hands. To the question of Job, "If a man die, shall he live again?" we answer: *"Yes, for the soul of man is, by its nature, immaterial, incorruptible, incapable of disintegration, can be annihilated neither by itself nor by any created power, and will not be annihilated by its Creator."* Here then is a purely rational, philosophic answer to a philosophic question.

Universal Belief in Immortality

We come now to a consideration of a less technical character. While simple, it is none the less weighty and impressive.

The belief in a future life is among the most universal beliefs of mankind. It ranks alongside the belief in a Supreme Being. It has been found among tribes and races of every degree of civilization or barbarism in every part of the world. "The notion of the survival of the spirit after death in some form, whether clear or vague," says Henry Frank, "has ever existed in the human mind from the most primitive times to the present hour." [2] Referring to this belief in the immortality of the soul, Plutarch observes: "This belief which we hold, is so old that we cannot trace its author or its origin, and it dates back to the most remote antiquity." [3]

Similar is the testimony of Sir James G. Frazer: "The question whether our conscious personality survives after death has been answered by almost all races of men in the affirmative. On this point skeptical or agnostic peoples are nearly, if not wholly unknown. . . ." [4] Later in that same work, Frazer points out how impressive is that widespread belief, saying: "It is impossible not to be struck by the strength, and perhaps we may say the universality, of the

[2] *Modern Light on Immortality*, p. 35
[3] *De Consol. ad Appolonium*
[4] *The Belief in Immortality*, vol. I, p. 33

natural belief in immortality among the savage races of man-kind. With them a life after death is not a matter of specula-tion and conjecture, of hope and fear; it is a practical cer-tainty which the individual as little dreams of doubting as he doubts the reality of his conscious existence." [5]

While a few have questioned the existence of such a be-lief in Buddhism, Frazer, Max Müller, Rhys David, and other careful investigators are unanimous in affirming its "belief in the existence of the human soul after death." [6] In fact, Metchnikoff's painstaking study caused him to conclude that Buddhism "is so persuaded of survival after death as being the rule, that it grants only to rare and elect souls the privilege of at length laying down the burden of continuous life." [7]

Confucius mirrors the belief of the Chinese in the inde-structible character of the human soul. "Death," he says, "is not destruction properly so-called, but a decomposition which resolves each substance into its natural state. The in-tellectual substance again ascends to heaven from which it came, the animal spirit, *khi*, unites with the aërial fluid, and the terrestrial and aqueous substances turn once more to earth and water." [8]

At one time the Jews were behind the other nations in the distinctness of their belief in personal immortality. This seems to have been traceable to the intensity of their con-viction that obedience to Jehovah's commands would bring them national victory and agricultural prosperity. The bit-ter experiences of the exile shattered this illusion and later we find some of the noblest proclamations of a future life coming from the lips of Jewish sages.

[5] *Ibid.*, vol. I, p. 468
[6] *Ibid.*, p. 26
[7] *Ibid.*, p. 148
[8] *Modern Light on Immortality*, p. 37

Plato Champions Immortality

The Greeks appear to have been among the first to attempt a systematic philosophical treatment of immortality. While belief in a future life is evident in Homer, the conception of immortality is more distinct and also more spiritual in Pindar. It is, however, at the hands of Plato that the doctrine attained its most elaborate philosophical exposition and defence. He treats it in virtually all his writings but especially in *Phaedo*. Not less than eight different lines of evidence are adduced to establish the deathless character of the human soul. "Man," he taught, "consists of soul and body. The soul alone constitutes the self to which the body is only externally appended. So conceived the immortality of the soul is beyond all doubt, for the essence of life lies beyond all temporary change." [9]

Among the Romans, Seneca is emphatic in proclaiming a life beyond the grave. "As the mother's womb," he observes, "holds us for ten months, making us ready, not for the womb itself, but for life, just so, through our lives, we are making ourselves ready for another birth. . . . Therefore look forward without fear to that appointed hour—the last hour of the body, but not of the soul. . . . That day, which you fear as being the end of all things, is the birthday of your eternity." [10] Equally explicit is Ovid, who declares: "In my better part I shall be raised to immortality above the lofty stars." [11] So likewise Horace affirms:

> I shall not wholly die; large residue
> Shall 'scape the queen of death. [12]

[9] *We Believe in Immortality*, edited by S. Strong, p. 127
[10] *Epistulae ad Lucilium*, Epis. c. 11, sec. 23
[11] *Metamorphoses*; Bk. XV, l. 875
[12] *Odes*, Bk. III, ode 30, l. 6

Vying with these two in proclaiming the immortal character of the human soul is Cicero. "Whatever that may be," he asserts, "which feels, which has knowledge, which wills, which has the power of growth, it is celestial and divine, and for that reason it must of necessity be eternal." [13] As modern and up-to-date as today's newspaper is the answer he gives to those people to whom "the immortality of the soul seems incredible because they cannot conceive what kind of a thing the soul can be when freed from the body."

To such persons, he replies: "Just as if they could really form a correct idea as to what kind of thing it is even while in the body; what its form, size, and location are. . . . This should be pondered by those who say that they are unable to conceive a soul without a body; they will then see whether they can conceive it when it is in the body. As for myself, when I reflect on the nature of the soul, it seems to me by far more difficult and obscure to determine its character while it is in the body, a strange domicile, than to imagine what it is when it leaves it, and has arrived in the empyreal regions, in its own and proper home." [14]

With the birth of the Christian religion, the doctrine of immortality assumed a new position in the world. It became the basis of the whole scheme of the Christian faith. The mists and the haze in which it had been enshrouded for both philosopher and peasant were removed and the doctrine was set forth in clear and simple terms. Christianity's emphasis on the priceless value and the everlasting character of the human soul was an important factor in establishing the equality of men and the liberation of the slave. The doctrine received its complete philosophical elaboration from St. Thomas.

[13] *Tusculanarum Disputationum*, Bk. I, ch. 27, sec. 66
[14] *Ibid.*, ch. 22

The Significance of This Belief

The universality of this belief and its persistence through all the ages is truly striking. "We may safely say," observes John Fiske, "that for much more than one hundred thousand years, mankind has regarded itself as personally interested in two worlds." [15] For a belief so universal and persistent, there must surely be a foundation in fact. True, many crudities are to be found in the conceptions of savages concerning the life beyond, just as there are to this day crudities in their conceptions of the sun and the heavenly planets. But who would expect to find among rude and savage peoples the same type of concepts as those obtaining among cultured and civilized nations? What is truly remarkable is that, in spite of all the diversity of concept, the same underlying belief in a future life is always present.

The universality of this belief raises the question: What is its origin? Thus Frazer, after raising the question, suggests an answer: "What then is the kind of experience from which the theory of human immortality is deduced? Is it our experience of the operations of our minds? or is it our experience of external nature? As a matter of historical fact —and you will remember that I am treating the question purely from the historical standpoint—men seem to have inferred the persistence of their personality after death, both from the one kind of experience and from the other, that is, both from the phenomena of their inner life and from the phenomena of what we call the external world." [16]

Since this belief is based upon both types of phenomena, it has a firmer basis than beliefs based solely on the observation of external phenomena—beliefs which could not be

[15] *We Believe in Immortality*, S. Strong, p. 127
[16] *The Belief in Immortality*, vol. I, p. 468

checked by comparison with the facts and experiences of man's inner life. Judgments concerning the apparent movement of the sun around the earth and other matters of natural science were on a different basis. Here peoples were without the scientific instruments necessary to arrive at the facts. They were moreover questions of a purely speculative nature, having no direct and immediate bearing on the life or destiny of mankind. Into such matters errors may creep all too easily. This is true not only among primitive peoples but among the civilized as well. But the question of immortality profoundly affects every human being, and like the existence of God, rests upon evidence drawn from the moral order, from the rational organization of the world, and from a scrutiny of the activities of the human mind with its sense of enduring personal identity amid the constant flux of ideas and experiences.

It is truly remarkable that while societies, in passing from rude and primitive conditions to civilization and culture, slough off many of their previous conceptions, the belief in immortality has not weakened but has grown in strength and in firmness. It would seem to be an apprehension of the human mind similar to the perception of the existence of a Supreme Being.

Thus Dr. J. D. Quackenbos rightly observes: "A psychological proof of *post mortem* existence has been found in the fact that immortality is an apprehension of human reason." [17] The argument from the universality of belief in a future life is certainly weighty and convincing. To say that all mankind in all ages and stages of civilization has been deceived is to impugn the validity of the human mind to distinguish truth from falsehood. Its scientific value is frankly acknowledged by Professor Gase-Des Fosse, who says: "If the name of science is given especially to all research based

[17] *Body and Spirit*, p. 262

on facts, it can be said that this argument in favor of the immortality of the soul has a scientific value, as all its strength lies in establishing a fact which is universally human." [18]

The Desire for Happiness

In mankind there is a deep-rooted and universal longing for happiness without alloy. So deeply implanted indeed in the heart of man is this craving, that he is compelled by his very nature to seek happiness. We frankly admit that this is one of the matters in which the will is not free. The mind and the will and the heart of man stretch out eager fingers seeking to grasp happiness. This craving for happiness is therefore an expression not merely of man's sensual appetite but also of his intellect and will. The desire for perfect beatitude, the striving for the possession of the infinite good, are the result not of a blind instinct but of an intelligent yearning. They are, in fact, an authentic expression of the rational nature of man, of that element which makes him specifically human.

A longing for happiness is peculiar to no man, but common to all mankind. Far from suppressing such desire, the development of the mental and moral faculties render more acute than ever that craving for the possession of the infinite good which alone can still the hungers in the restless heart of man. The more men seek to conform to the loftiest ideals of virtue, the less satisfied they become with the pleasures which do not minister to the deepest yearnings of their minds and souls. They want full and perfect happiness, without any admixture of pain, transiency or uncertainty.

Such is our major premise. It expresses a truth which no

[18] *The Proofs of Life after Death*, compiled and edited by R. J. Thompson, p. 206

man, who looks deeply into his own heart, or into other hearts, can really doubt.

Our minor premise asserts that such happiness cannot be found in this life. Our own experience, the testimony of our fellows, and the history of the human race show clearly that man's yearning for unalloyed happiness can never be satisfied in this vale of tears. Health, strength, beauty, riches, popularity, intellectual talents fall to the lot of few. But even to those few, they bring no exemption from the worries and trials which beset the footsteps of all mortals. Indeed, these possessions not infrequently increase nervous tensions and make the head rest less lightly on the pillow.

With half the world rising up periodically to destroy the other half, with blood, sweat and tears the order of the day for hundreds of millions, with the fear of ever bigger and better wars to plague our tomorrow, it is evident that anything like perfect happiness on this war-torn planet is beyond the wildest dreams of man. Fortunate are the mortals who manage to keep half a step in front of disaster ever snapping at their heels. Hence we are obliged to postulate a future life wherein man's universal and necessary yearning for happiness will find its fulfillment.

To deny this is to predicate both folly and cruelty on the part of God. Such a denial would mean a head-on collision with the great principle formulated by Aristotle: *Nature does nothing in vain.* Sir Thomas Browne characterized this as "the only indisputable axiom in philosophy." [19] Botanists, physiologists, and other searchers into nature have pointed out its detailed exemplification in their respective fields. The hunger for food, the thirst for water, the craving of the lungs for air, the yearning for sleep, the desire for companionship, all find their fulfillment in the world of reality.

Would it not be strange indeed if the desire for perfect

[19] *Religio Medici,* Ph. I, Sec. 15

happiness, the noblest of all the cravings that stir within the human breast, were planted in man only to mock and taunt him with its unattainability? Would it not be passing strange if this were the one blind spot in the cosmic eye, where vision is most imperative? Are we to believe that this region of man's highest hopes and deepest yearnings is the one place where Nature *does* something in vain? "We scale the ladder of creation," observes Dr. Richard Downey, "only to find it break at the topmost rung!" [20] This is an impossible conclusion. It runs counter to the very structure and constitution of our minds, hearts and souls, counter to nature, and counter to God, our Creator and our loving Father. Therefore we are compelled to conclude that there must be a life beyond, where the deepest cravings of man's nature, so universal and so inextinguishable, will find their fulfillment in an unalloyed happiness that knows no ending.

The Rational Organization of the Universe

The existence of life beyond the grave follows as a necessary corollary of the rational organization of the universe. The guarantor of the reasonableness of creation is none other than God, who is infinite justice and righteousness. Hence we may say that immortality follows as a direct and immediate consequence of the rational organization of the universe and indirectly and ultimately from the existence of an infinitely perfect God. He is the underwriter of the reasonableness of the cosmic scheme, the vindicator of the moral law written in the mind and the heart of man. The argument achieves its full cogency only when the appeal is carried to the Supreme Being, who is both the ultimate source and sanction of the moral order of the universe.

The reasoning runs as follows: God has written in our

[20] *Personal Immortality*, p. 23

rational nature the moral law, commanding us to do right and to abstain from wrong. As an infinitely wise, just, and holy lawmaker, He must have provided a perfect sanction for this law. But in this life there is no such perfect sanction. Therefore the soul must exist at least for some time after death.

We have already established, in our discussion of religion and morality, the necessity of sanctions to put teeth into the moral law here. It is sufficient to point out that no law is worth the paper on which it is written, if it does not provide sanctions in the form of rewards and penalties to secure its enforcement. No legislator who is in earnest about his law can allow it to be ignored with impunity. The failure to do so would indicate to young and old alike that the law is only a dead letter, which they can observe or violate as best suits their convenience and pleasure. God could not play the role of such an indifferent legislator. *If He makes a law for man, He must attach to it a proper sanction.*

The moral law, that good should be done and evil should be avoided, is universal among mankind. A study of the literatures, laws, and moral ideas of the nations of the world proves this abundantly. If such a law were without sufficient sanction, it would obviously be incomplete and inadequate, and consequently incompatible with the character of an infinitely wise and just lawmaker.

"The Bootlegger Grows Fat"

It is a matter of common observation that a sufficient sanction of the moral law is not found in this life. Virtue does not always receive its due reward, nor vice its proper punishment. While honesty is ordinarily the most profitable policy, there are numerous instances where its observance yields but a meager dividend, and its violation, riches and pleasures. The widespread graft and corruption, which honey-comb the politics of so many of our large cities, is concrete evidence that vast numbers do not believe in the remunera-tiveness of uncompromising honesty under all circumstances.

All too often the bootlegger, the gambler and the grafter grow fat and rich, and bask in the luxuries and pleasures which money can buy, while the scrupulously honest man grows thin and poor, with his nose to the grindstone, as he wears himself out trying to keep the wolf from the door. Al Capone with his winter home in Florida, with its Oriental rugs, its gold door knobs, with his yachts, his thick beef-steaks, his carnival of sensual pleasures, is the symbol of the man who grows fat upon the returns of his brothels and his other villainies. How many a Lazarus, reeling under the burden of providing the bare necessities for his family, must have looked wistfully at the sumptuous palace of this earthly Dives and hungered for a few scraps from his table groaning with delicacies garnered from far and near. No, a realistic view of the distribution of the good things of this earth, its pleasures and its luxuries, compels one to admit that they are not proportioned on the basis of virtue.

This is further confirmed by the fact that multitudes of virtuous people spend long years of their life on beds of pain, from which the only escape is death. Others are handi-capped by frightful deformities which rob them of the pos-sibility of marriage and of establishing homes of their own. One has but to visit a home for crippled children or an in-stitution for victims of incurable cancer to realize how hol-low and empty is the adage: virtue is its own reward. He realizes likewise how monstrously irrational is the cosmic scheme of things, if the flickering candle of life is forever extinguished in the damp darkness of the uncomprehending grave.

Father Damien of Molokai

Take, for instance, Father Damien laboring among the lepers at Molokai. Giving up home and family in Belgium to spend himself in ministering to these outcasts of humanity on a lonely island in the South Pacific, he eventually contracts the dread disease and dies. His life is a long martyrdom, motivated by a quenchless love for God and unflagging devotion to the most neglected of His children. In an open grave the lepers place the body of the man whom they love more than life itself. He was their spiritual shepherd, their physician, their nurse, their carpenter, their defender, the man who laid down his life for them. Stand by that open grave and say:

"Well, there's your six feet of earth. Soon the clay will close over you. The black silence of the grave will engulf you. The worms and the maggots will devour what the leprosy has left. You come to the same end as that of the villain, the knave, and the murderer. They come to it after trampling upon all the laws of God and man. You come to it over the *via dolorosa* of martyrdom for God and man. But the end, the goal, the reward is just the same."

Who is there who would not cry out in protest against such monstrous injustice? Who would not rebel against such utter irrationality? Who would not proclaim that such a common dénouement of virtue and vice brands the universe as a ghastly farce and life a tragic lie? Yes, we can go further, and affirm that such an ending would constitute a denial of the wisdom and justice and holiness of God Himself, and therefore of His very existence. Hence we are obliged to repudiate the monstrous conclusion that death is the end of all, the verdict meted out alike to sinner and to saint.

If there is a moral order in this world, as all mankind admits, then there must be a recompense in proportion to one's deserts. Back of that moral order stands its guarantor and vindicator, God, whose infinite justice equips it with adequate sanctions. Since these are not always applied in this life, there must be a life beyond, in which the gross and palpable inequities of the earthly scene will be rectified in a pattern of perfect justice. It is evident then that it is God Himself who constitutes the unshakable foundation and the ultimate basis for a future life.

A Demand of the Moral Order

The existence of such a divine Being, who will ultimately reward me for doing my duty or punish me for neglecting it, is a matter of life and death to the practical reason. Without God, the bottom falls out. "The whole system of our belief," points out Professor Henry Sidgwick, "as to the intrinsic reasonableness of conduct must fall, . . . without a belief in some form or other that the moral order which we see imperfectly realized in the actual world is yet actually perfect. If we reject this belief, . . . the Cosmos of Duty is reduced to a chaos, and the prolonged effort of the human intellect to frame a perfect ideal of rational conduct is seen to be foredoomed to inevitable failure." [21]

Immanuel Kant likewise insisted upon the immortality of the soul as a postulate of the practical reason. Man has no alternative to belief in an after life, he declared, except the impossible one of acting against his rational nature. We may thus summarize his argument: The law of duty postulates moral perfection or holiness. But such perfection is not attainable in this life. Therefore it can only be achieved by an indefinite progress. But such indefinite progress implies the persistence of the human personality after the disintegration

[21] *Method of Ethics*, Bk. IV, Ch. VI, 1st Edit.

of the body. This is but another way of saying that the human soul must be immortal.

The argument is a valid one. Its cogency lies in the obligation of man to act in conformity with the dictates of practical reason. This does not require us to agree with Kant's conception of the *autonomy of reason*. For we do not weaken the cogency of the argument, but strengthen it, when we push the sanction for the moral law to a source beyond reason, to its ultimate source and final sanction, God, its author and vindicator. The gist of this argument is contained in the simple statement of von Hartmann: "The bare fact that we possess moral instincts is, even taken by itself, the refutation of all anti-teleological views of the universe." [22] By anti-teleological views von Hartmann means views which would regard the universe as without meaning or purpose.

A Stairway Leading Where?

It is to be noted that the argument for the immortality of soul as a postulate of practical reason is in reality but a corollary of the rational organization of the universe whose guarantor is God Himself. Scholars who have thought deeply on the problem, though they may differ in other respects, have not failed to perceive God's rational organization of the cosmos as the ultimate grounds for the belief. Thus John Fiske declares: "I believe in the immortality of the soul . . . as a supreme act of faith in the reasonableness of God's work." [23] "You ask," said Goethe, "what are my grounds for belief in immortality. The weightiest is this: We cannot do without it." Dr. Joseph Fort Newton asserts: "Manifestly the soul is as immortal as the moral order which

[22] *D. sittl. Bewusstsein*, p. 465
[23] *We Believe in Immortality*, ed. S. Strong, p. 59

inhabits it, else morality were a mockery." [24] E. Y. Mullins goes to the heart of the matter when he declares: *"The universe is a stairway leading nowhere unless man is immortal."* [25] The stairway of duty, if the universe is organized on rational lines, must lead to God. Says George H. Carruthers:

> The picket frozen on duty,
> The mother starved for her brood,
> Socrates drinking the hemlock,
> And Jesus on the rood;
> The millions, who humble and nameless,
> The straight, hard pathway trod,
> Some call it consecration—and others call it God.

Yes, God is the beginning and the end, the alpha and the omega of all our striving, the guarantor of our unending life, the haven of all our anxious hopes and eager yearnings.

One of the shining merits of the doctrine of immortality is that it harmonizes so well with the reasonableness of creation. The two doctrines support each other, and neither could stand without the other. While God and the rational organization of the cosmos constitute the ultimate grounds of our belief in a future life, the demand of our moral nature for a divine remunerator, who will rectify in a future life the inequalities of the present, is one of the most forcible proofs of God's existence. Thus do these truths fit together into a pattern, which satisfies the demands of our rational nature and gives meaning and purpose to human existence. With any one of these missing, life would be a mere jigsaw puzzle, which would remain forever unsolved.

"On the supposition of universal mortality," observed Professor Hastings Rashdall, "the contrast between the capacities of human nature and its actual destiny, between the

[24] *Ibid.,* p. 155
[25] *My Idea of God,* p. 199

immensity of the man's outlook and the limitations of his actual horizon, between the splendour of his ideals and the insignificance of his attainment, becomes such as to constitute, in a mind which fairly faces it, a shock to our rational nature sufficient to destroy belief in the rationality of things, and to imperil confidence in the authority of Moral Reason as a guide to human life. To those who have once accepted the rationality of things, and most emphatically to those who have once accepted the faith in a personal God, the improbability that a being of such capacity should have been created to be simply the creature of a day, that 'cometh up, and is cut down, like a flower, and never continueth in one stay,' has almost invariably amounted to an absolute impossibility. It is the favourite argument alike of reasoned Philosophy, and of the intensest moral intuition." [26]

"I Would Go Mad!"

Let us illustrate these abstract truths with an example. Some time ago we had occasion to prepare for death a mother who had been bed-ridden for several years because of a serious spinal injury. Widowed after the birth of her fifth child, she had worn herself to the bone to keep her little brood together, a roof over their heads, and clothes on their backs. After some seventeen years of incessant labor, which included taking in washing, ironing, sewing, and all manner of other work, she suffered an injury that made her a hopeless invalid with half of her body paralyzed.

In the last year cancer had set in. Always cheerful, never complaining, she bore her burden like the Christian heroine that she was, in spite of the intense pain caused by the inroads of the cancer. The joys, which every mother craves, of nestling in the home she has made, of leaning proudly on

[26] *The Theory of Good and Evil*, vol. 2, p. 265

the arms of her stalwart sons, of listening to the tender confidences of her lovely daughters, aglow with the meaning and the mystery of life at the threshold of romance, were to be denied her. The sequel to her seventeen years of unremitting toil and of four years of invalidism, she knew full well, would be death.

One day when we visited her, the dread carcinoma was eating like a glutton into her emaciated body and her failing strength told her that the end could not be far off. Out through the hospital window, she could see people passing, happy, gay, and free from care. Fighting to hold back the tears, she said to us: "Father, these last four years have not been easy. At times the pain has been almost unbearable. I've worked so hard for my children. I love them, and I hate to leave them now. But God knows best. And I bow to His will. *But if I did not believe there is a God and a future life, I think I would go mad.*"

God and an After Life

In those simple words, she summed up the case for an after life with a directness and pregnancy greater than that found in the treatises of all the philosophers. For she expressed the irrepressible demand of the practical reason of all mankind, of all the men and women whose cross is heavy and whose road is steep. Is that not the conviction burnt into the souls of the millions of American sons who fought, suffered and died for what they believed to be a better world? Had you said to the soldier who had endured months of nameless suffering, as he lay dying in his lonely foxhole:

"Soon the water and the mud will cover you with its pall of death. That will be the end of you and all your dreams. Your love for your wife and children, your devotion to your country, your sacrifice for human freedom, and all the high hopes and ideals which surged within your soul, all perish with you beneath the oozing slime. Like a candle snuffed in the night, your flickering light goes out. The end for you is darkness, silence, and the uncomprehending mud which covers you and all your hopes and dreams."

Would not he, like the mother just mentioned, have said: "If I were to believe that life is such a ghastly farce, that the sufferings and the life, which I offer up on the altar of my country's cause, bring me no reward, that there is no God, no hereafter, I would go crazy." Yes, God and an after life are necessary to satisfy the demand of our moral nature that the universe be organized on rational lines and is not a crazy quilt of patterns running at cross purposes and leading only to idiocy. "Can it be fancied," asks Edgar Allan Poe, "that the deity ever vindictively made in His image a mannikin merely to madden it?"

"I Shall Emerge One Day"

The hypothesis that death completely destroys the human personality, renders the universe monstrously irrational. According to that hypothesis, points out Dr. Harry Emerson Fosdick, "one generation of incomplete, aspiring persons is wiped off the earth, as a child erases unfinished problems from his slate, that another generation of incomplete, aspiring persons may be created—created and then annihilated. Nothing ever is finished anywhere. God, like a half-witted artist, amusing himself with tasks that have no meaning, paints pictures in which he barely outlines forms of beauty, full of promise, only to erase them and begin again. Aspiring characters, as an agnostic said, are trying to get music out of sackbuts and psalteries, that never were in tune and seemingly never will be, and our social labors simply build transient oases in a desert world, empty of spiritual meaning—oases that in the end the desert will consume in burning sand." [27]

The mere exposition of the consequences of such a theory is sufficient to show its untenable character. On that theory, the thief, the sensualist, the murderer, are wise, while the saint, the sage, the martyr are fools. If there was ever a *reductio ad absurdum*, here is one.

The necessity for an after life, as a consequence of the rational organization of the universe, is so clear and so overwhelming that it is difficult to see how anyone who has followed with open mind the course of the argument, can entertain any serious doubts. It is not too technical nor too abstract for a child to understand. The conclusion which we have reached is the only one which accords with our minds, with our moral nature, and with the very instincts of our nature. It is not mere egotism, nor selfishness. It is in harmony with the noblest part of our nature. "The cry of the human," declares Henry van Dyke, "for a life beyond the grave comes from that which is noblest in the soul of man." [28] Robert Browning but expresses the conviction of mankind the wide world over in his lines: [29]

> If I stoop
> Into a dark tremendous sea of cloud,
> It is but for a time; I press God's lamp
> Close to my breast; its splendour, soon or late,
> Will pierce the gloom: I shall emerge one day.

A Few Analogies

We offer now a few analogies which are suggestive and helpful in our thinking about the survival of the human personality after the disintegration of the body. Look at

[27] *The Assurance of Immortality*, Harpers, N.Y.
[28] *Greatest Thoughts on Immortality*, p. 68
[29] *Paracelsus*, Pt. V

nature in the dead of a northern winter. How drab and life-less appear the gaunt skeletons of leafless trees, the flowers long faded and gone, the grass, sere and dead. What a picture of death all nature presents! Yet how quickly the trees, the flowers, the grass, respond to the kiss of the spring sunshine and leap from the dark abyss of death to the multi-colored pageant of life. How speedily the gaunt skeletons of the trees shoot forth bud and leaf, the flowers find their colors and their fragrance, and the grass its verdant blade, all throbbing and aglow with the mystery of a resurrected life.

Take the case of the cocoon and the butterfly. In the larva stage the butterfly is shut up in a cocoon. It is without the power of movement, and bears no resemblance whatsoever to the shimmering fleet-winged insect it is soon to be. Let a stranger scrutinize that bit of formless matter and he will find nothing therein to tell him of the slender-bodied, wide-winged, roving insect that is to emerge from the chrysalis, and haunt us with its gorgeous coloring and tremulous beauty as it flits from flower to flower. Here is a transformation which mirrors in a small and feeble manner the still more marvelous emergence of the resplendent soul of man from the disintegrating prison house of the body.

Take the case of man himself. He begins his earthly pilgrimage as a unicellular organism, a tiny fecundated ovum. If not informed beforehand, who, gazing upon that microscopic bit of protoplasm, would ever suspect that from it would emerge a Plato, a Shakespeare, an Einstein? What could be more unlike a fully developed human being, whose mind can penetrate to the distant stars, trace their orbits and measure their mass, than such a microscopic bit of formless matter? Here is a miracle of nature, a miracle which prepares our minds for that climactic event in the life of man when the soul wings its way from its bodily cocoon to roam the untrammeled world of the spirit.

All of these illustrations help us to look beyond the mere appearance of things to appreciate the higher forms of life to which they finally arrive. They all help us better to appreciate the truth of that profound principle laid down by Aristotle: "We judge the nature and the worth of a being not by its origin but by the goal at which it finally arrives."

We have now completed the presentation of all the principal lines of evidence and of reasoning of a philosophical character to establish the immortality of the human soul. All the important considerations proposed by philosophers and scientists will be found in summary form in this treatment. We have not presented evidence from spiritualistic performances or psychic research, because we believe that up to the present, none of these investigations have yielded results which are conclusive and capable of objective verification by impartial investigators under controlled conditions. Nor is any such evidence at all needed. We have confined ourselves to the solid ground of philosophic reasoning where the capacity to think straight is the only passport required for participation. The evidence for an after-life is clear, cogent, and conclusive before the court of the human intellect.

Evidence from Divine Revelation

We could rest our case here. But there is a final line of evidence which lifts the conclusion to still higher grounds of certitude, namely, divine revelation. This line assumes of course the existence of God and the fact [29a] of a revelation from Him. But as these truths have already been established by proofs of a rigorously philosophic character, there is no

[29a] This evidence is presented in detail in Ch. XXVIII.

reason why we should not avail ourselves of this supreme evidence. It places upon our conclusion the seal of divine approval, and gives us the highest form of certitude possible, namely, the assurance of God Himself. This gives to humanity, toiling, sweating, and busy in a thousand pursuits, a certainty and a comfort which they could never obtain from the reasoning of philosophers.

Furthermore, almighty God gives us this comforting assurance in such clear and simple terms as to dissipate all doubt and uncertainty. It is to be noted too that while philosophy can prove conclusively that the soul must survive the body at least for some time, it cannot, strictly speaking, demonstrate from reason alone that such a survival is everlasting. Here is where divine revelation supplements our reason with the knowledge that the soul upon leaving the body passes on into *everlasting* life. This means that the soul is immortal—as immortal as the God who brought it into being out of the abyss of nothingness.

Let us now look at the evidence offered by divine revelation. "The souls of the just," says the Book of Wisdom, "are in the hand of God, and the torment of death shall not touch them. In the sight of the unwise they seemed to die, and their departure was taken for misery. . . . But they are in peace, and their hope is full of immortality." [30] Similar is the testimony of Ecclesiasticus: "The dust shall return into its earth from whence it was, and the spirit to God who gave it." [31]

Fifteen hundred years before Christ, Job predicts the resurrection of the dead as he looks forward to the coming of the Redeemer. "I know," he says, "that my Redeemer liveth, and in the last day, I shall rise out of the earth, and I shall be clothed again with my skin, and in my flesh I shall

---

[30] *Wisdom* 3, 1–4
[31] *Eccles.* 12, 7

see my God." [32] This prophecy of the patriarch is confirmed by the Redeemer Himself who says: "All who are in the graves shall hear the voice of the Son of God, and they who have done good, shall come forth unto the resurrection of life." [33] One of the most comforting utterances that ever fell from the lips of Christ is that which He addresses to Martha: "I am the Resurrection and the life; he that believeth in me, although he be dead, shall live." [34]

St. Paul appeals to the fact of immortality as basic in the teaching of Christ. "The body," he says, "is sown in corruption, it shall rise in incorruption; it is sown in dishonor, it shall rise in glory; it is sown in weakness, it shall rise a spiritual body. . . . For this corruptible shall put on incorruption; and this mortal shall put on immortality. But when this mortal shall have put on immortality, then shall be brought to pass the saying which is written: Death is swallowed up in victory." [35]

In a second letter to these same Corinthians, the Apostle again reminds them: "For we know that if our earthly house of this dwelling be destroyed, we have a building from God, a house not built with hands, everlasting in the heavens." [36]

People asked then, as they ask now, for a detailed picture of the felicity which the souls of the just will enjoy in Heaven. St. Paul tells both them and us that it is beyond the reach of human experience and above the power of the mind to conceive. "Eye hath not seen," he declares, "nor ear heard, neither hath it entered into the heart of man what things God hath prepared for those who love Him." [37]

[32] *Job* 19
[33] *John* 5
[34] *John* 11:25
[35] 1 *Cor.* 15
[36] 2 *Cor.* 5, 1
[37] 1 *Cor.* 2

It is as difficult for one born blind to picture all the beauty of a mountain landscape or for one born deaf to catch all the varied notes and tones of a great symphony as it is for a pilgrim in this earthly valley to conceive all the joys and bliss in the world of spirit. We know in a general way that the essential beatitude of the righteous will consist in the beatific vision, wherein they shall see God not through a mirror darkly, as in this life, but face to face. Then they shall know even as they are known. For Christ Himself has said: "Blessed are the clean of heart for they shall see God." [38] In the possession of God, Who is infinite truth, beauty, goodness, the human soul will find the answer to all its restless questing.

Among the supreme joys of life is that which comes from the discovery of truth. How deeply that quest grips the mind and the soul of man, and how indescribable the thrill of joy that comes from its attainment! When the Greek mathematician, Archimedes, finally achieved the solution of a problem on which he had long been absorbed, he ran through the streets of Syracuse, shouting: "Eureka! Eureka! I have found it! I have found it!" Who will describe the ecstasy that must have flooded the souls of Marie and Pierre Curie, when after hundreds of discouraging efforts, they finally succeeded in isolating and in giving to the world the unknown element of radium with its almost miraculous power of healing.

Similar joys have come to Pasteur, Newton, and to all the noble souls who pushed back the frontiers of our darkness and brought the light of new discoveries into our world. Happiness scarcely less profound must likewise have flooded the souls of all the men and women whose patient labor, unflagging perseverance and creative insight have produced masterpieces of music, painting, sculpture and literature.

[38] *Mat.* 5

What could engross the mind and thrill the soul more profoundly than the progressive attainment of truth, which would make the soul more and more like unto God?

It is in terms such as these that St. Thomas seeks to portray the felicity of heaven. Nor must we overlook, while stressing the pleasures of the intellect, the source probably of the greatest joy to most people, the joy of love. All the rapture and the ecstasy of love which human beings have ever experienced in this life will certainly continue to flood the souls of the just in ever-increasing measure. The mind and the heart and the soul of man will find the answer to their endless gropings and searchings in the mind and the heart of God.

A Great Responsibility

The fact of immortality places upon man a great responsibility. It is that of using well the fleeting moments of this earthly life that he may spend his eternity with the just and righteous in Heaven. The decision rests with each of us. For we ourselves must decide whether we shall be, in the words of the Apostle Jude, "wandering stars for whom the storm of darkness is reserved forever," [39] or whether we shall be as stars that shine forever in the unfading glory of God. The attainment of that goal of eternal felicity is life's supreme triumph. The loss of it is life's ultimate and irrevocable tragedy.

This was the thought in St. Paul's mind when he wrote to the Galatians: "What things a man shall sow, those also shall he reap. For he that soweth in his flesh, of the flesh also shall reap corruption. But he that soweth in the spirit, of the spirit also shall reap life everlasting." [40]

[39] *Jude* 1
[40] *Gal.* 6, 8

The secret of the power of the saints to resist temptation is their ability to view a proposed act *sub specie aeternitatis,* that is, in the light of its eternal consequences. This is the touchstone which has never failed them. If those consequences mean the loss of God and of their everlasting happiness, they set their face like flint against the act. If they mean bringing the soul nearer to God and to the attainment of life's supreme goal, they are willing to go through hardship, humiliation, fire and death to accomplish that act as a step toward their great goal.

This is illustrated by an incident in the life of St. Thomas More. While imprisoned in the Tower of London by Henry VIII for refusing to take the oath that would put loyalty to his king before loyalty to his God, he was visited by his wife.

"Why, Mr. More," she said bluntly, "I marvel much that you who have hitherto been taken for a wise man, will now so play the fool as to lie here in this close, filthy prison, shut up with mice and rats, when you might be abroad at your liberty enjoying the favor of the king and council. You might dwell in peace in your fair house at Chelsea with your library, gallery, and garden, and be merry in company with me, your good wife, your children and household."

"Why, good Alice," he said with a winning smile, "is not this prison as near heaven as my own house?"

"Oh! tilly vally! tilly vally!" she replied with a sneer of contempt.

"Nay, then, Alice," More continued, "how long, think you, one might live to enjoy this house of ours?"

"Perhaps some twenty years."

"Well, now, my good Alice, he were a very bad calculator that, for a hundred or a thousand years, would risk the loss of an eternity." [41]

[41] *Walter's Life of Sir Thomas More,* ch. VIII

In a Nutshell

The survival of the soul after the death of the body is a truth of philosophy and as such can be established by appropriate evidence. We do not establish philosophical truths by the methods of demonstration common to mathematics and the physical sciences but by philosophical facts and reasoning. This is as valid a method for its subject matter as are the methods of mathematics and of the physical sciences for theirs. A recognition of this elementary truth, often overlooked by untrained investigators, will prevent confusion, misunderstanding, and futility on the part of the investigators, and disappointment on the part of the readers. Immortality cannot be adequately treated if torn from its roots in the immateriality and incorruptibility of the soul and in the rational organization of the universe. From these two antecedent truths the necessity of an after-life follows with invincible logic.

Referring to the immaterial nature of the soul, we showed that it could not be subject to death. For death means the disintegration of something into its parts. But since the soul is simple and immaterial, it is not composed of parts and therefore cannot disintegrate nor die. We then pointed out that the soul can be annihilated neither by itself, nor by any earthly power, and that God, who alone could do so, will not undo the noblest work of His hands.

We then showed that mankind in all ages and in all conditions of civilization and barbarism has believed in a life beyond the grave. To say that all mankind is in error is to impugn the capacity of the human mind to know. We pointed out that this is a matter not merely of speculative interest but also of vital concern for every human being.

We have shown that the desire for perfect happiness planted in the breast of every human is understandable only if that desire can at some time be fulfilled. Since it cannot be completely satisfied in this earthly life, there must be a future existence wherein it can be realized.

We showed that an after life follows as a corollary from the rational organization of the universe, whose author and guarantor is God. If there be no future life, in which the gross inequities of the present can be rectified, then stark madness glowers over the cosmic scene. The voice of our moral nature demands that virtue receive a recompense different from vice, and that the saint and the martyr receive a verdict different from that meted out to the thief and the murderer. God, infinitely just and holy, stands in the last analysis as the supreme and ultimate grounds for the existence of a future life.

This conclusion of our rational nature is confirmed by the voice of divine revelation, which lifts the truth of the immortality of the human soul to a still higher plane of certitude. Backing the verdict of our own reason is that which mankind craves most of all, the assurance of God Himself. It is the possession of an immortal soul that renders man a being of unique dignity and of transcendent worth. It imposes on him the supreme responsibility of so living that he will spend eternity with God and with the just and righteous in a felicity that knows no ending. To achieve that goal is life's supreme triumph, to miss it is irretrievable tragedy. Man will not fail to gain that goal, if he walks in the footsteps of the divine Master and spends himself in deeds of love and service for God and man. On this blended note of faith and hope and cheer, as sounded by William Ellery Channing,[42] we end our odyssey:

> I laugh, for hope hath happy place with me,
> If my bark sink, 'tis to another sea.

[42] *A Poet's Hope*

PART IV

THE BIBLE AND SCIENCE

The Origin of Man

The origin of man is a question of absorbing human interest. Hundreds of volumes have been written upon it . . . and the end is not yet in sight. It has been the subject of excited debate and of acrimonious controversy. Much of the excitement has now subsided, and it is possible to discuss the subject in a calm, dispassionate manner. This we propose to do.

It is of unique interest to all educated people because it stands at the focal point in the relations between the Bible and science. Here the twain meet. We propose to give each a friendly hearing, welcoming the light which each can throw upon the subject. It is only by welcoming this twofold light that the full, rounded picture can be obtained.

We know in advance that there is a unity to all truths since they all stem from the mind of God. The truths discovered by the scientist from the vast book of nature and those revealed in the Bible can no more contradict one another than God can contradict Himself. What is of enormous importance, and what has been too frequently neglected in the past, is to ascertain precisely what truths science has discovered and what truths the Bible does disclose. When this is accomplished, the problem of harmonizing the two solves itself.

CHAPTER XXVI

CREATION AND EVOLUTION

In the beginning God created heaven and earth.
—*Genesis* 1:1

ONE of the most important theories formulated by science in the last hundred and fifty years is the principle of organic evolution. It has profoundly influenced speculation and research in biology, comparative anatomy, embryology, anthropology, genetics, and paleontology. It has had far-reaching repercussions in the fields of philosophy and of religion. It is because of its bearing upon conceptions in these latter domains that we discuss it here.[1]

Our purpose is neither to prove nor to disprove the theory of evolution. Neither do we intend to go into an exhaustive presentation of the scientific data upon which the generalization is based, but rather to review those findings briefly and then to analyze and interpret their bearing upon theistic philosophy and religious thought and belief. Because we are writing from the viewpoint of a philosopher and not of a scientist, we shall refrain from entering into the arena of the latter to dispute with him the accuracy of the alleged findings—a function for which no philosopher *as such* is trained or qualified. This is the function of other scientists—to check and verify to the hilt the evidence reported by their colleagues.

[1] For an exhaustive treatment of this subject, see the author's book, *Evolution and Religion*, distributed by Our Sunday Visitor Press, Huntington, Ind., pp. 247 ff., 1932, $2.50.

This we cheerfully leave to them, confident that it will be done with painstaking precision and thoroughness. Those who are accustomed to find in the treatment of evolution by a philosopher or theologian biting criticism, frequent minimizing of the evidence as well as occasional bursts of spleen and ridicule, will find none in this discussion. We seek light, not heat; truth, not a dialectical victory. Confining ourselves to the role of a philosopher, we propose to analyze and interpret in a calm, dispassionate manner, the implications of this great scientific finding upon the origin and development of life, the creation of man, the interpretation of the story of creation as narrated in the Book of Genesis, and the larger problem of the methods employed in the divine administration of the universe.

Writing as a philosopher, we are not called upon to decide whether or not evolution has been definitively established as a scientific fact. We express no judgment on that point. If it be granted, however, simply for the sake of the discussion, that the data establish evolution as a scientific generalization, tentative and subject like all the laws of science to modification upon the discovery of new evidence, we ask: Does evolution conflict with the Bible, with belief in a divine Creator of the universe and of all forms of life therein, with the spiritual nature of man, the freedom of the will, and the immortality of the human soul? Does it lessen in any way the need of a directive Intelligence behind the universe and all its vast network of natural law? Does evolution alter man's essential origin or his destiny? These are the questions which evolution has raised for more than a century in the minds of thinking people throughout the world.

When the findings of the evolutionary sciences were first being unfolded to an awed and bewildered world, these questions aroused violent and bitter controversy which continued for several generations. Fortunately, the strong feelings and the excitement have abated, permitting the public to get a better view of the real issue and to rule out the many misunderstandings and misapprehensions which obscured the vision and prejudiced many good people against the evolutionary theory.

The Meaning of Evolution

The fundamental meaning of evolution is that there has been a development from simple rudimentary organic life to higher and more complex forms. Functions which were originally performed by a single protoplasmic cell are now discharged by separate organs, highly specialized for that specific task. Thus an amoeba, a unicellular organism that floats about in a drop of water, so infinitesimally small as to be invisible to the naked eye, manages with its one cell to assimilate food and to propagate its kind, though it is completely lacking in the special organs which are usually associated with such functions. Evolution represents a progressive march upwards from simple, rudimentary, homogeneous organisms to higher, complex, heterogeneous organisms with specialized organs for different functions. That, in brief outline, is the general picture of evolution.

Darwinism, which in the mind of the layman is generally synonymous with evolution, is used by the scientist to describe the particular *causal* agency advanced by Darwin to explain evolution, namely, Natural Selection. While the majority of scientists today no longer admit the sufficiency of natural selection alone to explain evolution, and may be said therefore to have discarded Darwinism, there is probably no scientist of repute in the world today who does not admit the fact of evolution in the sense of a progressive development to higher and more complex forms of life.

Evolution cannot be demonstrated in the same manner as a principle of mathematics or a theorem of geometry. It is arrived at inferentially as a result of the observation of a great number of facts scattered over many fields. It gives unity and significance to data in such widely different fields as paleontology, embryology, comparative anatomy and biology, which otherwise would be incoherent and meaningless. As most of the evidence relates to changes in the remote past, it must by its very nature be indirect and largely circumstantial, since no living eye-witness was present to note the happenings, and no documents were then written in human language. Corroborative evidence is gleaned from changes which are occurring in living species within our own day, but most of the data must be dug from the strata of the rocks in the form of the fossil remains of plants and animals.

Evidence from Paleontology

Paleontology, which probably offers the strongest evidence for evolution, has clearly established the existence of a gradual progression from simple rudimentary organisms to higher and more complex forms as one advances from lower to higher strata of rock. The evidence indicates that higher structures of animal life, such for example as the vertebrates—animals having a backbone—did not exist during the early stages of animal life, but made their appearance only at a comparatively recent date.

Old estimates as to the age of the earth and of life upon it must be revised radically in the light of recent scientific evidence. According to the most recent computations based on the rate of radium emanation, a period of approximately 1,000,000,000 years has elapsed since the earth attained its present diameter. Estimates concerning the length of time that has elapsed since life first appeared upon the globe range from 50,000,000 years upwards to approximately ten times that figure. These are, of course, only estimates, but they represent the general drift of scientific thought on the subject and the writer sees no reason for seeking to minimize them.

The age of the earth and of life upon it, no matter what antiquity be imputed to both, does not disturb any principle of the Christian faith or of the Biblical revelation when the latter is properly understood. This reference to the age of the earth and of life upon it is made to show that geology offers abundant time for the slow, gradual transition to constantly increasing higher forms of which the paleontologist finds a fossil record, and for each step of which he postulates vast periods of geological time.

Evidence from Comparative Anatomy

Comparative anatomy reveals that in the animal kingdom there are several distinct main types of architecture, each of which characterizes one of the main divisions of the kingdom. "Within each of these great assemblages of animals characterized by a common plan of organization," says Professor H. H. Newman, Professor of Zoology at the University of Chicago, "there are almost innumerable structural diversities within the scope of the fundamental plan. These major or minor departures from the ideally generalized condition remind one of the variations upon a theme in music; no matter how elaborate the variation may be, the skilled musician recognizes the common theme running through it all. This fundamental unity amidst minor diversity of form or of function is looked upon as a common inheritance from a more or less remote ancestor. In animals belonging to the same group and therefore having the same general plan of organization we find many organs having the same embryonic origin and the same general relation to other structures, but with vastly different superficial appearance and playing quite diverse functional roles." [2]

Vestigial structures which are found both in animals and in man point significantly to an ancestorship in which these were functional and useful. They are meaningless and incoherent except on the assumption of evolution. Few laymen realize how numerous these lingering echoes of a remote past are in the body of man. According to Widersheim there are "no less than 180 vestigial structures in the human body, sufficient to make of a man a veritable walking museum of antiquities. Among these are:—the vermiform appendix; the abbreviated tail with its set of caudal muscles; a complicated set of muscles homologous with those employed by other animals for moving their ears, but practically functionless in all but a very few men; a complete equipment of scalp muscles, used by other animals for erecting the hair but of very doubtful utility in man even in the rare instances when they function voluntarily; gill slits in the embryo, the homologues of which are used in aquatic respiration; miniature third eyelids (nictitating membranes), functional in all reptiles and birds, greatly reduced or vestigial in all mammals; the lanugo, a complete coating of embryonic down or hair, which disappears long before birth and can hardly serve any useful functions while it lasts. These and numerous other structures of the same sort can be reasonably interpreted as evidence that man has descended from ancestors in which these organs were functional. Man has never completely lost these characters; he continues to inherit them though he no longer has any use for them. Heredity

[2] H. H. Newman, Chapter on Animal Evolution in *Contributions of Science to Religion,* edited by S. Mathews, Appleton, New York, 1927, p. 176

is stubborn and tenacious, clinging persistently to vestiges of all that the race has once possessed, though chiefly concerned in bringing to perfection the more recent adaptive features of the race." [3]

Evidence from Embryology

Embryology is the science which studies the various stages through which the individual passes in its development from a single-celled fertilized ovum to its appearance at birth. Students of this science have long noted that members of closely related adult species keep step most of the way through their ontogenies and diverge only toward the end of their courses. On the other hand distantly related species diverge early in their developmental paths, while unrelated forms usually have little or nothing in common from the beginning.

In the embryonic development of members of the higher species, a sort of rough repetition of the characteristic features of many lower groups has been noted. This has been embodied in the so-called biogenetic law: ontogeny is a recapitulation of phylogeny. In less technical language this means that the different stages in the development of the individual reflect in a dim vestigial manner some of the principal ancestral forms from which the species is descended, the earliest embryonic stages resembling the most remote ancestors. Professor H. H. Newman phrases it thus: "The developmental history of the individual may be regarded as an abbreviated resumé of its ancestral history."

There is no denying that there are many gaps and ragged edges in the evidence on which the so-called biogenetic law is based. Probably the most that can be said for the embryological evidence is that it is suggestive in a general way

[3] H. H. Newman, op. cit., p. 179

and not demonstrative of ancestral relationships. It is to be observed, however, that the resemblances noted have little meaning or coherence save on the postulate of an evolutionary past.

"The embryology of man," says Professor Newman, "is now pretty thoroughly known in spite of the great difficulty of obtaining the early stages. Step for step it is almost precisely like that of other primates, especially like that of the anthropoids, and it is only in the latest stages that it takes on distinctly human characteristics. This is not equivalent to saying that the expert embryologist is in any doubt as to the diagnosis of a human embryo no matter how early the stage, for there are specific features about all embryos from the egg stage on to the end of development that may be distinguished by anyone sufficiently versed in the subject. In spite of these specific differences, however, there can be no question that the embryology of man and that of any of the anthropoid apes show the closest of resemblances at every stage and diverge sharply only in the late stages of prenatal life. So close a resemblance in developmental histories is found only in species that are members of the same ancestral stock, for they have both inherited the characteristic features of their development from their common ancestors." [4]

The Fossil Pedigree of Man

Opponents of evolution often refer to it derisively as "the monkey theory" of man's descent. But no scientist of repute in the world today maintains that man is a lineal descendant from the monkey, the ape, the gorilla or the chimpanzee. The commonly prevailing scientific view is that both branched off long ages ago from a common stock.

[4] H. H. Newman, *op. cit.*, p. 193

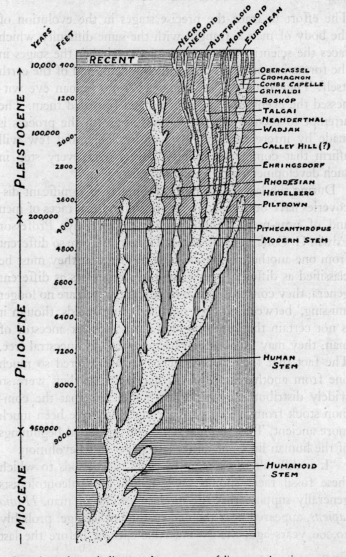

Genealogical tree indicating the ancestry of living and extinct races of mankind. On the left are given estimated depths of the more recent geological deposits and of the time occupied by their accumulation.—Reproduced with permission from *The Antiquity of Man.* by Sir Arthur Keith. Williams and Norgate, Ltd., London

The effort to trace the precise stages in the evolution of the body of man is fraught with the same difficulty which faces the scientist who tries to piece together the stages in the formation of mountains and continents and of the earth itself. They occurred at a time when no human eye witnessed the events and no human hand recorded them. The attempt to reconstruct the various stages in the process is made by inference from the data available, and few will affirm that complete certainty hovers over every step in such developments in the dim and misty past.[4a]

During the last half century a number of significant discoveries have been made in regard to the fossil races of men and of near-men. "These ancient types," says Professor Edwin G. Conklin of Princeton University, "are so different from one another and from modern man that they must be classified as different species and in some cases as different genera; they constitute six distinct links, which are no longer 'missing,' between modern man and anthropoids, though it is not certain that any one of them is a direct ancestor of man; they may be collateral branches of our ancestral tree. The fact that these forerunners of man differed so much one from another and the further fact that they were so widely distributed over the earth indicates that the common stock from which they sprung must have been much more ancient. They do not represent the actual beginnings of the human line, but rather late stages in its evolution.

"It is difficult to estimate in years the periods to which these fossil races should be assigned, but paleontologists generally suppose that the modern species of man, *Homo sapiens*, appeared near the end of the last ice age, probably 20,000 years ago; the Neanderthal species, before the last

[4a] For a splendid presentation and analysis of the data on this point, see Raymond W. Murray, *Man's Unknown Ancestors*, Bruce, Milwaukee, 1943

ice age, from 50,000 to 100,000 years ago; the Heidelberg species during the second interglacial period, at least 300,-000 years ago; the Piltdown species during first interglacial period, say 400,000 years ago; while the Java man probably preceded the first ice age, and therefore lived at least 500,-000 years ago. There are many evidences that the human stock, the *Hominidae*, goes back to a much greater antiquity than half a million years; among these evidences are the striking differences in these fossil species, the fact that their remains have been found so far apart as western and southern Europe, Palestine, Rhodesia, Java, and China, and especially the fact that crude stone implements, known as eoliths, have been found in still older strata. Prevalent opinion among paleontologists and anthropologists is that the *Hominidae* separated from the *Simiidae* not less than one or two million years ago. This immensely long period is only about one thousandth part of the time which has elapsed since life first appeared on the earth." [5]

While the fossil remains relating to prehistoric man and to the alleged transitional forms through which man emerged from animal ancestors have received divergent interpretations at the hands of various scientists, this should not blind us to the fact that there is practically unanimous agreement among them that the evidence points clearly in the direction of such a transition. There is disagreement as to the interpretation of the details in the story, but no substantial disagreement as to the general direction in which the evidence points.

Additional evidence of the fact of evolution might be drawn from: (1) taxonomy, the science of classification; (2) serology, the science of blood tests; (3) geographic dis-

[5] E. G. Conklin, *Principles and Possibilities of Human Evolution*, International Clinics, vol. I, series 40, J. B. Lippincott Co., Philadelphia, Pa., 1930

tribution, the study of the horizontal distribution of species upon the earth's surface; (4) genetics, the analytic and experimental study of evolutionary processes going on today. It is thought, however, that the evidence which has been briefly outlined from paleontology, comparative anatomy, and embryology will be sufficient to indicate the chief lines of converging data which have led many scientists to regard evolution no longer as a conjecture or a hypothesis, but as a principle inferentially but validly established.

Origin of Evolution Theory

The basic idea of evolution, that the present forms of life have developed from lower and more rudimentary forms, was first definitely proposed by the French scientist, Lamarck, in 1809. His theory seems to have attracted but little attention from scientists generally. Most people looked with suspicion upon ideas which sought to find a natural explanation for occurrences which were generally attributed to the supernatural. If they had possessed greater familiarity with the writings of Augustine and of Gregory of Nyssa in the fourth century and with the principles of scholastic philosophy generally, they would have experienced less difficulty in harmonizing the new ideas with the ancient tradition.

It was not until Charles Darwin published his *Origin of Species* in 1859 that the theory of evolution became of engrossing interest to the scientific world. The great popularizer among the English speaking peoples of Darwin's technical writings and work was Thomas H. Huxley. An agnostic himself, his interpretation of the bearing of Darwin's findings upon creation, a personal God, and religious conceptions generally, was strongly colored by his own sceptical views.

The outstanding popularizer of Darwin's book, in the German-speaking world, was Ernst Haeckel. A blatant atheist himself, he loudly proclaimed that the new findings banished completely such treasured beliefs of Christianity as a personal God, a spiritual soul, freedom of the will, and immortality. He used the reported facts of evolution to bludgeon the ancient faith from the minds of men. Others, obsessed with the power of the new findings to explain all the works which religious people had attributed to God, spoke and wrote of evolution as sounding the death knell of belief in the Bible and in a personal deity.

Religious Leaders React

It is not surprising, then, that the evolutionary theory aroused violent hostility among the religious leaders of the day. To many of them it seemed not only as an impious assault upon the Mosaic account of creation but a conspiracy to substitute natural law for the action of God. *The Dublin University Magazine* accused Darwin of seeking "to displace God by the unerring action of vagary" and with being "resolved to hunt God out of the world." As the champion of Protestant orthodoxy in England, Mr. Gladstone, in an address at Liverpool, declared: "Upon the grounds of what is called evolution, God is relieved of the labour of creation; in the name of unchangeable laws he is discharged from governing the world."

In a sermon at the University of Oxford, the Dean of Chichester warned the students that "those who refuse to accept the history of the creation of our first parents according to its obvious literal intention, and are for substituting the modern dream of evolution in its place, cause the entire scheme of man's salvation to collapse." These utterances are typical of the view expressed by many divines of the day, that a person must choose between God and evolution, that belief in both was impossible.

Much water has run under the bridge since 1859. The controversy has long since died. Peace has come to the opposing camps. The last convulsive gasp of the controversy occurred at the Scopes trial at Dayton, Tennessee, in 1925, when the legislature, as the result of agitation led by William Jennings Bryan, an ardent fundamentalist, sought to ban the teaching of evolution as a fact in the tax-supported schools. Most of the country looked upon the trial with amusement, as a relic of a long outmoded past, that had no place in our day. People had long since laughed off the idea, once so feverishly held, that evolution is a denial of the authority of the Bible and of the Creator. Perhaps the outstanding fact brought out by the trial was that not a single scientist of eminence could be found to take up arms against evolution or to dispute its well authenticated findings in all its far-flung fields.

Both Sides at Fault

As we look back over the controversy that raged so furiously for more than half a century, we see now that both sides were at fault. The principal mistake made by the scientists, or more frequently by their followers and interpreters, was in drawing philosophical and religious inferences and deductions unwarranted by the data of science. Many of them went outside their own domain and, invading the domains of the philosopher and of the theologian, gave forth pronunciamentos on God, the human soul, the freedom of the will and immortality. Ernst Haeckel is the classic example of this type. He had legions of imitators. The drawing of the philosophic and religious implications of the raw data of natural science is a fine art which demands professional training. If the scientists and their popularizers had simply stated their findings and had allowed time for the analysis and interpretation by competent scholars of their bearing upon religious conceptions, much of the controversy could have been avoided.

The chief mistake of the religious leaders was in appealing to the Bible as a textbook of science, as a revelation concerning biology, geology, paleontology and other sciences totally alien to the religious scope and purpose of the Scriptures. Interpreting in a literal sense the Mosaic account of creation, they sought to refute the findings of the biologist and the geologist. This was a grievous error.

Warning of Augustine

They had forgotten the wise admonition given by Augustine back in the fourth century to his fellow Christians against lecturing the naturalist on the phenomena of nature: "It very often happens that there is some question as to the earth or the sky, or the other elements of this world —respecting which one who is not a Christian has knowledge derived from most certain reasoning or observation, and it is very disgraceful and mischievous and of all things to be carefully avoided, that a Christian speaking of such matters as being according to the Christian Scriptures, should be heard by an unbeliever talking such nonsense that the unbeliever perceiving him to be as wide from the mark as east from west, can hardly restrain himself from laughing.

"And the real evil is not that a man is subjected to derision because of his error, but it is that to profane eyes, our authors (that is to say, the sacred authors) are regarded as having had such thoughts; and are also exposed to blame and scorn upon the score of ignorance, to the greatest possible misfortune of people whom we wish to save. For, in fine, these profane people happen upon a Christian busy in making mistakes on the subject which they know perfectly; how, then, will they believe these holy books? How will they believe in the resurrection of the dead and in the hope of life eternal, and in the kingdom of heaven, when, according to an erroneous assumption, these books seem to them to have as their object those very things which they, the profane, know by direct experience or by calculation which admits of no doubt?

"It is impossible to say what vexation and sorrow prudent Christians meet with through these presumptuous and bold spirits who, taken to task one day for their silly and false opinion, and realizing themselves on the point of being convicted by men who are not obedient to the authority of our holy books, wish to defend their assertions so thoughtless, so bold, and so manifestly false. For they then commence to bring forward as a proof precisely our holy books, or again they attribute to them from memory that which seems to support their opinion, and they quote numerous passages, understanding neither the texts they quote, nor the subject about which they are making statement." [6]

Summing up his exposition of this important principle for the interpretation of the Bible, Augustine says: "The gospels do not tell us that our Lord said, 'I will send you the Holy Ghost to teach you the course of the sun and the moon'; we should endeavor to become Christians and not astronomers."

A similar note of warning was sounded by Cardinal Bellarmine in 1616 anent the Galileo controversy when he said: "I say that if a real proof be found that the sun is fixed and does not revolve around the earth, but the earth round the sun, then it will be necessary, very carefully, to proceed to the explanation of the passages of Scripture which appear to

[6] *De Genesi ad litteram*, lib. I, cap. XIX

be contrary, and we should rather say that we have misunderstood these than pronounce that to be false which is demonstrated."

It was the failure of the religious leaders of Darwin's day, excited by the violent attacks made on religion by the apostles of evolution, to remember that the Bible is a revelation of spiritual verities, not a textbook of natural science, which was in no small part responsible for the fury and length of the controversy on evolution. Indeed, this failure has played a part in almost every conflict, or rather in every imagined conflict, between science and religion. It is necessary to remember that while the sacred writers communicate great spiritual and religious truths, they reflect merely the views on natural science prevalent in their day.

The Biblical Story

Let us now turn to the Biblical story of creation. The first chapter of Genesis tells us: "In the beginning God created heaven and earth. And the earth was void and empty, and darkness was upon the face of the deep; and the spirit of God moved over the waters." On the first day, God made light. On the second, He separated the land from the waters. On the third, He caused the earth to bring forth the green herb. On the fourth day, He set the sun, the moon and the stars in the heavens. On the fifth, God said: "Let the earth bring forth the living creature in its kind, cattle and creeping things, and beasts of the earth."

Coming then to the creation of man, the sacred author continues: "And He said: Let us make man to our image and likeness: and let him have dominion over the fishes of the sea, and the fowls of the air, and the beasts, and the whole earth . . . and God created man to His own image; to the image of God He created him; male and female He created them." . . . And God saw all things that He had made, and they were very good." In the second chapter, seventh verse, there is a further reference to the creation of man. "And the Lord God formed man of the slime of the earth: and breathed into his face the breath of life, and man became a living soul."

The whole account is presented in simple, non-technical language which would bring it easily within the understanding of all. What, one might ask, was the purpose of the detailed declarations of the sacred writer? Father J. A. Zahm answers as follows: "The Hebrew people had lived among idolators and were surrounded by people who gave divine worship to many of God's creatures. Moses wished to impress upon their minds that neither the sun, nor the moon, nor the stars, neither any animal, nor the earth which affords its nourishment, nor any of the elements, are God, as was supposed by the Sabianism of the Orient, especially of Chaldea; by the worship of animals in Egypt; by the divine honors paid to the earth by the Romans, Pelasgians, and Germans; and by the cult of fire-worshipers of Greece and Persia. All these things, the objects of the adoration of the heathen, are the works of God. There is no power opposed to God which is equal to Him. Neither is matter, as such, according to the later opinion of the Platonists, the seat of evil. Everything is the work of God, and everything therefore is good."

It is obvious then that the truth which the author is seeking to convey is a religious one. "From the foregoing," continues Father Zahm, "it is manifest that the prime object of the Mosaic narrative, like that of all revelation, was a religious one. 'The Gospels,' says St. Augustine, 'do not tell us that our Lord said, I will send you the Holy Ghost to teach you the course of the sun and the moon; we should endeavor to become Christians and not astronomers.' So it is with the Mosaic account of creation. Its purport is not to teach geology, physics, zoology, or astronomy, but to affirm in the most simple and direct manner the creative act of God and His sovereignty over all creatures. Its object is not to anticipate any of the truths of science or philosophy, but to guard the chosen people of God against the pernicious errors and idolatrous practices which were then everywhere prevalent." [7]

Interpreting Genesis

In interpreting the Genesiac account of creation, it is well to keep in mind the warning of Augustine, of Cardinal Bellarmine, and of the scholarly Pontiff, Leo XIII, in his encyclical on Holy Scripture: "It should be borne in mind, first that the sacred writers, or more truly the Holy Spirit who spoke through them, did not wish to teach men those things (namely, the inmost constitution of visible things) which would be in no wise profitable unto salvation." In formulating this principle of exegesis, Leo XIII quotes the very words of St. Augustine, and thus reëchoes in the modern age the warning issued by the learned Bishop of Hippo in the fourth century but which was so generally ignored throughout the intervening ones.

In applying this principle, whose soundness will be recognized by scriptural scholars and scientists alike, to the interpretation of Genesis, Dorlodot says: "Henceforth then it is no longer allowed to violate this principle, and when our excellent apologists of the nineteenth century come again to us and say that 'Moses was either inspired, or else he was naturally conversant with the latest discoveries of modern science,' it is our duty to retort that if their interpretation of Genesis really implies such a consequence, then

[7] Zahm, *Bible, Science and Faith*, p. 33

this interpretation is certainly false. And speaking generally, we must reject *a priori* any interpretation which would make a text of Holy Writ a Divine instruction upon a subject belonging to the physical or natural sciences." [7a] In other words, if a person comes with some scientific speculation and offers as the solitary proof of its correctness some stray passage from the Bible, we can generally reject such a scientific theory without further investigation because it is based upon a false conception of the Bible as a divine revelation of the truths of natural science instead of truths of a religious character.

In the light of this basic principle of Biblical exegesis, we ask: What, then, is the outstanding religious truth taught us in Genesis? Simply this: The universe and all living things owe their existence in some way to the creative power of God.

> *The earth is the Lord's and the fulness thereof:*
> *The world and they that dwell therein.*

The detailed processes by which the planets were formed, the hills fashioned, and living creatures brought into being, are part of the legitimate subject-matter of natural science. In other words, Genesis is no textbook of geology, astronomy, botany or zoology or any of the other sciences. Certainly no person who is even slightly familiar with the findings of geology thinks of creation as completed in six literal days.

Evolution of Man

How about evolution when applied to man? Here a distinction is necessary. In regard to the soul of man, it is the common teaching of theologians that God creates directly

[7a] *Darwinism and Catholic Thought*, Benziger Bros., N.Y., 1922, p. 11

and immediately the soul of each individual human being. In regard to the body of man, the evidence of evolution from antecedent animal life is most impressive, and in the judgment of most scientists, overwhelming. The Church leaves the individual free to accept or reject this view in accordance with his judgment as to the weight of evidence behind it. The attitude of the Catholic Church, ever the friend of science, and hospitable toward its every discovery, is summed up admirably by Rev. Dr. E. C. Messenger as follows: "The Church says:

'1. There is nothing in this notion intrinsically repugnant either to the Scriptures or to Faith.

'2. She will not affirm it, even supposing it were true, because it is not her business to make such affirmations.

'3. Taking it as a "possible hypothesis" (as derivative creation applied to animals lower than man is taken for a "probable hypothesis"), Catholics may freely work toward its establishment, by research and discussion.

'4. If any one chooses to make it a purely personal belief, he may.' " [8]

Discussing the attitude of the Church toward evolution, Rt. Rev. Msgr. U. A. Hauber observes: "Most of her spokesmen tend toward acceptance of a moderate form of the theory, and one of them at least (Canon de Dorlodot of Louvain) outdoes Darwin in his enthusiasm for the theory of absolute natural evolution. As long as they leave Almighty God in His place and admit that the human soul is radically different from the animal soul, the Church does not interfere, the matter is outside the sphere of religion." [9]

In his article on Transformation in the *Dictionnaire Apologétique de la Foi Catholique*, the great French theologian, Père de Sinéty, S.J., declares: "If anyone should

[8] E. C. Messenger, *Evolution and Theology*, Macmillan Co., N.Y., 1932, pp. 250 f.
[9] *Creation and Evolution*, Paulist Press, New York, p. 25

find it more satisfying for the scientific mind to think that the Creator, in order to constitute the body of the first man, utilized matter already organized, and that He more or less profoundly transformed this organism, by the very infusion of a spiritual soul, we do not see that this could be objected to from the theological point of view. The Church has never pronounced, either directly or indirectly, on the state of the matter which, according to the text of Genesis itself, served for the constitution of the human body."

The character of that matter, whether it was simple organic matter or a living animal body, points out the noted Dominican exegete, P. F. Ceuppens, Professor of Old Testament Exegesis in the Collegio Angelico in Rome, is not a question of exegesis but of anthropology.[9a]

To the same effect is the observation made back at the turn of the century by the learned Jesuit, Father J. Donat: "In itself the theory of evolution, which asserts the variability of species of animals and plants, is by no means opposed to religious truths. It neither includes a necessity of assuming the origin of the human soul from the essentially lower animal soul, nor is it an atheistic theory. On the contrary, such an evolution would most clearly testify to God's wisdom in laying such a wonderful basis for the progress of nature, provided this theory could be proved by scientific facts; indeed, for an evolution within narrow limits, circumstantial evidence is not lacking." [10]

Referring to jubilant anti-evolutionist cries that arise from time to time in certain quarters, the late Bertram Windle issued a warning which cannot be too often repeated: "Such anti-evolutionary cries should never, under any circum-

---

[9a] *"Utram materia illa organica, vivens, fuerit animal vivens, quaestio ista non ad exegesim sed potius ad anthropologiam pertinet."* De Historia Primaeva, *Collegio Angelico*, Rome, 1934

[10] J. Donat, S.J., *The Freedom of Science*, J. F. Wagner, Inc., N.Y., 1914, p. 223

stances, come from the Catholic ranks. Of all people we can afford to survey this scene of conflict with complete calm, for we know that God's two books of revelation and nature cannot possibly contradict each other. Hence, as Leo XIII told us, and as common sense dictates, we should rejoice in any new discovery, whether it tells for or against evolution; for the truth is what we are looking for, and not victory over our supposed antagonists. The fact is, that this exultation on the part of anti-evolutionists leads their opponents very naturally and logically to conclude that these would-be defenders of religion believe that the establishment of evolution as a fact would mean the destruction of the Christian faith, whereas nothing could be more untrue or more ridiculous." [11]

It is well to note that among the scientists carrying on original research are a number of Catholic priests who rank among the highest authorities in their field. In Europe the findings of Abbé Breuil and Father Hugo Obermaier have attracted world attention. In China the paleontological research of the Jesuit Fathers Licent and Teilhard de Chardin has greatly increased our knowledge of early man.

In Protestant circles the fundamentalist groups, who are wedded to a literal interpretation of the Bible touching on matters of natural phenomena, and regard the Scriptures as a textbook of natural science as well as a divine communication of religious truth, have been slow to recognize the discoveries of science in the field of evolution. Among the Protestant groups wherein the Bible is not regarded as revealing truths of natural science, the theory of evolution has gained general acceptance. Discerning leaders of most faiths are unwilling to make orthodoxy hinge upon adherence to outmoded systems of biology. In their ears there still reverberates the warning sounded by Erasmus: "To

[11] *Fortnightly Review*, Oct., 1931, p. 235

identify the new learning with heresy is to make orthodoxy
synonymous with ignorance."

Augustine's View

Among Catholics, Canon Dorlodot is not alone in holding to a theory of absolute natural evolution. Back in the
fourth century the great Augustine, by one of those daring
flights of sheer genius, likewise conceived of God as per-
forming a single *direct* creative act, producing the potentialities (*rationes seminales*) of all forms of life. Such at least
is the conclusion reached by Dorlodot, who has made a most
exhaustive study of Augustine's writings. All students of
the philosophical and religious implications of evolution will
be interested in the process of reasoning which led this great
speculative genius back in the fourth century to arrive at
the daring and sublime conception of creation, not as a
series of special interventions, but as an orderly evolution
proceeding according to definite laws.

In his great treatise on Genesis, Augustine repudiates the
crassly anthropomorphic concept of the Creator, saying:
"To suppose that God with bodily hands formed man from
the dust is very childish. . . . God neither formed man
with bodily hands nor did He breathe upon him with throat
and lips." [12] According to Dorlodot, the learned Bishop
of Hippo held to a form of absolute natural evolution. He
maintained that at the beginning God created living creatures only in their causes—*rationes seminales*. "The terrestrial or aquatic matter which He created at the beginning
virtually contained all living beings just as a seed contains
a plant virtually, and it was only later, as time went on,

[12] See *De Genesi contra Manichaeos*, lib. ii, cp. 14, in Migne xxxiv, 188—
lib. v, cap. 5 and cap. 23—and lib. vii, cap. 1. See also Osborn, *From the
Greeks to Darwin*, Chas. Scribner's Sons, New York, 1894, Chapters II
and III.

that the different organized beings, including the human body, appeared, or, to use his own expression, 'came forth from their causes' by a natural evolution of inorganic matter." [13]

Declaring that creation took place in the mathematical instant at the beginning of time, Augustine maintained that the "continued work can only mean the government of the world (that is, the conservation of things by God, and His *concursus* with secondary causes). *Hence, there has been no other intervention since the moment when God created the world.* God, therefore, has not made any species which was not virtually contained in the inorganic world as He had created it at the beginning, and this applies to *the body of man* as well as to the other living beings. . . . As to the *soul* of the first man, Augustine, faithful to his principle concerning God's repose, holds also that it was created at the first instant of time. Later on, when the body had reached, by natural evolution, a suitable state of organization, the soul united itself to the body by a kind of natural inclination." [14]

It will be noted that this view of St. Augustine represents a more thoroughgoing and radical form of evolution than that held by Charles Darwin and Alfred Russell Wallace, who postulate the intervention of God for the special creation of the first form or forms of life. According to Augustine, God did not interrupt the unbroken reign of natural law to create directly and immediately the beginnings of life, nor even the body of the first man, but created them in their causes or germinal powers (*rationes seminales*) and then caused them to be evolved in accordance with the operation of the laws of nature of which He is the ultimate author.

[13] Dorlodot, *Darwinism and Catholic Thought,* translated by E. C. Messenger, Benziger Bros., New York, 1922, p. 142
[14] Dorlodot, *ibid.,* p. 143

It will be a matter of surprise for many to learn that this view of absolute natural evolution under the leadership of Augustine and Gregory of Nyssa prevailed, according to Dorlodot, as "the common opinion of the Fathers, at least up to the eighth century and probably to the end of the twelfth." [15] That it was subjected to notable modifications in the thirteenth century at the hands of Thomas Aquinas and others was due, not to scriptural or dogmatic reasons, but to considerations of a scientific nature drawn largely from the physics of Aristotle.[16]

Needless to say, the physics of the ancient Stagirite has long since been outmoded, and nothing in the advanced science of the present day would demand a serious modification in the Augustinian principle of absolute natural evolution. On the contrary, the developments of modern science enable us to appreciate, as never before, the magnificent daring and sublimity of that view which fifteen centuries ago envisaged the Divine Omnipotence as acting not by special interventions for the creation of species and genera, but as uniformly operative through all the vast uninterrupted sweep of natural law. It reduces the bewildering multiplicity of phenomena to the unity of natural law through which the Divine Power is uniformly operative. It is a conception as brilliant as it is profound, and gives probably the noblest and most exalted of all the interpretations of the expression of God's creative power. While at present it does not represent the common view of theologians, it is not unlikely that it will continue to win many additional adherents in the years ahead. Certainly, it fits in perfectly with all the findings of science and renders it unnecessary to postulate what philosophers, theologians and scientists are agreed

[15] Dorlodot, *op. cit.*, p. 151

[16] Dorlodot, *op. cit.*, see appendix IV, "Evolution of Ideas in the Thirteenth Century under the Influence of Aristotle's Physics," pp. 152 ff.

should be avoided, if possible—special, extraordinary acts of divine intervention in the world of nature.

Evolution—God's Method of Creation

To localize the causes of misunderstanding between scientists and Scriptural scholars and to hold them up to the light of impartial scrutiny from both sides is usually not only the first but the most effective step in eliminating the misunderstanding itself. In the light of the foregoing discussion it should be evident that there is no real ground for warfare between the scientist and the theologian on the subject of evolution. That there is no conflict between religion and science on the matter of evolution is the conviction not only of Christian philosophers and of Biblical scholars but of the outstanding leaders in science as well. In a Joint Statement upon the Relations of Science and Religion, issued in 1923 and signed by such eminent scientists as Millikan, Pupin, Noyes and Birkoff in physics, Campbell in astronomy, and Osborn, Welch, Coulter and Conklin in biology, these outstanding leaders conclude: "It is a sublime conception of God which is furnished by science, and one wholly consonant with the highest ideals of religion, when it represents Him as revealing Himself through inbreathing of life into its constituent matter, culminating in man with his spiritual nature and all his Godlike powers."

That is why there are practically no scientists of repute in the world today—Millikan said he knew of none—who regard the materialistic interpretation of life and the universe as offering any satisfaction to the thinking mind. That is why the theistic philosophy which assigns an adequate and proportionate cause for the design and purpose and plan in nature, and recognizes the presence of a great Intelligence behind the laws and the processes and the framework of the universe is held by the scientists of eminence throughout the world. Under this conception *evolution is but the process or the method by which God brought the various forms of life into being.*

For, by creating the first germinal forms of life and endowing them with potentialities which would evolve into successive higher forms in accordance with definite laws which He infused into them, God remains the Creator and Author of all living organisms just as truly and as really as if He had created them all at once in their different species and genera. Indeed, this concept of creation as a continuous unfolding and a ceaseless climbing to higher and higher forms of life, eternally marching upward, is of far greater grandeur and sublimity than the concept of creation which was completed in the instant it was begun and then remained static and unchanged throughout all time. Far then from lessening the creative power of God, or minimizing the need of His presence in the universe, evolution exalts His power and renders the pageant of progressive botanical and zoölogical life upon this planet forever inexplicable without His guiding presence.

In causing the body of man to be evolved from lower forms of animal life and then when the physical organism had attained an appropriate stage of neurological development and brain capacity, infusing into it a spiritual and immaterial principle called the human soul, God would be the Creator just as truly as if He had caused man to spring forth suddenly full-blossomed from the dust of the earth. Nor is there any reason to feel that the animal origin of the human body disparages the dignity of man. For in the hierarchy of values, living creatures certainly rank far higher than the dust of the earth. Instead then of lessening the dignity of man's origin, evolution actually exalts it, by placing it far above the moistened dust or mud of the earth to living creatures endowed by God with sentiency and a form of intelligence. Thus when analyzed and viewed in the calm light of reason, this old sentimental objection to evolution is seen to have no basis in either fact or reason.

Use of Secondary Causes

Moreover, evolution fits in admirably with the principle of the divine utilization of secondary causes to attain a purposed end—a principle generally accepted by the greatest theistic thinkers. In simple language this means that God is not to be conceived as constantly interfering with the laws and processes of nature to attain the objectives purposed in the divine plan, but that He endows nature and her laws with a potency and direction adequate to achieve her ends. In accordance with this principle the concept of biological evolution on our earth and the evolution of the entire universe into a harmonious whole under the reign of natural laws would admirably reflect the unity, power, and wisdom of the Divine Being.

St. Thomas Aquinas gives a terse but lucid statement of this principle so far-reaching in its philosophical consequences: "The potency of a cause is greater, the more remote the effects to which it extends." [16a] Thus a billiard player who with one stroke of his cue knocks the fifteen pool balls into their pockets displays vastly greater power and skill than the player who requires fifteen separate strokes to accomplish the same result. The great theistic philosopher Suarez expresses the same principle when he says: "God does not interfere directly with the natural order, where secondary causes suffice to produce the intended effect." [17]

In commenting upon this principle so clearly enunciated

[16a] *Summa c. Gent.*, III, C.lxxvii
[17] *De opere sex dierum*, II, C. X, n. 13

by St. Thomas Aquinas and Suarez, the great modern scientist and philosopher, Father Erich Wasmann, declares: "In the light of this principle of the Christian interpretation of nature, the history of the animal and vegetable kingdoms on our planet is, as it were, a versicle in a volume of a million pages in which the natural development of the cosmos is described, and the finger of God is evident throughout." [18]

The continued onward sweep of science has pushed farther back the frontiers of knowledge, and with each enlargement of the horizon has come a new and a more enrapturing vision of the Creator. More and more as science unravels the tangled skein of nature's network of laws, and probes deeper and deeper into the amazing complexities which characterize the organization of living matter even in its lowest form, does the human mind catch glimpses of the workings of that Supreme Intelligence which lies behind the framework of the material universe and yet permeates its every particle from the infinitesimal proton to the largest star with the omnipresence of law.

"No Fear of Science"

"Religion," declared Pope Pius X, "has no fear of science. Christianity does not tremble before discussion, but before ignorance." Thus forcefully and eloquently does the Pontiff express the mind of the Church that no mistake could ever be more disastrous for the cause of religion than to oppose the continued march of science on the ground that it blurs the vision of God and tends to remove Him from the universe. On the contrary the free and untrammeled prosecution of scientific research, resulting in continued new discoveries, is the most effective stimulus to a growing knowledge of God, for it sketches upon the canvas of the universe

[18] *Cath. Ency.* article on *Evolution*, Vol. V, 655

the lineaments of a Supreme Intelligence that not only transcends the cosmos, but is also immanent in its every part.

It is evident then that evolution presents no grounds whatsoever for disquietude or doubt as to God's place in the universe. Far from taking God out of the universe it gives us a more sublime conception of God's creative act, and of His superintending providence in every blade of grass, in every leaf on the tree, in every flower that grows, in every nook and corner of the universe. Furthermore, it will be remembered that the Bible gives no revelation concerning the subject matter of science but reveals only spiritual and religious truths. Thus it does not encroach in any way upon the freedom and autonomy of the human intellect in its investigation of the structure, organization, and functioning of the material universe and of the laws which are embedded alike in the grain of sand and in the most distant star. Evolution may well serve as a ladder upon which the student of nature climbs to secure a deeper and more penetrating insight into the creative power of God that unfolds itself in every living creature from the lowest to the highest.

Charles Darwin tells us that before he began to study the secrets of nature and the mysteries that lie locked up in the petals of a rose, the words of Wordsworth applied to him as they apply to most people today:

> A primrose by the river's brim
> A yellow primrose was to him
> And it was nothing more.

Only Rational Explanation

After he began his investigation of the secrets of nature, he found it a veritable fairyland where more poetry, romance and adventure were woven into the stamens and pistils and petals of the flowers than could be found in any book written by human hands. He saw, as every student of nature to this day sees, the picture portrayed in lines of simple beauty by a writer of our own day, Augustus Wright Bornberger:

> There's part of the sun in an apple,
> There's part of the moon in a rose;
> There's part of the flaming Pleiades
> In every leaf that grows.
>
> Out of the vast comes nearness;
> For the God whose love we sing
> Lends a little of His heaven
> To every living thing.

The creative power of God constantly operative in the evolutionary process disclosed by scientific research, offers the only rational explanation of the universe. The acceptance of a self-existent, omnipotent and omniscient Being can alone serve as the foundation for any system of cosmogony which satisfies our intellectual need of causation. The nature of this Being, while necessarily beyond the scope of our physical senses, can be known by us indirectly through the effects of which He is the cause.

A conclusion such as this was reached by the great scientist Lamarck, the real father of the theory of organic evolution, who said: "Nature, not being intelligent, not even a being, but an order of things constituting a power subject to law, cannot therefore be God. She is the wondrous product of His almighty will, and for us of all creatures she is the grandest and the most admirable. Thus the will of God is everywhere expressed by the laws of nature since these laws originate from Him."

God—Alpha and Omega

Evolution renders more imperative than ever before the need of a great intelligence to explain the progressive march of life from the lowest to the highest forms. Instead of the crude concept of a Deity working as a master mechanic constantly interfering with natural processes to make needed adjustments, evolution gives us a more sublime concept of a God who operates through the laws of nature which He has established and which hold universal sway throughout the entire universe from the tiny amoeba to the most distant star. Instead of the old picture of a world created in six days, evolution, if proven, discloses a far grander panorama of the creative power of God unfolding itself in the gradual development of the world and of all living creatures.

As the tiny mountain rivulet as well as the majestic lake and river, after many windings and turnings, all trace their course at last down to the ocean's mighty shore, so all things and all living creatures, great or small, all trace their origin and existence back to God, their Creator, for He has said: "I am the beginning and the end, the Alpha and the Omega." This is the lesson taught by the grain of sand, the blade of grass, the leaf on the tree, and by the meanest flower that grows. It is the refrain sung for us with exquisite melody by the perfume of the violet, the white chastity of the lily, and the pensive beauty of the foliage in its autumnal coloring of crimson and gold, sighing its requiem over the death of summer.

Thus we see that nature is one grand cosmic book describing the power and the majesty of God and bearing on its title-page those memorable words of Genesis which express so beautiful and so sublime a truth: "In the beginning God created heaven and earth."

of life from the lowest to the highest forms. Instead of the crude concept of a Deity working as a master mechanic constantly interfering with natural processes to make needed adjustments, evolution gives us a more sublime concept of a God who operates through the laws of nature which He has established and which hold universal sway throughout the entire universe from the tiny amoeba to the most distant star. Instead of the old picture of a world created in six days, evolution, if proven, discloses a far grander panorama of the creative power of God unfolding itself in the gradual development of the world and of all living creatures.

As the tiny mountain rivulets as well as the majestic lake and river, after many windings and turnings, all trace their course at last down to the ocean's mighty shore, so all things and all living creatures, great or small, all trace their origin and existence back to God-their Creator, for He has said: "I am the beginning and the end, the Alpha and the Omega." This is the lesson taught by the grain of sand, the blade of grass, the leaf on the tree, and by the meanest flower that grows. It is the refrain sung for us with exquisite melody by the perfume of the violet, the white chastity of the lily, and the pensive beauty of the foliage in its autumnal coloring of crimson and gold, sighing its requiem over the death of summer.

Thus we see that nature is one grand cosmic book describing the power and the majesty of God and bearing on its title-page those memorable words of Genesis which express so beautiful and so sublime a truth, "In the beginning God created heaven and earth."

PART V

JESUS CHRIST: THE FOUNDER OF THE CHRISTIAN RELIGION

His Character and Revelation

The purest among the strong and the strongest among
the pure, Christ lifted with his wounded hands empires
from their hinges and changed the stream of ages.

JEAN PAUL RICHTER

There are many truths about God and religion which man by his unaided reason would never be able to discover, and without them he would be groping in the mists of uncertainty. Jesus Christ dispels the darkness and presents the fulness of divine revelation. The voices of prophets and seers find their fulfillment in Him. He is God incarnate. In Him we secure an authentic picture of the love and mercy of God. For Jesus is the untarnished mirror of the Most High. For twenty centuries His winsome personality has held His followers in thralldom.

By word and deed Jesus Christ proved His divinity, and affirmed it under dramatic circumstances before Caiphas. Not even the threat of death could stay His testimony. The revelation of Jesus is transmitted to mankind chiefly through the Gospels. These are historic documents whose genuineness and reliability have withstood the acid test of repeated scientific investigations. We end our study by presenting the distinctive message of Jesus, the message of an all-embracing love. In that message alone Jesus discloses that He is truly the light of the world, and that anyone who follows Him walks not in darkness but in the light of Truth and Life.

CHAPTER XXVII

THE DIVINITY OF CHRIST

OF ALL the teachings of Christ, there are none more important or with such far-reaching consequences as those concerning His own divine nature. If Christ be not God, but a mere man, then the religion which He founded has no divine authority behind it, no finality to its moral code, no uniqueness to its teachings, no mark which differentiates it essentially and generically from Hindooism, Mohammedanism, Confucianism, or the other religions of the world. In short, the authoritativeness of the Christian religion stands or falls with the divine character of its Founder.

What now is the evidence concerning Christ's divinity? Let us examine the plain teachings of the Saviour on this point as recorded in the Gospels. For the purpose of this study, it will not be necessary to regard the Gospels as divinely inspired documents, but simply as truthful narratives. Surely every person who knows something of history will grant that the evangelists did not invent the character of Jesus, but that they recorded the truthful story of His life and teachings.

For the sake of brevity, we shall pass over the evidence which implies the deity of Jesus, such as the passages wherein He speaks not as an ambassador but in His own name and by His own authority. We shall come at once to the direct and explicit teaching of the Master that He is in literal truth the Son of God, consubstantial with the Father in Heaven.

341

The first scene occurs at Caesarea Philippi. Christ asks the disciples: "Whom do men say that the Son of man is?", But they said: "Some John the Baptist, and other some Elias, and others Jeremias, or one of the prophets." [1] Not satisfied with these responses, Christ asks the disciples: "But whom do you say that I am?" It is at this time that Peter makes his memorable profession of faith in Christ's divinity, saying: "Thou art Christ, the Son of the living God."

Peter's Testimony Upheld

Does the Saviour tell Peter that he is mistaken, that he has been carried away by his enthusiasm, and that he attributes to his Leader a divine nature which the latter does not really possess? If Peter were mistaken, it would have been the duty not only of Christ, but of any honest man, to correct Peter and to remove a false impression under which he was laboring. Does Christ tell Peter he is mistaken? On the contrary, the Master confirms the truth of Peter's statement by assuring him that his answer was divinely revealed unto him, and by rewarding him in a striking manner for his profession of faith:

And Jesus answering, said to him: "Blessed art thou, Simon Bar-Jona: because flesh and blood hath not revealed it to thee, but my Father who is in heaven. And I say to thee: That thou art Peter, and upon this rock I will build my church and the gates of hell shall not prevail against it. And I will give to thee the keys of the kingdom of heaven. And whatsoever thou shalt bind upon earth, it shall be bound also in heaven; and whatsoever thou shalt loose on earth, it shall be loosed also in heaven."

Here then is a dramatic scene in which the Master with the skill of a great teacher carefully prepares the background

[1] *Matt.* 16:13-14

which makes Peter's unequivocal profession of faith in Christ's divinity stand out like a flash of lightning against a darkened sky. It is obvious that this Sonship of Christ is not used here in the vague sense, in which all good Christians are sons of God by grace and adoption. It is clear that Christ is infinitely more than that—namely, the Son of God by nature, that is, consubstantial with God. For this reason, Christ is declared by St. John to be "the *only-begotten* of the Father, full of grace and truth." [2]

Christ before Caiphas

Not less lucid, nor less dramatic than the scene of the profession of Christ's divinity which occurred at Caesarea Philippi was that which had its setting before the Sanhedrin, the Supreme Court of the Hebrews in which not Peter but Christ Himself is the speaker. The Master is charged with the crime of claiming divine honors, that is, with claiming to be the Son of God. Among the Jews this offence was punished with death. Caiphas the high priest addressed Christ in the solemn words: "I adjure thee by the living God, that thou tell us if thou be Christ the Son of God." [3] Jesus knew full well that if He answered in the affirmative, He would be signing His own death warrant. Does He seek to escape the impending doom by giving an equivocal or misleading reply? Does He seek to escape by the simple expedient of denying His own divinity?

On the contrary, without a moment's hesitation, without the slightest equivocation, He answers simply and clearly: "Thou hast said it." This is the Hebrew manner of saying: "Thou hast spoken the truth: I am in very deed." Immediately upon hearing this reply, Caiphas rent his garments,

[2] *John* 1:18
[3] *Mat.* 26:63

saying: "He hath blasphemed; what further need have we of witnesses? Behold, now you have heard the blasphemy; what think you?" But they answering, said: "He is guilty of death." The fact that the Sanhedrin accused Christ of *blasphemy* showed that they regarded Him as claiming *true* sonship, and not merely the Messiahship. For the false claim to the latter would have been mere prevarication and not blasphemy.

In literal truth, therefore, it can be said that Christ went to His death upon Calvary's gibbet rather than deny, or even equivocate concerning His own divine character. How is it possible then for any person, much less a Christian, who regards the gospels even as historical documents, to doubt or to deny the plain teaching of Jesus Christ concerning His own divinity?

Confirmed by Miracles

The Master not only declared that He was divine, but He confirmed it with signs and miracles, especially the miracle of His resurrection. Thus on more than one occasion, He appealed to the Jews to believe His works, if they would not believe His words. "The works themselves which I do, give testimony of me, that the Father hath sent me." [4] And again He says to them: "Believe you not that I am in the Father, and the Father in me? Otherwise believe for the very works' sake." [5]

St. Peter merely followed the example of his Master in appealing to the wonderful works of the latter as the convincing evidence of His Messiahship and of His divine Sonship. Thus on the first Christian Pentecost morning, when the Apostles are starting out on their sublime mission of win-

---

[4] *John* 5:36
[5] *John* 14:11-12

ning the world for Christ, St. Peter addresses the Jews: "Ye men of Israel hear these words: Jesus of Nazareth, a man *approved of God among you, by miracles, and wonders and signs, which God did by him,* in the midst of you, as you know." [6]

The effect made not only upon the disciples but also upon the multitudes who witnessed the miracles wrought by Jesus is reflected in the words of Nicodemus: "We know that Thou art come a teacher from God; for no man can do these signs which Thou doest, unless God be with him." [7] Indeed, St. John says explicitly that he has recorded the miracles of Jesus for the express purpose of enabling his readers to believe in the deity of Christ. "Many other signs," he says, "also did Jesus in the sight of His disciples, which are not written in this book. But these are written *that you may believe that Jesus is the Christ, the Son of God;* and that believing you may have life in His name." [8]

Even if there remained any traces of uncertainty in the minds of any of the disciples as to the deity of Jesus after witnessing the numerous miracles He had wrought, surely those vestiges must have been dispelled by the stupendous miracle of the Resurrection. This occurrence, confirmed by such an abundance of testimony, including that of the Apostles who spoke with the Master after His Resurrection, would seem to have removed the last vestige of uncertainty from the minds of the disciples as to the divine Sonship of Jesus. Even the centurion who had assisted in the crucifixion of the Master felt compelled by the signs and wonders occurring at the time of the Saviour's death, to cry out his belief in the divinity of Jesus. "Now the centurion," says St. Matthew, "and they that were with him watching Jesus,

[6] *Acts* 2:22
[7] *John* 3:2
[8] *John* 20:30

having seen the earthquake, and the things that were done, were sore afraid, saying: Indeed this was the Son of God." [9]

In the light of all the evidence thus far presented, which indeed is but a fragment of the great mass filling the Gospels, it would not seem to be too much to say that if Christ be not divine, then the New Testament, considered not only as an inspired document, but even simply as an historical work, falls to the ground and with it the whole superstructure of traditional Christianity reposing upon it. For the only way to escape from belief in the divine Sonship of Jesus is by impugning the historical truthfulness of the gospel—a procedure for which there is no scientific justification.

Christ of the Early Church

The early Christians were explicit in proclaiming their faith in the divinity of Jesus. The teachings of the early Church can best be perceived from the profession of faith required by converts to her fold. From the very first, it was the custom to require such a profession before the converts were admitted to baptism. To secure uniformity, a set formula was adopted which reflected the most fundamental articles of the faith then taught by the Church. The formula in general use during the first three centuries has been preserved for us, at least in part, by Tertullian,[10] by St. Justin [11] and by St. Irenaeus.[12] All these lived and wrote in the second century. Even hostile critics now generally admit that this formula traces its origin to a period not later than the first century, and that it was common to the Church both in the East and in the West.

In this formula, belief in the divinity of Christ is thus ex-

[9] Mat. 27:54
[10] De Praescript. c. 36
[11] Apol. I, 61
[12] Adv. Haer. I, 10

plicitly set forth as a necessary condition for entrance into the fold: "I believe in God the Father Almighty, and in Jesus Christ, His only Son, our Lord, who was born by the Holy Ghost of the Virgin Mary." It is identical with the corresponding article of the Apostles' Creed which we Christians of the twentieth century recite, thus professing the same faith as our co-religionists of the first and second centuries. Nineteen hundred years have not altered either our faith in the divine Sonship of Jesus or its external expression.

Testimony of the Fathers

The writings of the Fathers of the early Church abound in references to this central article of their faith. St. Clement of Rome, St. Ignatius of Antioch, and St. Justin Martyr lay special stress upon it. In his Apology to the Roman Emperor, written toward the end of the second century, Athenagoras of Athens writes: "Not only is the Father God, but also the Son and the Holy Spirit. In these three divine persons there is unity of Godhead, and in this unity of Godhead there is distinction of persons." [13] St. Irenaeus of Lyons writes at about the same time: "If Christ forgives sins, if Christ is Mediator between God and man, this is because He is really a divine person." [14]

It was to the universal belief of the early Christians in this great truth that St. Polycarp in the middle of the second century bore witness when, bound to the stake to be burned alive, he cried out: "For all things, O God, do I praise and bless Thee, together with the Eternal and Heavenly Jesus Christ, Thy well-beloved Son, with Whom, to Thee and the Holy Ghost, be glory, both now and forever. Amen." [14a]

[13] C. 30
[14] Adv. Haer. III, 9, 2
[14a] Mart. Polyc. c. 14

The same great truth was also emphasized by St. Hippolytus of Rome, by Tertullian of Carthage, by Origen and Clement of Alexandria, by St. Methodius of Tyre and by Melito of Sardis. Indeed, every writer of the period who referred to the matter, and whose writings have been preserved, taught the same doctrine.

That the mind of the infant Church was very definitely made up on the matter is evident likewise from her manner of dealing with heretics who presumed to deny the true and absolute divinity of Jesus Christ. Thus when Cerinthus, toward the end of the first century, proclaimed that Jesus was only the son of Mary and Joseph, and not of God, and that He was not, therefore, true God, the whole Church rose up in protest against his heresy and shunned him as an apostate.[15] The same vigorous condemnation was sounded when the Gnostics, and later on the Arians, assigned to the Saviour a middle place between the highest angels and the Supreme God, and thus reduced Christ to a sort of inferior deity. Without hesitation, the Church promptly branded them as heretics who departed from the faith delivered to them by the Apostles.

So universal was the belief in the divine Sonship of Jesus among the members of the early Church that they looked upon this as the distinguishing mark of the true Christian. Thus Canon Liddon accurately mirrors the faith of the Church in the first three centuries when he testifies that "the truth of Christ's absolute Godhead was beyond doubt the very central feature of the teaching of the ante-Nicene Church, even when Church teachers had not yet recognized all that it necessarily involved, and had not yet elaborated the accurate statement of its relationship to other truths around it."

---

[15] St. Irenaeus, Adv. Haer. V

Origen Replies to Celsus

The Christians of the first three centuries not only believed in the divinity of Jesus, but translated their belief into action by worshipping Him as God. This fact stands out with special clearness from the charges of polytheism and even of idolatry brought against them by their enemies. Thus Celsus, a scoffing pagan philosopher of the third century, contended that the Christians had no right to criticize the polytheism of the pagan world, since their own worship of Christ was essentially polytheistic. "The Christians," he declared, "worshipped no God, no not even a demon, but only a dead man. If they do not wish to worship the pagan gods," he said, "why should they not rather pay their devotions to some of their own prophets than to a man who had been crucified by the Jews?"

Origen, the greatest of the early Christian writers, defended the Christians from the attacks of Celsus. This he did, not by denying the charge that they worshipped Christ, but by showing that the Saviour was worthy of such adoration because He was God. "The gods of the pagans," he answers Celsus, "were unworthy of worship; the Jewish prophets had no claim to it; on the other hand, Christ was worshipped not as a mere man, but as the Son of God, as God Himself. If Celsus," he continues, "had understood the meaning of this, 'I and the Father are One,' or what the Son of God says in His prayer, 'As I and Thou art One,' he would never have imagined that we worship any but the God who is over all, for Christ says, 'The Father is in Me, and I in Him.' " [16]

The evidence of the belief of the early Church in the divinity of Jesus would be sadly incomplete, however, if we did not consider the testimony of the Christian martyrs.

[16] *Contr. Cels.* VIII, 12

They speak to us not merely with words, but with the far greater eloquence of their sufferings and their deaths. Gladly did some permit their bodies to be coated with pitch and tar to be burned alive to illumine the gladiatorial contests of the Romans. Others surrendered themselves to be torn limb from limb by the wild lions in the sand-covered arena. Still others placed their heads upon the swordsman's block, while their companions were nailed in ignominy to the cross. These tortures and others more excruciating still, they suffered cheerfully and with joy, rather than save their lives and gain the promised preferments by denying their God and Saviour, Jesus Christ.

Voices of the Martyred

They speak to us with voices that thunder in our inner ear. Their life's blood has placed upon their faith the seal of a conviction which neither time nor eternity can break. Instead of growing weaker with the lapse of centuries, their voices grow in volume and in strength, so that he must be deaf indeed who does not hear their thunderings: "We suffered and died for no mere man, but for our God and Saviour, Jesus Christ!" In their accents the attentive ear can discern the echoing of the voices of the Apostles and of Christ Himself.

In order to realize what it meant for the martyrs to profess their belief in Christ as true God, and seal that faith with their life's blood, it will be helpful to read the account of their ordeals as handed down by an eye-witness. Many such accounts have been preserved. The following one, which all scholars admit to be genuine, will serve as a sample. Before the tribunals of the prefect Calvisianus, there had been brought Euplius, a deacon of the Church at Catania, on the charge of being a Christian. According to the usual custom, the prefect endeavored to persuade the prisoner to renounce Christ and offer sacrifice to the pagan gods, promising him freedom for so doing. Perceiving that his entreaties were in vain, he ordered the prisoner to be stretched upon the rack. An eye-witness thus narrates what followed:

"And while being racked, Euplius said: 'I thank Thee, O Christ, Guard Thou me, who for Thee am suffering thus.' The prefect interrupted him, saying: 'Cease, Euplius, from this folly. Adore the gods, and thou shalt be set at liberty.' Euplius answered: 'I adore Christ; I utterly hate the demons. Do what thou wilt: I am a Christian. Add yet other tortures: I am a Christian.' After he had been tortured a long while, the executioners were bidden hold their hands. Then the Prefect said: 'Unhappy man, adore the gods. Pay worship to Mars, Apollo and Aesculapius.' Euplius replied: 'I worship the Father and the Son and the Holy Ghost. I adore the Holy Trinity, beside Whom there is no God. Perish the gods who did not make heaven and earth, and all that is in them. I am a Christian.'

"The Prefect again said: 'Offer sacrifice, if thou wouldest be set at liberty.' But Euplius answered: 'I sacrifice myself only to Christ my God: more than this I cannot do. Thy efforts are to no purpose; I am a Christian.' Then orders were given that he should be tortured again; and whilst every bone was wrenched from its socket, he cried out: 'Thanks to Thee, O Christ. Help me, O Christ! For Thee do I suffer thus, O Christ.' When finally all his strength had left him and his voice was gone, he still repeated these same exclamations with his lips only." [17]

In the dying words of Euplius, there is echoed the confession of faith in Christ's divinity that came from the lips not of hundreds but of thousands of martyrs. With their last

[17] *Ruinart, Acta Mart.* p. 439, as quoted by B. J. Otten, S.J., in *The Reason Why*, p. 264

breath, they breathed the name of their Lord and Master, Jesus Christ. That long line of martyrs, consisting of men, women and children, who withstood the allurements of the prefects and the refined cruelties of the executioners, who poured out their treasures and their life's blood for their Saviour, reveal to us the faith of the infant Church with a clarity and a certainty that far transcend the power of mere words to express. Their profession of faith is written in the deathless language of immortal deed.

The Same Reply

Christ remains the most potent influence in the life of the world. As Richter has said so beautifully of Him, "The purest among the strong and the strongest among the pure, Christ lifted with His wounded hands empires from their hinges and changed the stream of ages." Even the sensual Rousseau perceives the lineaments of the divine in the character of Christ as depicted in the Gospels, and gives expression to his conviction in the following striking lines:

"I confess to you that the majesty of the Scriptures strikes me with admiration, as the purity of the Gospels has its influence on my heart. Peruse the works of our philosophers, with all their pomp of diction; how mean, how contemptible they are, compared with the Scriptures! Is it possible that a book, at once so simple and sublime, should be merely the work of man? Is it possible that the sacred personage whose history it contains should be himself a mere man? Do we find that He assumed the tone of an enthusiast or ambitious sectary? What sweetness, what purity in His manners! What an effecting gracefulness in his delivery! What sublimity in His maxims! What profound wisdom in His discourses! What presence of mind in His replies! How great the command over His passions! Where is the man, where is the philosopher who could so live and so die, without weakness, without ostentation? . . . Yes, if the life and death of Socrates were those of a sage, the life and death of Jesus were those of a God." [18]

To the query which Christ addressed to the Pharisees nineteen centuries ago, "What think you of Christ? Whose Son is he?" the Christian Church replies in the twentieth century in the words uttered by Peter in the first: "Thou art Christ, the Son of the living God."

[18] *Emile*, book 4

CHAPTER XXVIII

REVELATION: ITS NATURE AND PURPOSE

THE goodness and the love of God shine forth in the revelation which He has vouchsafed to mankind. Unwilling to allow His creatures to be without a knowledge of truths which surpass the capacity of the unaided human mind to discover, the Creator has mercifully drawn aside the curtain of darkness from our eyes, permitting us to peer into the radiance of divine truth. While our minds are finite and cannot penetrate to the very depths of the mysteries of religion, they can catch glimmerings of mighty truths which exalt, strengthen and inspire us. For example, we would never know the great truth of the Blessed Trinity if it were not revealed to us. Through revelation God brings us closer to Him in knowledge and in love.

All the works of creation may be said to constitute a revelation of the mind and the will of the Creator—a natural revelation. By the study of such works, we come to the knowledge of the truths of natural religion. But the revelation of which we speak is a supernatural one. By a supernatural revelation we mean the communication of some truth by God to a rational creature through means which are beyond the ordinary course of nature.

Revelation may be supernatural *in manner*, but not *in substance*. For example, man can deduce the existence of God from a study of the works of creation. This naturally known truth is also supernaturally revealed. Such revelation is supernatural only *in manner*. The revelation of the triune nature of God, however, is supernatural *in substance as well as in manner*.

From the existence of a personal God and of a rational creature, the possibility of revelation is apparent. To say that God created man and then cut His creature off from all possibility of receiving a communication from his Maker is monstrous. As a father can communicate with his children, so the Creator can speak to His creatures. What would we think of a father who would never speak to his son? How unnatural would be the son who would never turn a listening ear to the tender and kindly voice of his sire?

God's love for His children far surpasses that of any human father. He manifests that love and solicitude by communicating to His children the deposit of divine truth in all its beauty and radiance. Instead of leaving man at the mercy of his own intellectual faculties, so often impaired by pride, sloth, and passion, to discover all the truths even of natural religion, an all-merciful Father has disclosed these to us with a certainty that removes all vacillation and doubt. The disclosure of supernatural truths is a further beautiful and touching manifestation of the Creator's love for His children, made in His image and likeness.

Christ—The Bearer of Revelation

Who was the bearer of this revelation to mankind? It was His own divine Son, Jesus Christ. Partial revelations had been delivered to the patriarchs and prophets to prepare the way for the full and universal revelation which God was to give us through His Son. Many prophecies had been made concerning the coming of Christ so that He would bear the credentials of His messiahship. His mission was to redeem mankind and to banish the darkness from the souls of men. He was the Light of the world, the Light that was to illumine the mysteries of life and death and show men the unfailing path to Heaven.

The revelation which Christ delivered to the world is supported not by a single miracle or prophecy, but by a multitude whose cumulative force cannot fail to carry conviction to the honest mind. That revelation is reënforced by the great web of Messianic prophecies. It is certified by the manifold miracles of Christ during His early mission and by the climactic miracle of His resurrection from the dead. It is supported by the marvelous spread of Christianity throughout the world, constituting a miracle of the moral order. It is further authenticated by the miraculous nature and vitality of the Christian Church which has triumphed over the determined efforts of mighty empires to destroy her.

Thus the Vatican Council teaches: "In order that the obedience of our faith might be agreeable to reason, God has willed that to the internal aids of the Holy Spirit, there should be joined external proofs of His revelation, namely, divine works, especially miracles and prophecy, which inasmuch as they manifestly display the omnipotence and the omniscience of God are most certain signs of a divine revelation and are suited to the understanding of all."

How may a revelation be known? By certain marks which show forth its divine origin. These are as follows: (1) The message must not be unworthy of its alleged Author. It must not be ambiguous or trivial. It must be noble, elevating, agreeable to reason, satisfying to human aspirations, and beneficial to society. (2) It must be confirmed by miracles or prophecies. That the good tidings which Christ brought to the world bear the first mark is evident to all who have read the Christian gospel. That His message is authenticated abundantly by prophecies and miracles, we shall now proceed to show.

The Proof from Prophecies

A prophecy may be defined as the definite prediction of events which depend for their occurrence on the exercise of free will, whether it be the free will of God or of rational creatures, and which are of such a character as to be beyond the possibility of guess work or of human prevision.[1] It is only God who knows beforehand what a free agent will do. That is why a prophecy, if fulfilled, is as conclusive a mark of divine authority as a miracle. The latter is an expression of God's omnipotence, the former of His omniscience. Both are seals, affixed by the hand of God Himself authenticating the work as His.

The web of prophecies running through the Old and New Testaments is so extensive as to preclude escape from the conviction that this is a seal of the divine authority behind the revelation. The prophecies are numerous, abound in detail and circumstance, and are literally fulfilled. Thus the date of the Redeemer's coming was foretold,[2] as was the fact that He was to be *born of a virgin*,[3] of the tribe of the *family of David*,[4] at Bethlehem,[5] and that kings would come offering gifts.[6]

Our wonderment is further increased when we discover that: the name of the Saviour was foretold; His passion and death were described; He was to be sold for thirty pieces of silver; His hands and feet were to be pierced; His garments were to be distributed and His outer garment assigned by lot; He was to rise from the dead and found a kingdom that would not be destroyed. All these detailed facts and a

[1] Cf. Archbishop Sheehan's *Apologetics*, Gill & Son, Ltd., Dublin, 1939, p. 70
[2] *Daniel* 9:24
[3] *Isaias* 7:14
[4] *Jeremias* 23:5
[5] *Micheas* 5:2
[6] *Psal.* 71:10; *Is.* 60:3–6

multitude of others were foretold in the Old Testament from 400 to 800 years before they occurred.

In the New Testament we find prophecies not less striking. Thus Christ foretold the manner and time of His death, His resurrection, His ascension. He foretold that Judas would betray Him, that Peter would deny Him thrice before the cock would crow twice, that His disciples would forsake Him, that the Holy Ghost would descend upon the apostles. After peering into the future to see the events that were to transpire after His death, Christ foretold the destruction of Jerusalem, the razing of the Temple, the dispersion of the Jews, the growth of His Church, and the preaching of the Gospel to all nations. Thus vividly do these prophecies attest the supernatural and divine character of the revelation of Christ.

Proof from Miracles

A miracle may be defined as an occurrence outside the course of nature, perceptible to the senses, and explicable only as the direct act of God Himself. We might more accurately term the miracles of which we are here speaking *evidential* to distinguish them from miracles not apparent to the senses. A miracle in the strict sense of the term constitutes clear proof of the divine origin of the doctrine in support of which it is wrought. It is a credential, certifying to the truthfulness of the doctrine as well as to its divine authority.

No one who admits the existence of a personal God can question the possibility of miracles. The Creator who fixed the course of nature can change, suspend or supersede it as He deems wise. A human legislator can modify or suspend his law. Who will deny the Author of the laws of nature the same power? Indeed, if He could not modify the work of His own hands, how could He be said to be omnipotent? The question, then, in regard to miracles is not whether God *could* work a miracle, but whether in any given case a miracle has occurred or not. In other words, the question of miracles boils down to a matter of evidence.

There is no denying, however, that there has been created in the minds of many people a prejudice against the possibility of miracles and a consequent distaste for their use as evidence in the establishment of the divine character of the Christian revelation. This is traceable to the oft-repeated assertions of scientists that the laws of nature are fixed and immutable and admit of no exceptions. They have created the widespread impression that science frowns upon the possibility of miracles. To be in step with the scientists, people generally have felt that they too must regard the possibility of miracles as disproved by the advance of modern science.

Let us now examine the line of reasoning of the scientists that would outlaw the possibility of miracles. Briefly it would run: Physical science declares that nature acts not capriciously but uniformly in accordance with definite laws. But the doctrine of miracles denies this. Therefore the believer in miracles must reject the outstanding generalization of modern science.

We reply by pointing out that we do not differ with scientists in regard to the law-abiding character of nature's operations. Indeed, we are at one with them in holding to the general law of nature that the same physical cause in the same circumstances will produce the same effect. We maintain, however, that when God intervenes, the circumstances are no longer the same, because a new force has been introduced. Even man can introduce a force which will alter the course of nature's operation.

Thus a baseball player who catches a fly ball prevents the

law of gravity from pulling it to the earth. Does he destroy the law of gravity? Not at all. He simply exercises a force sufficient to counteract the pull of gravity. When an airplane leaves the ground, is the law of gravity annulled and the uniformity of nature's operations impaired? Not at all. A contrary force sufficient to overcome the pull of gravity is introduced. When I swim in a stream, am I destroying the law of gravity? No, I am simply applying a force sufficient to counteract it and thus keep afloat.

Similarly in the case of miracles, we do not imply that the laws of nature are destroyed or rendered inoperative. We simply affirm that a greater force has been introduced, a force sufficient to bring about a different resultant. Far from nullifying the laws of nature, properly understood, miracles may be said to attest their validity. For surely it is a law of nature, and one of the most basic of all her laws that, when two opposing forces are brought into operation, the greater will always prevail over the lesser. As God is stronger than any force, it follows that His force will always prevail. To deny God the power to apply a force necessary to attain a desired end is to deny the existence of God as a personal, free agent.

Laws of Nature

Let us penetrate a little more deeply into the meaning of the laws of nature, a term which scientists use with such frequency. When we investigate what scientists mean when they speak of the laws of nature, we find that they mean so many uniform modes of action, invariably observed by natural causes in the production of their proper effects. Thus they say it is a law of nature that bodies attract one another, that fire burns, that the human body, once dead, never revives. According to scientists, then, the laws of nature are nothing else than the whole collection of similar uniform acts grouped under a general proposition.

Yet if we subject that concept to careful analysis we find that these uniform acts are not laws, strictly speaking, but the *effects* produced by laws. For a law is a *principle* of action, not the act itself. The fact that in America we drive on the right-hand side of the road is not a law. It is the result of a law which exists independently of whether an individual observes the law or violates it. So it is in nature. The fact that fire burns is not a law. It is the result of a law from which combustion proceeds as a uniform occurrence. Hence the laws of nature can only be the will of the divine Lawmaker as expressed in natural causes.

"As these natural causes are devoid of freedom," as B. J. Otten points out, "the will of the lawgiver can find expression in them only by means of predetermined forces; so that the laws of nature are objectively nothing else than the forces with which God has endowed His creatures, and by reason of which they must, when left to themselves, always act the same way if placed under the same circumstances." [7] Hence it is evident that the uniformity of the so-called laws of nature has its ultimate reason only in the will of God. When scientists penetrate beyond the superficial view of the laws of nature as mere uniform modes of action to the ultimate principle underlying all such laws they will perceive that it is none other than the will of the divine Legislator who has brought the universe into being and framed all its laws. Thus may the laws of nature be said to be the objectified thought of God.

[7] *The Reason Why*, B. Herder Book Co., St. Louis, 1921, p. 152

Hume's Objection

We should refer here to the objection of Hume which caused a considerable stir back in the eighteenth century. "A miracle," he says, "is a violation of the laws of nature; and as a firm and unalterable experience has established these laws, the proof against a miracle, from the very nature of the fact, is as entire as any argument from experience can possibly be imagined." [8] The explanation which we have just given shows that a miracle need not, and indeed should not, be viewed as a violation of the laws of nature. It involves simply the introduction of new force sufficient to change the resultant.

Hume's objection is vitiated by another fallacy, namely, the assumption that mankind has no experience of miracles. This is not only a begging of the point to be proved but is also a flying in the face of the testimony of both scientists and laymen alike. The only relevant testimony concerning the occurrence or the non-occurrence of a miracle is that of eye witnesses. Let us take the incident of Christ's walking upon the sea of Galilee. Hume argues that millions of people will testify that they have never seen anyone walking upon water. Granted. But that testimony is totally irrelevant and would be thrown out by any court of evidence.

We are not arguing that people generally walk upon water or that any appreciable number have ever done so. We are contending simply that Christ on one specific occasion did so. Now the only testimony that is relevant to that incident is the testimony of those who were present and who witnessed such an occurrence. The testimony of those who lived centuries later and who never witnessed such an

---

[8] *Hume's Works*, ed. 1770, Vol. III, p. 178. Cardinal Newman gives a complete refutation of this objection in his *Grammar of Assent*, pp. 306. 307

occurrence is completely beside the point. When carefully analyzed, Hume's objection is thus seen to be vitiated by a twofold fallacy. It is little more than a piece of artful pettifoggery.

Facing the Facts

In recent years something of the old prejudice against miracles has begun to wane. Many scientists are now willing to look into the cases of alleged miracles with open minds and allow the facts to write their own verdict. This change of attitude is due in no small part to the eminent medical scientist, Dr. Alexis Carrel. In his widely read *Man—The Unknown*, Dr. Carrel called attention to the impressive and carefully documented evidence of miracles at Lourdes. He pointed out that the scientific attitude is not to wave that evidence aside and formulate a judgment which amounts only to a pre-judgment—the root meaning of prejudice. The scientific attitude is to investigate the evidence, examine the actual facts, and arrive at a judgment on the basis of the verified data.

More and more is his wise counsel being followed. The scoffing of the cynics and the doubting of the incredulous are vanishing before the impressive evidence so carefully documented in the *Annals of Lourdes* by medical authorities of every shade of religious faith and of no faith at all. In that work are recorded the sworn testimony of physicians who examine a patient before he invokes the intercession of Our Lady of Lourdes, and the sworn testimony of the same physicians after the patient is instantly cured. Their testimony is corroborated by clinical data, X-ray photographs taken before and after, and by all the elaborate checks and controls devised by scientists.

The cures cover the widest assortment of human ills, including tuberculosis, organic lesions, paralysis, blindness, running sores, and cancer. Some of the miracles involve an instantaneous lengthening of bone structure—as shown by actual X-ray pictures. Before recording a cure as miraculous, physicians and surgeons are enlisted in the endeavor to find any natural explanation. Only when every natural factor has been ruled out is the case adjudged to involve the expression of supernatural power. It has been the frank facing of this evidence that has caused an ever-increasing number of scientists to abandon their attitude of incredulity and to admit not merely the possibility but the fact of miracles. Many came to scoff, but remained to pray.

We have beheld the great assemblage of crutches, wheel chairs, plaster-of-paris casts, and other evidences of invalidism which patients, miraculously cured, have left at Lourdes as mute symbols of their gratitude. It is difficult to gaze upon this tell-tale evidence and to read the sworn testimony of physicians—Protestant, Catholic, Jewish, and non-believers —certifying in the *Annals of Lourdes* to the complete and instantaneous cure of maladies deemed incurable, and understand how any normal mind can question the fact of miracles.

The best cure for scepticism on this subject is not argument, not theory, but a generous dose of the actual facts. For against a fact all argument collapses. "The man of theory," observes Carlyle, "twangs his full bent bow; nature's fact ought to fall stricken, but does not; his logic-arrow glances from it as from a scaly dragon and the obstinate fact keeps walking its way. How singular!"

While the evidence at Lourdes is most impressive and its bureau for the scientific investigation of miraculous cures is perhaps best organized, the searcher for evidence of this nature need not travel to Europe. He can find here on our own continent, at the Shrine of Our Lady of Guadalupe in Mexico, at the Oratory of St. Joseph at Montreal, and at the Shrine of St. Anne at Beaupré, Canada, irrefragable and convincing evidence of miracles in our own day.

Christ Appeals to Miracles

After this exposition of the possibility, the nature, and the fact of miracles, we return now to point out the demonstrative force of miracles in establishing the divine character of the Christian revelation. Christ Himself appealed time after time to His miracles as blinding evidence of His divine mission and of His divine message. "The *works* themselves which I do," he said, "give testimony of me, that the Father hath sent me." [9] Note the manner in which He appealed to His restoration of Lazarus to life as convincing evidence of His divine mission.

Lazarus, a man of great virtue, fell sick and died. He was a close friend of Christ, as were also his two sisters, Martha and Mary. During his illness, his sisters had sent for Christ. But he remained away purposely, as the Evangelist St. John tells us, to deepen the faith of His followers by a striking miracle. When He finally arrived in Bethania, Lazarus had been dead four days and was already interred. Nevertheless Christ assured the sisters that their brother would rise again. Going to the grave, Christ ordered them to open the tomb. They objected on the ground that the body was already undergoing putrefaction. At Christ's insistence, however, they opened the grave and exposed the body to the assembled multitude.

Then "Jesus lifting his eyes, said: 'Father, I give Thee thanks that Thou hast heard me. And I know that Thou hearest me always; but because of the people who stand about have I said it, that they may believe that Thou hast sent me.' When He had said these things, He cried with a

[9] *John* 5:36

loud voice: 'Lazarus, come forth.' And presently he that had been dead came forth, bound feet and hands with winding bands; and his face was bound about with a napkin. Jesus said to them: 'Loose him, and let him go.' Many therefore of the Jews, who were come to Mary and Martha, and had seen the things that Jesus did, believed in Him." [10]

What is to be noted particularly in this case is the explicit statement of Christ as to why He was about to perform this miracle: "Father . . . because of the people who stand about have I said it, that they may believe that thou hast sent me." Here Christ appeals to the miracle as the unmistakable credential of his oft-asserted, divine mission. It was God's seal upon the divine revelation which He had brought them.

Other miracles He had already wrought. He had fed five thousand persons with five loaves of bread. [11] By a mere word He had healed a person who had for thirty-eight years been sick with an incurable disease. [12] He had given sight to the man that was born blind. [13] He had walked on the surface of the storm-tossed sea. [14] These miracles had produced their effect upon His disciples and upon the people and now He wished to deepen that effect by a still greater miracle, the raising of Lazarus from the dead. Thus it was by the constant appeal to miracles that Christ drove home to the people the important truth of His divine mission and the divine character of the revelation which He was giving to them.

From all this it is evident then that miracles and prophecies are a seal, placed by God's own fingers upon the revelation brought to the world by Jesus Christ, certifying to its supernatural and divine character. In that communication from on high there are contained the imperishable truths

[10] *John* 11:41-45
[11] *Mat.* 14:17
[12] *John* 5:7
[13] *Mark* 10:52
[14] *Mat.* 14:26

which will guide all who believe and live them, to the harbor of eternal life. In bequeathing that revelation to man there is mirrored the solicitude and the love of God who lights our way through the valley of life to the mountain peaks of eternity. Like a good shepherd, He hungers for the safety of all His sheep, and sends His only-begotten Son to shepherd us on the way lest any be lost. That deposit of divinely revealed truth is our cloud by day and our pillar of fire by night, and no one who follows it will perish in the darkness.

CHAPTER XXIX

THE HISTORICAL CHARACTER OF THE GOSPELS

But the word of the Lord endureth for ever. And this is the word which by the gospel has been preached unto you.—*1 Peter* 1, 25

THE Christian revelation comes to us through two channels, tradition and the New Testament. By tradition is not meant the haphazard handing down of a doctrine from father to son, from generation to generation. It means the word of God that was not committed to inspired writings, but was preserved in writings of historical value, in the preaching and practice of the Apostles, in the sacramental and liturgical life of the Church. The writings of the Fathers of the Church, reflecting the teachings and practices of the Apostles and disciples, are rich sources of tradition. They are, of course, supplementary to Holy Scripture.

The New Testament may be viewed from two aspects: (1) as a collection of ordinary historical documents; (2) as a group of divinely inspired books, having God as their principal Author. By inspiration is meant an influence breathed forth by God on the soul of the writer so that he expresses what God wishes him to express. It does not imply a divine communication of knowledge to the writer. It is not perceptible to the senses. It does not modify the style or manner of expression of the writer. It moves him to write certain truths which he already knows and safeguards him from error in his writing. The fact that certain writings are inspired was made known by the early Christian Church, divinely appointed to teach all the nations of the world.

We shall make no further reference to inspiration in this discussion. We shall treat the four Gospels from a human point of view and undertake to prove from reason that they are trustworthy, historical documents. That is all that is necessary to establish the truth that they present in a reliable manner the revelation of Christ. While the Acts of the Apostles and the Epistles throw additional light upon the contents of divine revelation, the Gospels present the good tidings in sufficient detail for our purposes. We shall accordingly focus our attention upon them, contenting ourselves with the general observation that the historic validity of the other books of the New Testament can be established by similar lines of reasoning and of evidence.

A work must be accepted as historical in the sense that it is a trustworthy record of past events if it meets these three conditions:

1. It must be genuine in the sense that it is the work of the author whose name it bears.

2. Its author must be reliable in the sense that he is well informed and truthful.

3. It must be intact in the sense that the text is substantially as it left the author's hand.

All these conditions, as we shall show, are fulfilled in the Gospels, the four fundamental books of the New Testament.

How Written

Before presenting the evidence of the genuineness of the Gospels, we shall say a word about how the Gospels were written and copied. The entire New Testament was written in Greek with the single exception of the original of St. Matthew's Gospel. This was first composed in Aramaic, a language similar to Hebrew then current in Palestine, and the tongue which Christ Himself used. The Gospels, like the other books of the New Testament, were without punctuation and lacked the division into chapters and verses which we find in our modern printed Bibles. The original documents were written on papyrus, which served as "paper" at that time. The pages were gummed together into a long roll which was wound on two cylinders. Some idea of the bulkiness of their written material may be gained from the fact that the *Acts of the Apostles*, numbering fifty pages in a modern Bible, formed a roll about thirty feet long.

The Synoptic Gospels

The first three Gospels, Matthew, Mark and Luke, are written along similar lines and cover to a considerable extent the same general ground. They present more particularly the ministry of Christ in Galilee. The similarity or parallelism obtaining among the first three has caused them to be called the Synoptic Gospels. *Synopsis* is a Greek term for looking at and comparing two or more things together. The literary relationship of these Gospels to one another is a highly complicated technical question which has given rise to an enormous literature.

Numerous theories have been developed to explain the degree of dependence on one another, on a common oral tradition, and on other sources, but much uncertainty still clouds the picture. In general, critics, both conservative and radical, hold that the Synoptic Gospels were written somewhat earlier than the fourth Gospel, that of St. John. While in general agreement with the first three, the latter stresses for the most part the acts and utterances of Christ, which are omitted in the Synoptics, and treats mainly of His ministry in Judea.

If we consider the subject matter in the Synoptic Gospels as containing one hundred sections, the following percentages will show the amount of matter common and proper to each: [1]

	Proper	Common
Mark	7%	93%
Matthew	42%	58%
Luke	59%	41%
John	92%	8%

The percentages show that Mark has but little material, just about one-tenth, that is not contained in Matthew and Luke. The additional material in the first and third Gospels consists largely of the utterances of Jesus. In the fourth Gospel there are few passages which coincide with the narrative of the other three. In fact, aside from the account of the Passion, there are but three facts which St. John narrates in common with the other Evangelists—the feeding of the five thousand, the storm on the Sea of Galilee, and the anointing of the Lord's feet by Mary. While the Synoptics depict the life of Christ chiefly in Galilee, St. John follows Him into Judea, and relates how Christ journeyed to Jerusalem for the prescribed feasts. The only satisfactory explanation for this is that St. John, writing last of all, toward the close of the first century, was familiar with the other Gospels, and purposely abstained from writing anew what was recorded by them.

[1] Cf. Voste, J., *De Synopticorum*, 9

The Genuineness of the Gospels

External Evidence. That the Gospels are genuine is proven
by external and internal evidence. The external evidence
consists of the testimony of Christian and non-Christian writers of the first two centuries, showing that the Gospels were
widely known, diligently studied and treated with the utmost reverence throughout the Christian world. Within one
century following the death of the Apostles, the Gospels
were in practical use in all the churches. Wherever Christians assembled for the celebration of the Holy Mysteries,
selections from the Gospels were read. They constituted the
basis for the instructions and sermons preached to the wor-
shippers.

Is it believable that the Apostles or their successors, who
gave their lives to testify to the truth of all the teachings of
the Gospels, would have permitted a series of forged documents to be palmed off as the inspired word of God? Is it
credible that Jewish converts, so jealous of the authority of
their own Old Testament, would have accepted without
question such forgeries? Is it likely that the Gentiles, so
many of whom were philosophers, scholars, and men of
culture, would have accepted a Gospel which inculcated
penance and self-denial in place of sensual gratification without previously assuring themselves of the genuineness of
such a Gospel?

Is it possible that pagan philosophers and heretics, seeking
to refute the Gospel teachings, would have neglected the
simplest and easiest way of all, namely, that of showing that
the Gospels themselves were forgeries? Are we to believe
that the faithful, at a time when being a Christian involved
the danger of being martyred for one's belief, would all have
been ready and willing to lay down their lives for the foist-
ing of an impious fraud upon their children? To raise these

questions is to answer them. Either the Gospels are genuine, authentic records of the life and teachings of Jesus or all Christianity is reduced to a series of ridiculous absurdities—a conclusion which does violence alike to nineteen hundred years of human history and to the dictates of human reason.

The existence and use of the Gospels in the earliest days of the Church is proven beyond a shadow of doubt by the Didache, the Epistle of Barnabas, Ignatius, Clement of Rome, Polycarp, the Shepherd of Hermes, Papias of Hierapolis, Aristides, the Diatessaron of Tatian, Justin, Irenaeus, the Muratorian Fragment, as well as by the writings of the heretics Basilides, Valentine, Heracleon and Marcion.

The custom of reading the Gospels as Divine Service is explicitly mentioned by St. Justin Martyr about the middle of the second century. In 441 the First Council of Orange ordered the Gospel to be read after the Epistle and before the Offertory for the benefit of the catechumens who had to leave before the Eucharistic service began. In the early Church the book of the Gospels was carried in procession to the altar before Mass. The liturgical rite of incensing the Gospel book is very ancient, the incense signifying the "good odor of Christ." For many centuries the faithful made the Sign of the Cross at the end as well as at the beginning of the Gospel. Formerly all the clergy present were accustomed to kiss the book of the Gospels, while now only the celebrant does so, saying: "By the words of the Gospel may our sins be blotted out."

The Gospel of Matthew

Let us now look at the external evidence of the authenticity of each of the Gospels. We shall begin with the first Gospel, that of St. Matthew. The classic text covering the authorship of the first Gospel as well as of the other three is from St. Irenaeus. Born in the first half of the second century in Asia Minor, Irenaeus was a widely traveled man, familiar with the territory from Asia Minor to France. His writings reveal an inquiring type of mind and historical sense. He died about 202. He writes as follows: "Matthew published his Gospel among the Hebrews in their own language, while Peter and Paul were preaching and founding the Church in Rome. After their departure (death?) Mark, the disciple and interpreter of Peter, also transmitted to us in writing those things which Peter had preached; and Luke, the attendant of Paul, recorded in a book the Gospel which Paul had declared. Afterwards John, the disciple of the Lord, who also reclined on his bosom, published his Gospel, while staying at Ephesus in Asia." [2]

Papias, Bishop of Hierapolis in Phrygia, a friend of Polycarp and the last disciple of St. John, testifies: "Matthew wrote the Oracles (Logia) of the Lord in the Hebrew language; but everyone interpreted them as best as he could." [3] By the term *Logia* (Oracles) Papias does not mean a mere collection of the utterances of the Saviour, but a work which is substantially identical with the Gospel of Matthew. The expressions, "Logia of the Lord" and "words and works of the Lord," are employed synonymously by Papias, as is evident from his remark about St. Luke. It was in this sense that St. Irenaeus understood him, as is clear from the quotation of his already presented.

Similar is the testimony of Origen, who died 232: "Matthew published the Gospel for the faithful from Judaism in the tongue of the Hebrews." [4] Eusebius records for all posterity the testimony of the Fathers and writers of the early Church concerning the authorship of the first Gospel in the

---

[2] Eusebius, *Hist. Eccl.* V. 8, 2–4

[3] Eusebius, *op. cit.*, III, 39, 16: "Ματθαῖος . . . Ἑβραΐδι διαλέκτῳ τὰ λόγια συνετάξατο."

[4] Eusebius, *op. cit.*, VI, 25, 4

following words: "Matthew, who had at first preached to the Hebrews, when he was about to go to other peoples, committed his Gospel to writing in his native tongue, and thus compensated those whom he was obliged to leave for the loss of his presence." [5]

St. Jerome, the great Biblical scholar of the early Church, likewise bears witness to this truth.[6] The Aramaic Gospel of Matthew was certainly written before the destruction of Jerusalem. While it is impossible to fix the precise date, the most probable one is A.D. 42–50, the writing being done in Palestine.

The Gospel of Mark

Mark, the author of the second Gospel, is disclosed to us in the Scriptures as the cousin of Barnabas and the companion and disciple of Peter. Writing to the Colossians, Paul sends greetings from "Aristarchus, my fellow-prisoner, and from Mark, the cousin german of Barnabas, touching whom you have received commandments; if he come unto you, receive him; and Jesus, that is called Justus: who are of the circumcision: these only are my helpers in the kingdom of God, who have been a comfort to me." [7]

After the release of St. Paul, probably in 63, St. Peter claimed the services of Mark. It was to the home of Mark that St. Peter went after his own miraculous deliverance from prison. In his First Epistle he sends greetings from Rome in the name of his "son Mark." [8] Upon being imprisoned a second time in Rome, St. Paul desired to have the faithful companion of his first captivity with him again.

---

[5] Eusebius, *op. cit.*, III, 24, 6: "Ματθαῖος ἐν τοῖς Ἑβραίοις τῇ ἰδίᾳ διαλέκτῳ καὶ γραφὴν ἐξήνεγκεν."

[6] *De Vir. Ill.*, III

[7] *Col.* 4:10–11

[8] 1 *Pet.* 5:13

"Take Mark," he writes to Timothy, "and bring him with thee (to Rome), for he is profitable to me for the ministry." [9] The early Fathers of the Church commonly refer to Mark as the disciple and interpreter of St. Peter.

The historical evidence of St. Mark's authorship of the second Gospel is overwhelming. The earliest witness is Papias, Bishop of Hierapolis and disciple of St. John. When Papias made inquiries of St. John about Mark, the aged Apostle replied: "Mark, Peter's interpreter, wrote down what the Lord had said or done—so far as he remembered it—accurately, but not in order. For he had neither heard the Lord nor followed Him, but later, as I said, he was a follower of Peter, who gave such instructions as circumstances required, and not an orderly account of the Lord's words. Hence Mark was not at fault in writing some things simply as he remembered them. For his one care was to omit nothing that he had heard, and to speak truthfully thereon." [10]

This explicit testimony is further confirmed by St. Irenaeus, a disciple of St. Polycarp of Smyrna and later Bishop of Lyons, whom we have already quoted on this point. An interesting light is thrown on the origin of St. Mark's Gospel by Clement of Alexandria, head of the famous Catechetical School of that city toward the close of the second century. "When Peter had preached the word in Rome," he says, "many there besought Mark, who had followed him of old and remembered his words, to write down what he had said; accordingly Mark composed the Gospel, and gave it to those who had made the request of him, and Peter, knowing of it, neither hindered nor encouraged him." [11]

[9] 2 *Tim.* 4:11
[10] Eusebius, *Hist. Eccl.*, III, 39, 4
[11] Eusebius, *Hist. Eccl.*, VI, 14

In his *Prologue to Matthew*, St. Jerome states that "Mark, the interpreter of Peter and the first bishop of Alexandria, who did not indeed see the Lord, narrated of the things which he had heard his master preach. . . . Asked to Rome by the brethren he wrote a short gospel." [12] In these words of St. Jerome there is mirrored the unanimous voice of the Fathers and writers of the early Church and of a tradition which goes back to the Apostolic period. Harnack places the composition of the Gospel in the period A.D. 65–70

The Gospel of Luke

The author of the third Gospel and of the *Acts of the Apostles* was a companion and disciple of St. Paul. Writing during his second imprisonment to Timothy, St. Paul says: "Luke alone is with me." Ancient tradition unanimously ascribes this Gospel to the "beloved physician, Luke." St. Irenaeus thus bears witness: "Luke, the follower of Paul, wrote down the latter's Gospel—preaching in a book." [13]

In the seventeenth century Ludovico Muratori discovered in the Ambrosian Library in Milan a canon or list of books of the New Testament. While its author is unknown, scholars are agreed that it goes back to about 170. The notes attached to each of the books are of the highest importance. Concerning the third Gospel, the canon, known as the Muratorian Canon, affirms: "Luke, the physician, composed a Gospel in the name of Paul and in accordance with his teaching." The authorship is further confirmed by Tertullian (*Adv. Marc.*, IV, 5), Origen (*Hom.* I, *in Luc.*), Clement of Alexandria (*Strom.*, I, 21), and by Jerome (*De Vir. Ill*,

---

[12] "*Secundus Marcus, interpres apostoli Petri et alexandrinae ecclesiae primus episcopus, . . . ea quae magistrum audierat praedicantem iuxta fidem magis gestorum narravit quam ordinem. . . Rogatus Romae a fratribus breve scripsit evangelium.*"

[13] Eusebius, *op. cit.*, V, 8, 3

VII). Thus Origen mentions the Gospel of Luke among the four "which alone," says he, "are admitted without dispute by the universal Church."

The Gospel itself confirms in a striking manner the witness of tradition. Throughout this Gospel we see the hand of a disciple of St. Paul in style, in vocabulary—eighty-four words are found in Luke and Paul only—in sentence structure and especially in the conception of Christ's mission on earth. In the Epistles of Paul and in the Gospel of his disciple, the kingdom of God is world-wide. Jews and Gentiles, publicans and sinners, rich and poor, bond and free, are all called. "God will have all men to be saved, and to come to a knowledge of the truth," [14] epitomizes the message of both Luke and Paul.

Internal Evidence of Genuineness of Synoptics

Let us now glance at the internal evidence of the genuineness of the Synoptics. A careful study of the texts shows that the writers were Jews, and were contemporaries, or in close touch with contemporaries, of the events described. The texts contain nothing contrary to the laws, usages, institution, tastes, and customs of the time in which they were composed. They mirror the religious and social conditions then prevailing in Palestine with accuracy and precise detail.

The writers were Jews. The Gospel of St. Matthew was originally written in Aramaic, the language of the country where our Lord lived. The other three were written in the colloquial Greek of the period, but show marked traces of Hebrew idiom. Scholars are agreed that this popular form of the Greek language was used as a literary medium by Jews during the first century of the Christian era, but not subsequently. Furthermore the authors display no acquaint-

14 *1 Tim.* 2:4

ance with Greek philosophy or literature, but intimate familiarity with the religion and customs of the Jewish people.

That the authors were eye-witnesses of the events which they describe, or were in close touch with them, is evident from the vividness of the accounts and from the wealth of detail. Moreover their countless references to topography and to the political, social, and religious conditions of Palestine at the time of Christ, are flawless. Such an intimate close-up of those conditions, peculiarly complicated and transient, could not have been given by a stranger to Palestine or by a later writer.

For example, the government of Palestine at that time was administered by a curious medley of elements. There were Roman officials and native officials, while at the same time, the Sanhedrin, the great religious council of Jewish judges, still insisted on carrying out its functions, though this spelled almost incessant friction with the civil authorities. Roman money was used in commerce, taxes were paid in Greek money, while dues to the Temple were paid in Jewish money. This complicated pattern of Jewish, Grecian, and Roman elements is vividly portrayed in all its detail in the Gospels, thus stamping the authors as contemporaries of the events described.

"In the first three gospels," observes Weinel, "so much local colouring attaches to the figure of Christ, and His native language, Aramaic, is everywhere so easily traced, that it would have been absolutely impossible for an Italian Greek of the second century to invent such a personality. Jesus is at home in Galilee and in real life, not at the Emperor's court, not in Rome during the second century, and not in the brain of some Hellenistic poet. His native place is near the sea, where the fishermen let down their nets and on the mountains, where the lilies blossom and the wind rustles through the corn in the evening, and the little birds

in the thickets sing the praise of their Creator; there Jesus
was at home, there He really lived." [15]

The Gospel of John

Let us turn now from the Synoptics to the fourth Gospel
which differs so markedly in style and in content from the
first three.

It has been called the "universal Gospel" because of its
profound appeal to all humanity. It brings peace and comfort to the peasants in their humble cottages while at the
same time it grips the minds of the greatest philosophers and
theologians with its sublime conceptions. "I meditate on the
Scriptures," declared the poet Wordsworth, "especially the
Gospel of St. John, and my creed rises up of itself with the
ease of an exhilaration, yet a fabric of adamant."

On the one hand, it stresses the relation of the individual
to the Saviour and to God. On the other, it stresses institu-
tional religion, with the establishment of a Church apart
from the world, with emphasis on its unity, a training of the
disciples to carry on their Master's work of forgiveness and
of shepherding His sheep with spiritual birth and nourishment provided by the sacraments. "The book is fighting,"
observes von Hügel, "more consciously than the Synoptics
for that inalienable idea of all deepest religion—unity even
external and corporate among all believers." [16]

In short, the fourth Gospel is a singular combination of
simplicity of style and thought with penetrating philosophic
insight and mystical depth. At times the author achieves
heights of sublimity of thought and expression which would
do justice to the greatest of speculative philosophers. The

[15] Weinel, *Jesus in the Nineteenth Century*, 1903
[16] "The Gospel According to St. John," in *A New Commentary on
Holy Scripture*, edited by Bishop Charles Gore, Macmillan Co., N.Y.,
1928, p. 240

discourses of our Lord are all presented in a solemn, sustained and majestic style which is in sharp contrast to the simple, vivid manner of speech which the Synoptics picture Him as using with the plain people of Galilee.

Every thoughtful reader of the fourth Gospel finds three questions arising in his mind: (1) Why is this Gospel so different from the first three? (2) Is a Gospel of such philosophic depth and majesty of diction the work of the "beloved Disciple" or of a philosopher of a later generation? (3) Are the discourses of Jesus recorded as they were delivered by Him or do they mirror chiefly the author's own reflections upon the original words of Jesus? These are the questions which constitute the Johannine problem. Thousands of books have been written about it and numerous speculative theories have been brought forth. In the nineteenth century the pendulum swung to far-fetched extremes with fancy substituted for fact. Under the stress of continued scientific research, the pendulum has now swung back to reinforce virtually all along the line the verdict of ancient Christian tradition. Dispassionate scholarly research enables us to provide satisfactory answers, we think, to the three preceding questions.

Keys to Understanding Differences

The purpose, which the author of the fourth Gospel had in mind, is explicitly stated in the concluding verses of the twentieth chapter: "Many other signs also did Jesus in the sight of the disciples, that are not written in this book; but these are written, that ye may believe that Jesus is the Christ, the Son of God, and that, believing, ye may have life in his name." Since the author was familiar with the first three Gospels, he would naturally wish to record such "signs" as bore directly on the divine Sonship of Christ and to reproduce only such miracles and discourses as were not already presented by the Synoptics. This is the key to the understanding of the selection and organization of his material—all designed for the achievement of his distinctive end. For this reason he reproduces the miracles of the multiplication of the loaves and the walking upon the sea, since they form the introduction to the supremely important discourse on the Holy Eucharist which was omitted by the other Evangelists.

So much for the difference in his subject matter. Now in regard to the difference of style in which the Saviour's discourses are presented. The Synoptics present Christ's ministry in Galilee. Here the simple, unlettered country folk required a simple, vivid discourse, abounding with concrete illustrations and parables. In Jerusalem, where the author of the fourth Gospel so frequently depicts Jesus, it was different. Here our Lord was constantly engaged in controversy with the theologically trained Scribes and Pharisees and doctors of the law. In this difference of audience is found the key to the understanding of the change of style, diction and content in His discourses.

Moreover it must be remembered that the author, faithful to his avowed purpose, chooses for the most part only such portions of our Lord's discourses as bear directly upon His divinity. Presenting this teaching to a Jerusalem audience, abounding with Scribes and Pharisees, would fittingly call for a sustained solemnity of language. The fourth Gospel, with its greater profundities of thought and its greater majesty of language, may be viewed as carrying the simple instructions of the Synoptics to a higher and more advanced stage. Christ's net must catch not only the simple peasants of Galilee but the proud Scribes and Pharisees of Jerusalem as well.

While the difference in the audiences to whom Christ

speaks in the Synoptics and in the fourth Gospel explains to a certain extent the difference in form, language and style, it is to be admitted with all candor that the respective author's own style enters into and colors all that he writes. No one contends that the Master's discourses are reproduced in their entirety, word for word, in modern stenographic form. The brevity of the recorded sermons indicates that the leading ideas of much longer speeches are presented in greatly condensed form.

The literary canons of the time allowed much greater freedom in reporting a discourse than obtains today. "At that time," observes Cardinal Newman, "the third person was not so commonly used in history as now. When a reporter gives one of Gladstone's speeches, if he uses the first person, I understand not only the matter, but the style, the words to be Gladstone's; when the third, I consider the style, etc., to be the reporter's own. But in ancient times this distinction was not made. Thucydides uses the dramatic method, yet Spartan and Athenian speak in Thucydidean Greek. And so every clause of Our Lord's speeches in St. John may be St. John's Greek, yet every clause may contain the matter which Our Lord spoke in Aramaic. Again, St. John might and did select or condense (as being inspired for that purpose) the matter of our Lord's discourses, as that with Nicodemus, and thereby the wording might be St. John's, though the matter might still be Our Lord's." [17]

External Evidence of Authorship

The most ancient tradition of the Church ascribes the fourth Gospel to St. John the Apostle. Most impressive is the testimony of Irenaeus, a disciple of Polycarp, who was a disciple of St. John himself. "Then, (i.e., after the other

[17] Quoted by W. S. Reilly, *The Gospel According to St. John*, p. xxxvi

three Gospels) John, the disciple of the Lord, who also leaned on His breast, himself published also a Gospel, while he was at Ephesus in Asia." [18] The testimony of Irenaeus is confirmed by Theophilus, Bishop of Antioch (168 A.D.), who quotes the fourth Gospel as "inspired Scripture" and ascribes it to John.[19]

Of unusual significance is the testimony of the learned Clement of Alexandria, who, writing at the end of the second century, tells us that "John, perceiving that the other Evangelists had set forth the human side of the Person of Jesus, at the instance of His disciples composed a spiritual Gospel." [20] He styles it spiritual ($\pi\nu\epsilon\upsilon\mu\alpha\tau\iota\kappa\grave{o}\nu$) because of its insistence on the divine Sonship of Jesus. Similar is the testimony of Ignatius in numerous places, of Justin,[21] and of the ancient Muratorian Canon.

Back of these specific witnesses is a tradition dating from the second century and stretching from Antioch and Ephesus in the Eastern Mediterranean area over Carthage and Alexandria in Africa to Rome and Lyons in Europe that affirms the fourth Gospel to be the work of John the Apostle. All the early manuscripts and versions ascribe it to him. Among the witnesses to his authorship are men close to him personally or in time, while others are closely associated with the section of Asia Minor where the Gospel was written. It is the unanimous verdict of scholars that the Gospel was written *after* the destruction of Jerusalem, probably toward the close of the first century. Irenaeus reports that it was written at Ephesus.

[18] Eusebius, *Hist. Eccl.* V, 8, 2–4
[19] *Apology to Autolycus*, II, 22
[20] Eusebius, *Hist. Eccl.* VI, 14, 7
[21] *I Apol.* LXI, Dial LXXXVIII

Internal Evidence of Authorship

The internal evidence strongly supports the external. The minute details reported by the writer and his complete familiarity with Jewish customs and the conditions then prevailing in Palestine stamp him as an eye-witness and a Jew of Palestine. The intimate details within the Apostolic College, especially the description of the Last Supper, show that the writer must have been one of the Apostles. While the author writes in Greek, the mode of thought is that of a Palestinian Jew—as John the Apostle was—and in some instances the construction is Aramaic.

The writer, moreover, manifests an intimate familiarity with Palestine. Thus he speaks of Cana as Cana in Galilee (II: 1; IV: 46) to distinguish it from another village of the same name in near-by Syria. He shows a first-hand acquaintance with the villages around the lake of Genesareth, the size of the lake, the mountain that borders it on the northeast (VI: 3, 15). He is aware that Ennon near Salim was a place which afforded plenty of water for John the Baptist to use in baptizing (III: 23). This very place was rediscovered in 1892.

These and many other details which the writer mentions in a casual, offhand manner show he is speaking as an eye-witness of the events which he describes. "As one reads the Gospel and the accompanying Epistle," observes Professor Charles Harris, "the conviction becomes irresistible that the author in all sincerity lays the greatest stress upon his having been an eyewitness of what he records; and this implies that he was one of the innermost circle of disciples, and therefore an Apostle, and also John the son of Zebedee." [22]

[22] *A New Commentary on Holy Scripture*, edited by Bishop Charles Gore, Macmillan Co., N.Y., 1928, p. 76

The frequent reference to an anonymous disciple or "the disciple whom Jesus loved," "who rested on His breast," leads to the inference that the author of the Gospel is this disciple. The correctness of that inference is explicitly confirmed by the author in the second to the last verse in his Gospel, wherein he states: "This is that disciple who giveth testimony of these things, and hath written these things; and we know that his testimony is true." Then frankly admitting that his narrative gives only a partial account of the life of Christ, the author ends his Gospel: "But there are also many other things which Jesus did; which, if they were written everyone, the world itself, I think, would not be able to contain the books that should be written."

The external and internal evidence, harmonizing so perfectly, constitute solid historical ground for the conclusion that the fourth Gospel is the work of St. John the Apostle. Such is the unbroken tradition of the Church from the earliest days down to the present time. That traditional belief has been powerfully reënforced and substantiated by the findings of modern Biblical research.

In closing this discussion of the authenticity of the Gospels, we present the impressive testimony of three Scriptural scholars. The first is Dr. J. P. Arendzen, who writes: "The Gospels rank among the best attested works of the Graeco-Roman world. They are better attested than the works of Pindar, or Xenophon, or Horace; of Pliny, Polybius, or Suetonius; of Terence or Plautus, Sophocles or Euripides, or of a score of others, the genuineness and authenticity of whose writings are cheerfully accepted by every classical scholar in the world. For instance: Is there a Greek historian more unquestionably received, more absolutely believed, more respected as an utterly reliable source of information than Thucydides? Yet, the first allusion to Thucydides as author of his works occurs some two hundred and twenty years after his death, in the pages of another historian called Polybius!" [23]

Similar is the conclusion reached by Renan: "In fine, I admit as authentic the four canonical Gospels. All, according to my view, go back to the first century." [24] Of special significance is the conclusion reached after a lifetime of research by Adolf Harnack of Berlin, whose outstanding scholarship is acknowledged by all: "All competent men must finally admit that the chronological order, according to which tradition has arranged the old monuments and records of Christianity, is quite accurate in its main lines, and consequently compels the historian to reject as false all hypotheses that have been devised in opposition to that order." [25]

In this connection it is well to point out that, while we have presented the historical evidence, overwhelming in its massive cogency, of the authenticity of the four Gospels, this would not strictly be required to establish their historic validity as channels of the Christian revelation. All that the latter would actually demand would be that the writers, whoever they were, were accepted by their contemporaries as competent and trustworthy reporters of the teachings of Christ and of the Apostolic Church. No student of the Scriptures, no matter how liberal or radical in his views, will hesitate in acknowledging the competency and the trustworthiness of the authors of the four Gospels. Their acceptance at so early a date by all the colonies of the infant Church is eloquent and convincing testimony that the writers were recognized as competent and trustworthy authorities on the life and teachings of Christ. As a matter of fact, however, we are able, as has been shown, to do more—to establish

[23] The Gospels—Fact, Myth, or Legend? Sands, London, 1923, p. 27
[24] Devivier-Sasia, Christian Apologetics, J. F. Wagner, Inc., N.Y., 1924, Vol. I, p. 345
[25] Devivier-Sasia, op. cit., Vol. I, p. 340

the authors of the Gospels to be none other than the Evangelists Matthew, Mark, Luke and John.

Well Informed and Truthful

Having demonstrated the authenticity of the Gospels, we come now to a consideration of the second condition necessary for the trustworthiness of a record of past events, namely, that the writer be reliable in the sense that he is well informed and truthful. It is obvious that since two of the Evangelists, Matthew and John, were Apostles, they were admirably situated to present eye-witness testimony concerning the life and teachings of their Master. The other two, Mark and Luke, were companions and disciples of the Apostles.

Over a long period Mark was the disciple and secretary of Peter, putting down in writing the teachings of his master. He was likewise in close touch with Paul at various intervals. He was with both Peter and Paul in Rome before their death. He was converted at Jerusalem in the first decade of the Church and was the cousin and companion of Barnabas. Mark's mother was a prominent member of the infant Church in Jerusalem. In her home Peter found refuge after he was released from prison in the year 42–43 A.D. Traveling with Peter, Paul, and later with Barnabas alone, Mark was in intimate personal touch with the Christian colonies in Jerusalem, Palestine, Rome and Asia Minor.

Luke was the companion and disciple of Paul. The latter was converted not later than 35 A.D. and made five visits to Jerusalem where he conferred with Peter and James. Intimately associated with Barnabas, Paul was in the closest personal touch with many of the earliest Christian communities, upon whom he left, by his preaching and writing, a lasting mark. In addition to his association with Paul, Luke also had contact with Mark at Rome. About the year 57, he dwelt in Jerusalem with Mnason, a disciple of our Lord, and had association there with the Apostle James. For a time he lodged in Caesarea with Philip, one of the seven who were chosen deacons in 33 A.D. It is significant that Luke mentions explicitly in the beginning of his Gospel that he was in touch with those "who from the beginning were eyewitnesses and ministers of the word" and that he "diligently attained to all things from the beginning."

It is evident, then, that the authors of the four Gospels were either eyewitnesses themselves or were in close and prolonged association with eyewitnesses. They wrote for a generation, hundreds and thousands of whom had seen and heard Christ in the flesh, and who would have quickly pounced upon any inaccuracy in the narrative. The Gospels are not therefore the crystallization of late traditions. They are the records of events which they either witnessed or learned from witnesses. Is there any ancient work of secular history which rests so solidly upon the concordant testimony of so many competent eyewitnesses and contemporaries as do the Gospels? History knows of none. No one disputes that Caesar was the author of the Commentaries on the Gallic Wars. Yet what is the evidence for it? Merely two scant references about a hundred years later in the writings of Plutarch and Suetonius.

The authors of the Gospels not only knew the facts but they reported them truthfully as well. They could have had no motive to engage in a conspiracy to foist a monstrous falsehood upon mankind. Men do not endure hardship, suffer persecution, and risk death for the spreading of a lie that brings them nothing but hardship in this world and eternal damnation in the next. Their holy lives and their miracles testify to their divine ambassadorship and to their truthfulness in recording the deeds and utterances of their divine Master. That the writers of the Gospels were sincere and truthful is denied by no Scriptural scholar, radical, liberal or conservative.

That the Evangelists wrote accurately and truthfully can be verified moreover by reference to contemporary historical documents. The findings of modern historical, archeological, and ethnological research have enabled us to reconstruct with amazing accuracy and vividness the life, customs, laws and culture of the peoples among whom Christ lived and taught. That period represented the flood time of the great Greco-Roman civilization. A mass of historical and literary writings of that period have come down to us and have been studied with meticulous care and accuracy. So vivid is the light which modern scientific research has thrown upon the life and customs of Palestine at the time of our Lord that we probably know more about its minute details than we do of the life and culture of our own American colonies prior to the Revolution.

The findings of research corroborate all along the line the record of events mentioned in the Gospels. It is true that very slight discrepancies appear at some times in the Gospel narratives. But these can be harmonized by careful study. If the Evangelists had been impostors, however, conspiring to deceive mankind, they would have avoided even the appearance of such divergences.

Then there is the character of Christ. That character is so original, so noble, so lovable, so tragic, so surpassingly beautiful, that viewed merely as an artistic creation, it was beyond the inventive capacity of men such as the Evangelists. That character ran, moreover, against the grain of their preconceived image of the Messias. The Jews of their day—and the Evangelists were Jews—thought of the Messias as coming to restore the kingdom of David. They pictured that kingdom, not as a spiritual kingdom, but as a temporal one. How different is the Christ of the Gospels from the Messias of their expectation. Sticking to the facts of His life, the Evangelists are compelled to portray a char-acter radically different in many respects from that which they had cherished in their Messianic expectations. They portray a Christ who teaches meekness, humility, the love even of one's enemies, and who leads a life of poverty and humiliation culminating in the ignominious death upon Calvary's Cross.

This truth has been strikingly put by J. J. Rousseau. "Consider," he says, "the gentleness of Jesus, the purity of His morals, the persuasiveness of His teaching. How lofty His principles! What wisdom in His words! How oppor-tune, frank and direct His answers! How can the Gospel history be an invention? My friend, forgeries are not of this kind, and the acts of Socrates, which no one doubts, are not so well attested as the acts of Christ. Besides, this only in-creases the difficulty. Far more inconceivable is it that several men should have combined to fabricate this book than that there should have been one living original whom they de-scribed. No Jewish author could have fabricated the tone or moral teaching of the Evangelists. So powerful, over-whelming, and inimitable is the impress of truth stamped upon the gospel, that its inventor would be a greater marvel than its hero." [26]

It is the character of Christ, as portrayed in the Gospels, that stamps them in the judgment of Harnack with a seal of indisputable authenticity. Listen to his testimony, both eloquent and profound: "Jesus Christ had been their life-experience, and in Him they had found the Messias. They were convinced that God had made Him Wisdom and Righteousness, Sanctification and Redemption. No hope but found its security in Him, no exalted thought but found in

[26] Arendzen, *op. cit.*, p. 4

Him a living reality. Hence they brought to Him all they possessed. He was all that the human mind could conceive as most High. Within two generations of His death all has been said of Him whatsoever men are capable of predicating of any one. Yea, even more, they actually experienced Him and knew Him as the Everlasting One, as the Lord of the World and as the energizing principle of the life of their own souls. . . . Only now after Christ had come, were they certain of the Resurrection and of Eternal Life, and thus the sorrows of this world disappeared as a cloud is dissolved by the sun, and the remainder of their earthly life was light as day. This set of facts ushers the story of the Gospel into this world, and is at the same time the highest thing and the most unique in kind which meets us in the history of Christian doctrine. This great fact is as it were its seal, and makes this history different from the history of any other of the world's religions." [26]

The Integrity of the Gospels

We come now to consider the integrity of the Gospels, in the sense that they have come down to us substantially intact. We begin by pointing out the deep attachment of the early Christians to the Gospel texts. They were read aloud in the churches, sung in the liturgies, committed to memory, and treasured in their hearts. Holding fast to the four Gospels, the infant Church rejected all others. Gospels ascribed to St. Peter, St. James, and St. Thomas were in circulation in the sub-apostolic age, but were suppressed as spurious.

With jealous care, the early Christians guarded their spiritual patrimony. Any attempt to introduce a substantial change in the text on the part of Christian, Jew, heretic, or pagan would have provoked instant and violent protests. Even trifling changes aroused opposition and brought rebukes. Thus Sozomenes tells us that Bishop Spiridion openly rebuked a fellow-bishop who, in quoting a text, substituted another word having the same meaning as the original, but which appeared more elegant.

It was with difficulty that Pope Damasus prevailed upon St. Jerome to revise the Latin version of the Bible, because of the latter's fear that he would be regarded by the people as a corrupter of the text, should they find some alterations.[27] That St. Jerome's fear was not unfounded was evidenced by a letter which St. Augustine wrote to him. "A bishop of our province," wrote the saint, "having begun to read your translation of the Bible in his church, came to a passage of the prophet Jonas, which you have translated differently from what was known to the memory and ears of every one, and sung during many generations. Thereupon a great tumult arose among the people, caused principally by the Greeks, who called out that the text was falsified. . . . The bishop, not to remain without a flock, after this great danger, was obliged to correct the passage as if it were a fault." [28] What verbal change aroused this protest? St. Jerome had used the word "ivy" for "gourd." The incident illustrates the jealous tenacity with which the early Christians clung to the exact text of the Scriptures.

We do not wish to imply from the foregoing, however, that in the many intervening centuries in which the Gospels have been copied thousands of times and translated into all known languages, that different readings, called *variants*, have not appeared. What has happened to all ancient manuscripts, which have been copied hundreds of times, has likewise happened to the Scriptures. Different readings of the works of Horace have furnished material for three large volumes. No book has been copied, translated, annotated,

[27] *Praefat. ad Evang. ad Dam.*
[28] *Epist.* 71, *ad Hieron.*

so frequently as the book of the Gospels. It was inevitable that slight divergencies in the thousands of copies would appear in the course of the centuries. Were we to expect God to work a continuous series of miracles to preserve the Gospels from a certain liability to changes in the phraseology of the text, when such changes do not alter the substantial meaning or message of the sacred books? By no means. Man has the power to detect and correct his own mistakes. Textual criticism by carefully studying the variants of the texts can generally eliminate the defective reading and thus restore the primitive text. In other words, the substantial tenor of the sacred text has not been altered and the good tidings of divine revelation have come down to us in all their essential fullness, even though doubt or obscurity may cloud here or there a part of the phraseology or passage in the text.

Let us look a little more closely into the abundant material by means of which Scriptural scholars arrive at the primitive text of the Gospel manuscripts and demonstrate their integrity. The first and most striking aspect of all the Gospel manuscripts, which have come down to us, is their substantial uniformity. There are nearly thirteen hundred manuscripts in Greek alone, besides many in other languages. Among the earliest and most important are the Vatican manuscript at Rome and the Sinaitic at Leningrad, both of the fourth century; the Alexandrian at London and the Codex *Ephraemi rescriptus* at Paris, of the fifth century; and the Codex Bezae at Cambridge, England, of the fifth or sixth century. As the Gospels were probably written on papyrus which is perishable, the originals must have worn out from frequent use in the early Church. The use of copies in the absence of the originals is true likewise in regard to the great classics of ancient times. Thus the earliest manuscript of Vergil, in the Vatican Library, dates from the fourth century A.D., while the earliest copy of Homer's *Iliad,* in the Ambrosian Library at Milan, dates back only to the fifth century.

The extant manuscripts of the Gospels agree as to text, and carry us back to the fourth century. This is about three centuries after the originals were written. How are we to bridge that gap? We can do so by going to the translations of the Gospels in other languages, the Syriac and the Latin versions dating back to the second century. Upon examining these, we find all in substantial agreement.

Moreover we can further check the text of the Gospel manuscripts through actual quotations therefrom in the writings of the Fathers of the infant Church. So numerous are these quotations that if all the manuscripts and translations of the Gospels were lost, it would be possible to reconstruct virtually all the text of the Gospels from the vast multitude of quotations in the early Patristic literature. The writings of Origen, Clement of Alexandria, Irenaeus, Tertullian and Cyprian, who were active in the second half of the second century and in the first half of the third, constitute a mine of direct quotations. For instance, in the writings of Irenaeus, we find besides the names of the four Evangelists, 234 texts quoted from Matthew, 13 from Mark, 125 from Luke, and 94 from John. In addition, his writings present an analysis of the Gospel of Luke which corresponds exactly with the third Gospel as it has come down to us. In the writings of Tertullian, who was active in Proconsular Africa, we encounter not less than 925 texts taken from the Gospels.

The discourses and writings of Justin, Papias, and Marcion, active around the middle of the second century, abound in quotations. We find additional quotations in still earlier Christian literature, such as the Second Epistle of Clement, the Epistle of Barnabas, the so-called Gospel of Peter, the

Teaching of the Twelve Apostles, the Pastor of Hermes, and the writings of Sts. Polycarp, Ignatius, and Clement, which date back from the middle of the second century into the fourth quarter of the first.

The manuscripts, translations, and quotations from the writers and Fathers of the early Church are in textual agreement and constitute such an impressive bulk of converging and cumulative evidence as to bring conviction to all. Scholars of different schools of thought, radical, liberal, and conservative, find themselves in agreement, except in regard to a rare phrase, or sentence, or passage, which material would constitute only about one to two percent of the entire text. Indeed, in regard to the whole New Testament, Alfred Durand states that "no serious doubts exist except concerning about one-sixtieth of the contents of the New Testament. Perhaps even the number of passages of which the authenticity has not yet had a sufficient critical demonstration does not exceed twelve, at least as regards substantial alterations." [29]

We may conclude this discussion of the integrity of the Gospels with the observation of the great Scriptural scholar, Cardinal Wiseman: "Though every available source of information has been resorted to: though all the interpretations and explanations of scriptural texts given by the Fathers of the first ten centuries, as well as the versions of nearly all languages, the Arabian, the Syrian, the Coptic, the Armenian, the Ethiopian, have been consulted, with the purpose of ascertaining the true meaning of those texts; though the manuscript copies of all countries and of all times, from the sixteenth century up to the third, have been diligently scrutinized by a multitude of learned scholars, anxious to seize on their hidden treasures; though many critics, after having exhausted the riches of Western lore,

[29] *Catholic Encyclopedia,* "New Testament," p. 534

traveled to distant countries in search of new testimonies; though they fathomed, as it is said of Scholz and Sebastiani, the depths of Mount Athos and the libraries of the desert of Egypt and Syria, yet, notwithstanding all these scrupulous researches of past records, they have not been able to discover one single version or copy, duly authenticated, that might throw even the shadow of a doubt on any passage, that, before all these minute investigations, was held as certain and decisive in favor of this or that part of sacred doctrine." [30] Hence we are forced to conclude that the historical value of the Gospels cannot be questioned by anyone familiar with the evidence.

Viewed simply as historical documents, the Gospels present in a trustworthy and reliable manner the revelation of Jesus Christ to mankind. They should be read and meditated upon daily by all who wish to grow in spiritual insight and in holiness of life. They should be reverenced and loved as constituting not only the heart of the greatest book in the world but also a most important part of the spiritual patrimony of mankind.

[30] *Oriental Studies,* Lecture 10. Quoted by Devivier-Sasia, *op. cit.,* pp. 344–345

CHAPTER XXX

THE DISTINCTIVE MESSAGE OF CHRIST

WE HAVE set forth the nature and purpose of divine revelation and the historical character of the documents embodying that revelation. What is the content of that revelation? That is best discovered by the careful reading of the New Testament, the greatest book in the world. To be unfamiliar with that masterpiece is to be spiritually illiterate. More than any other volume ever printed, it will repay daily reading. This is a practice which cannot be urged too strongly upon all who seek to grow in the knowledge and likeness of Jesus Christ.

While a detailed presentation of its great truths is beyond the scope of the present work, it is not out of place to conclude with a brief presentation of the distinctive message of Jesus, a message which runs like a thread of gold through all the pages of the New Testament. That message was preached in season and out of season by the divine Founder of the Christian faith who substituted for the old Mosaic law, "an eye for an eye and a tooth for a tooth," the new *law of love,* prompting the individual to do more than is required of him by strict justice.

After referring to the *lex talionis* just mentioned, Christ says: "But I say to you not to resist evil: but if one strike thee on thy right cheek, turn to him also the other. And if a man will contend with thee in judgment, and take away thy coat, let go thy cloak also unto him. And whosoever shall compel thee to go one mile, go with him two." [1] In the rendering of that superabundant service, more than the law of justice and equity could demand, in the rising above the merely human instinct to strike back, and in returning love for hatred, will be found one of the most important laws of the spiritual universe. In the measure in which individuals fulfill this law of surplus service, will be found the measure of the spiritual progress of mankind. It is the unfailing index of the race's progress in social altruism, the unerring gauge of the spiritual qualitativeness of human life.

The surplus that is rendered in helpful service, in kindliness, in love, is not lost but becomes part of the common spiritual treasury of the race. Like the Egyptian granary, filled at Joseph's order during the seven fat years, it tides mankind over the lean years of selfishness, war and spiritual famine. Like a mighty reservoir that holds the answer to the cry of all life in time of drouth, it rescues the race from extinction in periods of crass materialism and spiritual aridity, when man acts on the principle of "an eye for an eye," and measures his payments in terms of cold calculating justice, in which the dividends of generosity and love are conspicuously absent. Without that surplus, mankind but treads the weary treadmill of spiritual stand-pattism, stretching the status quo into the shadows of eternity, and anchoring the race in the bog of spiritual barrenness. It is the surplus in service, in kindliness, in love which constitutes the lifting power of the universe, the fulcrum which elevates human life from the lowly swamps of selfishness to the mountain peaks of magnanimity and nobility of character.

"Unprofitable Servants"

The insistence by Christ upon the necessity of doing more than is commanded if one is to achieve any marked spirit-

[1] *Mat.* 5:39–42

ual progress is brought out vividly in two further instances. After alluding to the servant who ploughed the field, fed the cattle, and performed nothing but the duties enjoined upon him, Christ turned to the disciples with the words: "So you also, when you shall have done all these things that are commanded you, say: We are unprofitable servants; we have done that which we ought to do." [2] The mere doing of what they "ought to do" established no claim to spiritual nobility or perfection of character.

They must do more than that. Only when the narrow channel of strict duty overflows with the surplus in generosity, in kindliness, in love, is there a contribution to the spiritual treasury of the race and a stimulus to its progress. Only when the *lex talionis* and the cold calculations of legalistic ethics are transcended in the surplus payments of a mighty and generous love that forgets the decimal points of strict justice, and pours itself out in torrents beyond all requirements, does one contribute to the spiritual dynamics which constitute the lifting power of the universe. Then and only then.

A second instance in which Christ emphasized the necessity of doing more than merely keep the commandments if one aspires to perfection, occurred during His encounter with the rich young man. In response to the query as to what he should do to enter into life, Christ tells him to keep the commandments. When the young man replies that he has done this from his youth, Christ declares: "One thing is wanting unto thee: go, sell whatsoever thou hast, and give to the poor, and thou shalt have treasure in heaven; and come, follow me." [3] It is to be noted here that the mark of Christ's discipleship is not the mere keeping of the commandments. It is the doing of the *more* than the law requires, the giving of

[2] *Luke* 17:10
[3] *Mark* 10:21

one's riches to the poor and the spending of one's life in the service of mankind.

The quality of doing more than is required is, then, the distinctive quality of the true Christian and the unfailing index of nobility of life. With his penetrating insight into human life, Shakespeare recognized this trait as the crown of the moral character. Thus in depicting the qualities of Desdemona in the ascending scale of their values, Iago places this as the crowning one, saying of her: "She is so free, so kind, so apt, so blessed a disposition, that she holds it a vice in her goodness not to do more than is requested." This is the attitude which Christ sought to make universal among His followers, and the distinctive mark of His discipleship —the attitude of regarding as a vice in one's goodness the failure to do more than is requested.

The men and women who have made the greatest contributions to human welfare, who have blazed new trails through ethical jungles, and have carved their names most deeply upon the grateful hearts of the race, are those who did not stop to count the cost in labor, in love, in sacrifice. They threw their lives upon the altar of mankind's progress, esteemed the sacrifice as naught, and regretted only that they had but one life to give.

"The men," observes Dr. Harry Emerson Fosdick, "who have struck humanity's life as the shaft of water strikes the turbine at Niagara, saying, 'Move,' have been men who knew that 'God does not always pay wages on a Saturday,' and so were willing to serve on through all hostility, to help the very humanity that cursed them while they blessed. The roll-call of the world's spiritual heroes reveals not a single one-mile man. For no man ever saved anybody, or served any great cause, or left any enduring impress who was not willing to forget indignities, bear no grudges, and, like Paul when the Jews had cast him out of their synagogues, had beaten, stoned, and all but killed him, say, 'I could wish my-self accursed for my brethren's sake, my kinsmen according to the flesh. . . . My heart's desire and prayer to God for Israel is that they may be saved.' The world's saviors have all, in one way or another, loved their enemies and done them good. All of saviorhood lies in the second mile." [4]

"Through the Black Face There Shines . . ."

Booker T. Washington, born in slavery and abandoned by a father whom he never saw, rising from slavery and lift-ing his people from a condition of intellectual, social and spiritual bondage, is an inspiring example of a man who did not stop to count the cost. When only ten years old, he was working in the coal mines of West Virginia, beginning at four A.M. and working till six P.M. for the princely sum of 25 cents a day. Seeing the number "18" on one of the barrels at the mine, his curiosity as to its meaning was aroused. Pro-curing a copy of Webster's Spelling Book, he mastered the mystery of the alphabet and learned to read. After getting as much education as a Negro could in those days, he came to Alabama to found the Tuskegee Institute. An appropria-tion of $2,000 had been granted by the State. But when he arrived, he found no land, no buildings, no pupils. Appealing to the legislature for additional funds to purchase land and erect buildings, he was opposed by a State Senator who publicly declared: "One Negro can go and hide behind a stump and whisper it to another. Negroes need no school-house."

For thirty-four years Booker T. Washington labored to make his dream of a great school for his people come true. With unflagging zeal he labored, begging for funds on his lecture tours, teaching, writing books, struggling against

[4] *The Second Mile*, Associated Press, N.Y.

frightful odds for the cause to which he had consecrated his life. On every hand he met racial prejudice and hatred. When Theodore Roosevelt received him at a luncheon at the White House, Southern Senators and Congressmen stormed in indignation, declaring the President had insulted the womanhood of the South, demanding an apology which, thanks to the courage of the President, was never forthcoming.

In the face of constant discrimination, social ostracism and scowling prejudice with the temptation to strike back ever present, Washington recalled the words of Christ: "The disciple is not above the Master. If they have persecuted me, they shall also persecute you." Rising above the human tendency to strike back, to return hate for hatred, Washington followed in the footsteps of the Master, writing in his diary: "No man either white or black, from North or from South, shall drag me down so low as to make me hate him."

Before his death, Tuskegee Institute had grown to be the largest Institute of its kind in America, with buildings costing $2,000,000 spread over 2000 acres, and an enrollment of 1800 students learning 47 trades taught in 100 buildings. When he died on November 14, 1915, Andrew Carnegie voiced the sentiment of millions of Americans who had followed the inspiring record of his career, when he said: "History will tell us of two Washingtons, one white, one black, both fathers of their peoples." Tuskegee Institute, continuing his work of intellectual and spiritual emancipation of the most neglected of God's children in America, will ever remain the lengthened shadow of a mighty character— mighty in its capacity to suffer, to serve, to sacrifice.

From the black depths of a West Virginia coal mine and the still blacker depths of a mind unillumined by even the rays of the alphabet to the sunlit mountain peaks of scholarly leadership and literary achievement—what a climb! What an achievement! Here was a life in which the turning of the other cheek, the walking of the second mile, the returning of love for hatred were of almost daily occurrence. Here was a life in which the surplus in service, in sacrifice, in love, flowed like a tidal wave over the banks of strict duty, enriching all mankind. Through the black face of Booker T. Washington shines a white light that will guide the groping feet of generations yet unborn.

The Alchemy of Love

What is the motive and the only motive that can supply the power necessary to enable a man to go the second mile, to do more than is required of him? Christ supplies the answer. Apparently as if in answer to the expressions of astonishment and incredulity on the faces of His disciples, Christ discloses the secret source of the power that will enable them to convert their compulsions into superabundant service joyously rendered. "You have heard," He says, "that it hath been said, Thou shalt love thy neighbor and hate thy enemy. But I say to you, Love your enemies: do good to them that hate you: and pray for them that persecute and calumniate you: That you may be the children of your Father who is in heaven, who maketh his sun to rise upon the good and bad, and raineth upon the just and the unjust."

The motive is love, a universal love, a love that embraces one's enemies. It is the only motive which can convert a work of drudgery grudgingly performed into a labor of love, done with eagerness and joy. It is the magical alchemist which alone can transmute the iron of heavy-footed drudgery into the gold of joyous service, poured out without stint and far beyond the limitations of mere duty. Christ here sounds the most distinctive note of all His teachings to mankind. Love is both the foundation and the apex of the Christian gospel. Without it the religion of Christ vanishes into thin air.

Christ not only discloses the secret source of the power which will enable them to go the second mile, but He points to it as the mark which will most clearly distinguish His disciples from the heathen. "For if you love them that love you, what reward shall you have?" He asks. "Do not even the publicans this? And if you salute your brethren only, what do you more? Do not also the heathens this? Be ye therefore perfect, as also your heavenly Father is perfect." There are no halfway measures with Christ, no compromises with the ideal such as the prudent and worldly-wise are fond of making. His followers are called to the noble ideal of the highest love, a love that embraces their enemies, a love that makes them share in a manner the perfection of God who is Infinite Love. It is only in proportion as they tap this source of spiritual power that they become able to convert their compulsions into streams of joyous service which overflow the narrow channels of strict duty and thus make gladsome the whole terrain of human life.

How weak is the life and fruitless the love of the soul that does not root itself in the Infinite Source of both is thus depicted by Frederick L. Knowles:

> O Love triumphant over guilt and sin,
> My soul is soiled, but Thou shalt enter in;
> My feet must stumble if I walk alone,
> Lonely my heart till beating by Thine own;
> My will is weakness till it rest in Thine,
> Cut off, I wither, thirsting for the Vine;
> My deeds are dry leaves on a sapless tree,
> My life is lifeless till it live in Thee!

Thornton Wilder opens *The Bridge of San Luis Rey* [5]

[5] Albert & Charles Boni, N.Y., 1936

with a brief account of the collapse of a bridge hurling to sudden destruction a little group of people crossing it. Then he goes back and sketches the life of each of the victims, searching for some clue to solve the riddle of why these particular individuals should have had their lives snuffed out so suddenly and with such apparently blind indiscriminateness. He ends his quest by pointing to the only factor he has been able to find, which gives meaning to life and constitutes the bridge even to those who are gone. It is the final sentence and the noblest line in the whole novel: "There is a land of the living and a land of the dead and the bridge is love, the only survival, the only meaning."

In his play, *The Servant in the House*,[6] Charles Rann Kennedy draws a vivid picture of the dwelling compounded out of the beating of human hearts, and embodying the noble deeds of generous service of all the illustrious dead —a house that symbolizes the hopes and groping aspirations of the race. Here is the scene:

Bishop. They say it's an enormous concern!

Manson. So it is.

Bishop. Well, what would such an establishment as that represent? In round numbers, now?

Manson. (calmly) Numberless millions.

Bishop. Numberless mil . . . ! (He drops his fork.) My dear sir, absurd! . . . Why, the place must be a palace— fit for a king!

Manson. It is! . . . You must understand, this is no dead pile of stones and unmeaning timber. *It is a living thing.* . . .

When you enter it you hear a sound—a sound as of some mighty poem chanted. Listen long enough, and you will learn that it is made up of the beating of human hearts, of the nameless music of men's souls—that is, if you have ears. If you have

[6] Harper Bros., N.Y., 1908

eyes, you will presently see the church itself—a looming mystery of many shapes and shadows, leaping sheer from floor to dome. The work of no ordinary builder! . . .

The pillars of it go up like the brawny trunks of heroes: the sweet human flesh of men and women is moulded about its bulwarks, strong, impregnable: the faces of little children laugh out from every corner-stone: the terrible spans and arches of it are the joined hands of comrades; and up in the heights and spaces there are inscribed the numberless musings of all the dreamers of the world. It is yet building—building and built upon. Sometimes the work goes forward in deep darkness: sometimes in blinding light: now beneath the burden of unutterable anguish: now to the tune of a great laughter and heroic shoutings like the cry of thunder. (Softer.) Sometimes, in the silence of the night-time, one may hear the tiny hammerings of the comrades at work up in the dome—the comrades that have climbed ahead.

A Cosmic Anchorage

While the love of friends is common to all mankind, the love of enemies is distinctively Christian. What is the incentive for a love that is certainly not rooted in human instincts, but rises in defiance of their clamor for vengeance, and exhausts itself in deeds of kindliness to those who hate us and in prayers for those who persecute and calumniate us? It is the consciousness that in so doing we are walking in the footsteps of the divine Master and are meriting a reward from Him who promised that not even a cup of water given in His name would pass unrequited. Human beings must have incentives equal to the tasks demanded of them. The doing of deeds of surplus service, the loving of those who hate us, praying for those who persecute and revile us, must be based upon something more real than fine words and glorious rhetoric. They must have a cosmic anchorage.

They must be rooted in the nature of the spiritual universe. They must have God as their Underwriter, the Guarantor of their worth.

It is only the sure consciousness that there is a Divine Being who witnesses the human scene, and reads the thoughts that pass unspoken in the kingdom of the soul, that can prompt a person to return love for hatred and, while burning at the stake, pray for his murderers. Take away that Divine Being, the unfailing source of mankind's hope of reward for unselfish love and heroic sacrifice, and the bottom falls out of the moral universe. The incentive has perished utterly. As water cannot rise higher than its source, neither can human conduct transcend its incentives.

This point was made simply and graphically by an American doughboy in World War II. "If there isn't a Being in the upper story," he said as he stood in a front line trench with wounded and dying comrades about him on every side, "who sees and rewards the deeds of bravery and devotion of those who never come back to get Congressional medals or hear themselves eulogized, then the universe is just plumb crazy and the coward and the cheat alone are wise. And I'd find suicide the easiest way out." More than fine words and pretty speeches are needed as incentives to deeds of unselfish love and heroic sacrifice for men who know they will never live to hear them. God alone constitutes the only firm foundation for the moral universe. Without Him, it is a topsy-turvy universe, "full of sound and fury, signifying nothing."

What Is the Incentive?

After enunciating the code of the second mile and pointing to a love that embraces enemies as its motive power, Christ then proceeds to disclose the incentive for such superabundant service and such transcendental love, namely, the sure reward of Almighty God. "Take heed," says He, "that you do not your justice before men, to be seen by them: otherwise you shall not have a reward of your Father who is in heaven. Therefore when thou dost an almsdeed, sound not a trumpet before thee, as the hypocrites do in the synagogues and in the streets, that they may be honored by men. Amen. I say to you, they have received their reward." Herein Christ discloses the weakness of all such motivation —it functions only when in the spotlight and under the stimulus of the praise of men. When the spotlight is absent, however, or when the crowds are present not to applaud but to condemn, to light the fagots that will burn you at the stake, the incentive to heroic sacrifice has strangely disappeared.

Inducements which are traceable to the desire of human applause are as fickle and unstable as the weather vane, veering in a different direction with each new gust of wind. But sanctions based upon the consciousness of divine approval are as constant as the North Star, which never ceases to shine and to guide the mariner safely over the storm-tossed sea. The incentive which is born of the consciousness that God who sees in secret will repay is alone capable of sustaining an individual to carry on in the face of the jeering and scoffing of the multitude, prompting him to return love for hatred and to face death with a smile. Only a divine sanction can enable weak human nature to transcend the instincts of the flesh, to stifle the cry for vengeance and to rise to the supernatural heights of praying for those who malign and persecute us.

Christ directs the disciples to act not for the praise of men, but for the approval of God Who alone can fittingly reward them. "But when thou dost alms," He said, "let not thy left hand know what thy right hand doth." Why this disregard

for the applause of men? Christ answers: "That thy alms
may be in secret, and thy Father who seeth in secret will repay thee." In purifying the motive by stripping it of the
hankering for human praise, the individual comes to act for
the highest and holiest motive—the approval of God and
of Him only. This motive alone covers the whole of human
life and grips the individual when removed from the eyes
of men as effectively as when he is in the limelight of this
world's gaze. It alone can convert weak flesh into muscles
of iron and nerves of steel and hold the individual to the
path of high nobility as unflinchingly as the magnet holds
the steel.

A Divine Approval

A study of the lives of the men and women who have
enriched human life most generously with their achievements discloses that they were not only heroes of the second
mile, but that they were more concerned in winning the approval of God than of men. When William Crawford
Gorgas, who had spent his life in waging a relentless warfare
against yellow fever, giving it no quarter but insisting upon
its eradication from civilized life, lay dying in London, he
was visited by the King. In recognition of his conquest of
this age-old disease which had taken annually thousands of
lives, George V knighted him and pinned upon him the
Harbin Gold Medal for his "services to mankind." After
expressing his appreciation, Gorgas added: "I hope, however, that my real decoration will not be lacking when I
pass on to the other world. My faith in God and in eternal
life is absolute." Here was the motive that sustained him in
his long struggle against one of the worst enemies of mankind.

Louis Pasteur has the unique distinction of being the Fa-

ther of three distinct sciences—bacteriology, physio-chem-
istry and bio-therapeutics. By universal acclaim his name
heads the list of all those geniuses who have made notable
contributions to medical science. Yet few know that the
motive which sustained him through the long years of unremitting toil, from early morning till late at night, wresting
from nature the secrets which she had shielded for uncounted ages and shoving back the frontiers of the unknown, was a living faith in God to whom he turned for
his reward. At the very peak of his scientific achievements
he wrote to his children: "The more I know, the more
nearly is my faith that of the Breton peasant. Could I but
know all I would have the faith of a Breton peasant's wife."

As he lay dying, he clasped in his hands his rosary while
they read to him the life of St. Vincent de Paul who did so
much for the orphans and the poor waifs of France. Oblivi-
ous of the applause of men, Pasteur looked forward to the
approval of his Maker as the recompense for one of the
most fruitful lives in human history. On his tomb at the
Pasteur Institute in Paris are carved the words he had written in one of his letters, which sound the keynote of his
life: "Happy the man who bears within him a divinity, an
ideal of beauty and obeys it; an ideal of art, an ideal of science, an ideal of country, an ideal of the virtues of the
Gospel."

For twenty-four years Jean de Brébeuf labored as a Jesuit
missionary among the Indian tribes of New France. A man
of culture and refinement, he lived in the wigwams of the
Indians, sharing their wretched food, enduring the cold that
at times split the bark on the trees, and suffering all the hardships of the untutored redmen. Many a time his eyes were
red and bleary from the smoke in the wigwam, a smoke
which almost suffocated him. One night as he looked at the
degraded lot of Indians huddled about him at the fireside,

and contrasted these ignorant, superstitious, treacherous, vermin-infected savages with the cultured companions to whom he was accustomed in France, the thought of leaving them and returning to his homeland occurred to him. Then he recalled the words of Christ: "He that shall lose his life for my sake shall find it." With the promise of Christ echoing in his ears, he beat back the temptation to leave, and wrote in his own blood a vow to remain at his lonely post of duty until death would call him home.

On March 16, 1649, he was taken prisoner by the hostile Iroquois and dragged to St. Ignace. On entering the village he was met with a shower of stones, beaten with clubs and tied to a stake to be burned to death. Remembering the calm fortitude with which Christ had permitted Himself to be crucified, Brébeuf kissed the stake that was to be his cross. While a fire was slowly kindled around his feet, his body was slashed with knives. Scalding water was poured over his head in mockery of baptism, a collar of red hot hatchets was placed around his neck, and a red hot iron was thrust down his throat. During all his frightful torments, Brébeuf uttered no single word of complaint. When at last he fell, the Indians, amazed at his incredible capacity to suffer, plucked the heart out of his body and ate it, thinking they might in this manner capture something of his bravery. No wonder it is that the memory of Brébeuf is cherished among the people of Canada more than that of all the other early missionaries.

What nerved Jean de Brébeuf to face without flinching the frightful tortures inflicted upon him? Pretty speeches? The applause of men? Worldly fame? How utterly meaningless these would have been to him as the flames leaped up around him in that far-off wilderness of the redmen. Only the sure consciousness that God would see and understand and be his unfailing reward could have sustained him not only in that hour of excruciating torture but all through the twenty-four years of his missionary labors, replete with hardship and sacrifice.

When Savonarola, the Dominican Prior of St. Mark's in Florence, was crossing the plank leading to the scaffold on which he was to be hanged and his body burned in ignominy, he was confronted by the bishop of Vasona who said to him: "I separate thee from the Church militant and from the Church triumphant." To which Savonarola replied: "Not from the Church triumphant. That is beyond thy power." The consciousness that God saw the purity of his motives and understood the nobility of his courageous struggle against the prevailing corruption in high places, sustained him to mount the gibbet and face death with a smile. Rising higher than the jeers of the mob was the voice of his own conscience speaking its approval of his conduct and echoing, he firmly believed, the approval of that divine Judge before whom the secrets of the heart are as the pages of an open book.

God—the Only Answer

No matter where we look, then, at the list of the heroes of the second mile, at the men and women who have borne their cross up Calvary's heights that the very multitudes crucifying them might be redeemed, we find that their appeal has been from Caiphas, from Pilate, from the mob, to God. They have been able to return love for hatred, to pray for those who persecuted and reviled them only because they found in the "Father who seeth in secret and will repay" the promise of their sure reward. God alone gives meaning to the universe and constitutes the only answer to the cry of every noble soul for strength to endure, to carry on, to scale the heights. "To know thee," cried the Psalmist, "is perfect righteousness; yea, to know thy dominion is the root of righteousness." It is in moments of "exceeding righteousness," of heroic sacrifice that mankind feels most sensibly the presence of God. That presence enables an individual to realize that God and one constitute a majority, and thus gives him new strength and courage. It renders him independent of the praise or blame of man, making the approval of God the mainspring and the end of all his actions.

The noblest definition of God ever given is that uttered by St. John when he said simply: "God is love." "If any one love me," said Christ, "he will keep my word, and my Father will love him, and we will come to him and make our abode with him." It was this vision of God as love which prompts old Sabre, one of the characters in A. S. M. Hutchinson's novel, *If Winter Comes*,[7] to point out the answer to the mystery and riddle of life. "I tell you, Hapgood," he cries, "that plumb down in the crypt and abyss of every man's soul is a hunger, a craving for other food than this earthly stuff. . . . Light, light—that's what he wants." . . .

"I've got the secret. I've got the key to the riddle that's been puzzling me all my life. I've got the new revelation in terms good enough for me to understand. Light, more light. Here it is: God is . . . *love*. Not this, that, nor the other that the intelligence revolts at, and puts aside, and goes away, and goes on hungering, hungering and unsatisfied; nothing like that; but just this; plain for a child, clear as daylight for grown intelligence: God is . . . *love*. . . . 'He that dwelleth in love dwelleth in God and God in him; for God *is* love.' Ecstasy, Hapgood, ecstasy! It explains everything to me. I can reduce all the mysteries to terms of that."

"I tell you . . . old Sabre, when he was telling me that, was a pretty first-class advertisement for his own revelation.

[7] Hodder & Stoughton, Ltd., London, 1933

He'd found it all right. The look on him was nearer the divine than anything I've ever come near seeing."

It was this vision of God as love which entered so deeply into the mind of Toyohiko Kagawa that it transformed him into one of the noblest ethical characters of Japan, an apostle of social justice, a defender of the rights of the poor and lowly, a pleader for peace amidst the raucous shouts of Nipponese for war. It caused him to share his little shack, about ten by eight, and his meagre food, with a beggar. In this little hut in the slum district of Osobe, he wrote his radiant songs of Jesus and his books which have carried the winsome picture of Christ into the hearts of hundreds of thousands of his countrymen. When confronted by a bully who demanded his few coins to buy liquor, Kagawa refused. Whereupon the bully rained blow after blow upon his face, knocking out several of his teeth and causing the blood to stream from his lips. But Kagawa did not strike back. His vision of Christ, buffeted, spat upon and saying, "If any one strike thee on the right cheek, turn to him the left also," restrained him. Terror-stricken at the strange spectacle, the bully fled in dismay.

For there is something deep down in the heart of man that crumples at the sight of a person who innocent, defenceless and unafraid bears the buffetings and blows heaped upon him without striking back. Physical force falls to its knees in awe when confronted with the moral might of the naked human soul. Kagawa has made the hearts of uncounted thousands in the Orient burn with a new love for Christ as he walks the second mile among them with a love that never stops to count the cost in labor, in kindliness, in sacrifice.

It was this vision which took possession of Albert Schweitzer, eminent in philosophy, theology, scripture and music. Learning of the plight of the natives of the Lambarene district in the Belgian Congo, with no doctor to minister to their many ills, he surrendered his chair at the University of Strassburg, studied medicine, and for twenty-four years has ministered as a physician to the most neglected of God's children in equatorial Africa. Upon the heartstrings of these people, he has played a nobler melody than ever he played upon the great organs of Europe—a melody singing into their hearts the thrilling song of Christ.

Love Opens Sightless Eyes

Newton D. Baker, Secretary of War in President Wilson's cabinet, tells an amazing story of the power of a mighty and a generous love that overflowed the bounds of duty with deeds of superabundant service and kindliness. While visiting the worst casualties of the American army in the federal hospitals, Mr. Baker came upon one that stirred him deeply. He was a veteran who would seem to have been as frightfully mutilated as any soldier that came out of the holocaust alive. Both legs were gone, one arm gone, blinded in both eyes, his face was terribly mutilated, and he was wheeled helplessly around the grounds of the hospital in a perambulator by a nurse. No one expected him to live. Meeting someone from the hospital later on Mr. Baker asked: "Did that young man live?" "Did he live?" echoed his friend. "Why, he's married his nurse." How marvelous, reflected Mr. Baker, is the capacity of women to love those who stand desperately in need of loving and who pour out their love for the sheer joy of giving.

Several years elapsed, and the incident had almost faded from his mind when Mr. Baker, as a trustee of Johns Hopkins University, received a letter from its president. The letter informed him of the plan of the University to do an unusual thing, to hold a mid-semester convocation to confer the doctor of philosophy degree upon a young man who, in spite of being heavily handicapped, had done one of the most brilliant pieces of research ever accomplished at the University. To his amazement the name was that of the crippled veteran—William Harrison Craig. Still incredulous, Mr. Baker investigated further and discovered that it was none other than the mutilated soldier whom nobody had expected to live, much less to shove back the boundaries of our darkness. When the crippled scholar was wheeled across the stage to receive the highest honor within the competency of Johns Hopkins to bestow, the students and faculty stood up and cheered as they had never cheered in all the history of the University.

As I read this story, I wondered: Was there not another person in that story who might well have received a doctorate? What about that gracious, kind and radiant nurse who did not stop with the routine duties of a nurse, but who bathed this helpless invalid with her love and tenderness? With all due credit to the plucky veteran for his magnificent achievement, is there anyone, I wonder, who can withhold his admiration from that great-hearted woman whose love opened those sightless eyes to ferret out new truth from nature's tangled skein, and who inspired him with the will to live, to struggle, to achieve.

An inspiring love like hers, that did not stop to count the cost, but poured itself out in torrential streams of devotion, service and sacrifice, is the hidden lining of the story of more superlative achievements than this world dreams of. Love that flows over the bounds of duty, that forgets itself in the ministry of others, that asks only the joy of giving, only the privilege of serving, sacrificing and dying for its beloved, is the one force which lifts the universe. It shines with the white radiance of eternity, and discloses to us most authentically the essential nature of God. For where noble, unselfish, sacrificial love is, there is God. Where God is, there is Heaven.

When Christ was dying upon the cross, He said: "I thirst." In answer to his plea, the executioners placed a sponge, dipped in vinegar and gall, to his lips to accentuate the thirst on his parched lips and tongue. Down at the foot of the cross, the Roman soldiers were casting dice for His garments. What a temptation to strike back, to invoke God's punishment upon His persecutors, His torturers! But no! Christ had taught His disciples to love their enemies, to pray for those who persecute and revile one unjustly. Here was the chance to exemplify that teaching under the most terrible circumstances. Raising His eyes to heaven, Christ said: "Forgive them for they know not what they do." [8] Seeing this, even the Roman centurion cries out: "Truly, this is the Son of God!" Here is the climactic expression of the religion of Christ. Here is the noblest note sounded in the diapason of history. Here is a love whose lifting power was thus described by Christ who was Love Incarnate: "I, if I be lifted up from the earth, will draw all men unto me." [9]

To conclude: The distinctive mark of the true Christian is his willingness to do more than is required, to travel the second mile in superabundant service. This spirit rises to a still higher and nobler expression in transcending the instinctive human clamor for vengeance and in returning good for evil, love for hatred, and in praying for those who persecute us. The motive is the consciousness that, in so doing, one merits a divine approval and a divine reward. In that magnanimity of love one feels most clearly the touch of God, the indwelling of Him who is Love Unutterable. There is a quiet joy in the heart, a peace that passeth understanding in the mind, a radiance that shines in the eyes, mir-

[8] *Luke* 23:34
[9] *John* 12:32

roring a divine Light which burns within the soul. Here is the unfailing mark of the true Christian. Here is a faith that moves mountains. Here is a love that constitutes the uplifting power of the universe.

HERE ENDS THE READING OF THIS BOOK
NOW FOR THE LIVING OF IT

A BRIEF BIBLIOGRAPHY

(Hundreds of detailed references occur in the text. The following books are cited for the convenience of the reader desirous of building up a working library on the subject.)

Arendzen, J. P., *The Gospels—Fact, Myth, or Legend?* Sands, Edinburgh-London, 1923

Barnes, A. S., *The Early Church in the Light of the Monuments*, Longmans, Green & Co., N.Y., 1913

Boedder, Bernard, *Natural Theology*, Longmans, Green & Co., N.Y., 1899

Brosnan, W. J., *God Infinite and Reason*, Fordham University Press, N.Y., 1924

Brown, C. R., *Why I Believe in Religion*, Macmillan Co., N.Y., 1924

Brown, W. R., *Pathways to Certainty*, Scribners, N.Y., 1930

Cooper, C. C., Ed., *Religion and the Modern Mind*, Harper & Bros. Co., N.Y., 1929

Cooper, J. M., *Religion Outlines for Colleges, Course 111*, Catholic Educational Press, Washington, D.C., 1930

Donat, Joseph, *The Freedom of Science*, Joseph F. Wagner, N.Y., 1914

Dorlodot, de Henry, *Darwinism and Catholic Thought*, Benziger Bros., N.Y., 1922

Driscoll, J. T., *Christian Philosophy—God*, Benziger Bros., N.Y., 1900

Duchesne, Msgr. L., *Christian Worship: Its Origin and Evolution*, Macmillan Co., N.Y., 1919

Fillion, L. C., *The Life of Christ*, tr. 3 vols. B. Herder, St. Louis, 1928

Garrigou-Lagrange, R., *God, His Existence and His Nature*, tr. B. Herder, St. Louis, 1934

Hocking, W. E., *The Meaning of God in Human Experience*, Yale University Press, New Haven, 1912

Jones, Rufus, *Pathways to the Reality of God*, Macmillan Co., N.Y., 1931

Joyce, G. H., *Principles of Natural Theology*, Longmans, Green & Co., N.Y., 1924

Lattey, Cuthbert, *The Religion of the Scriptures*, B. Herder, St. Louis, 1922

Lattey, Cuthbert, Ed., *God—A Symposium*, Sheed & Ward, N.Y., 1931

Macintosh, D. C., *The Reasonableness of Christianity*, Scribners, N.Y., 1926

Maher, Michael, *Psychology: Empirical and Rational*, Longmans, Green & Co., 1911

Mathews, Shailer, *The Growth of the Idea of God*, Macmillan Co., N.Y., 1931

Murray, R. W., *Man's Unknown Ancestors*, Bruce, Milwaukee, 1943

O'Brien, J. A., *Evolution and Religion*, Our Sunday Visitor, Huntington, Ind., 1931

O'Brien, J. A., *Religion in a Changing World*, Our Sunday Visitor, Huntington, Ind., 1938

O'Brien, J. A., *The Faith of Millions*, Our Sunday Visitor, Huntington, Ind., 1938

Otten, Bernard, *The Reason Why*, B. Herder, St. Louis, 1912

Pesch, Tilmann, *The Christian Philosophy of Life*, B. Herder, St. Louis, 1922

Schmidt, Wilhelm, *Origin and Growth of Religion*, L. Mac-Veagh, The Dial Press, N.Y., 1931

INDEX